THE INTELLIGENTSIA
AND THE INTELLECTUALS

THE INTELLIGENTSIA
AND THE INTELLECTUALS
Theory, Method and Case Study

Edited by

Aleksander Gella
State University of New York at Buffalo

SAGE Studies in International Sociology 5
sponsored by the International Sociological Association/ISA

For information address

SAGE Publications Ltd.
44 Hatton Garden
London EC1N 8ER

SAGE Publications Inc.
275 South Beverly Drive
Beverly Hills, California 90212

International Standard Book Number
0 8039 9958 5 Cloth
0 8039 9972 0 Paper

Library of Congress Catalog Card Number
38421

First Printing

Printed in the United States of America

CONTENTS

Preface 7

1 An Introduction to the Sociology of the Intelligentsia
Aleksander Gella 9

I THEORETICAL AND METHODOLOGICAL PROBLEMS
IN STUDIES OF THE INTELLIGENTSIA AND
THE INTELLECTUALS

2 Methodological Problems in Comparative Studies
of the Intelligentsia
Peter C Ludz 37

3 What Is an Intellectual?
Lewis S Feuer 47

4 Members of the Intelligentsia as Developers and
Disseminators of Cosmopolitan Culture
Helena Z Lopata 59

5 Changes in the Concept of Intellectuals
Tibor Huszar 79

6 The Roles of the Intellectual and Political Roles
Seymour M Lipset and Asoke Basu 111

II REVOLUTIONARY MOOD AMONG THE
CONTEMPORARY INTELLIGENTSIA

7   The Humanistic Intelligentsia
Harold M Hodges Jr   153

8   Filmmakers as Part of a Revolutionary Intelligentsia
Leonard Henny   173

III   **STUDIES IN THE NATIONAL INTELLENTSIA**

9   The Class of the Intelligentsia in Africa
Zygmunt Komorowski   201

10   The Development of the Intelligentsia Between the Wars:
The Case of Czechoslovakia
Jan Hajda   211

11   Soviet Scientific and Technical Intelligentsia and
Its Social Makeup
N N Bokarev and N B Chaplin   223

Notes on Contributors   233

PREFACE

Throughout the world, even in western societies, contemporary intellectuals and others whose work and interest involves them directly in the intellectual and cultural life of their society are inclined to identify themselves more with the community of those who participate in the creation and administration of cultural values and knowledge than with the traditional classes of their family origin. The controversy surrounding the concept *intelligentsia* and the growing significance of the world development of this substratum led me to organize a Round Table entitled 'Toward the Sociology of the Intelligentsia' for the VIIIth World Congress of Sociology, Toronto, August 1974. The number of candidates for participation in the panel was much greater than the limited time allowed. This fact as well as the considerable heat generated by our panel discussions confirmed my conviction that comparative studies of the intelligentsia on an international scale are needed. I hope that our Round Table discussion made a first step toward further systematic research and comparative study on the subject.

The present volume is a direct result of the panel's discussion. The 12 panelists represented eight countries: Canada, Czechoslovakia, Germany, Holland, Hungary, Poland, the Soviet Union,* and the United States.

This book is not of a monolithic character; on the contrary, it represents highly divergent opinions. It reflects the great controversy between various liberal approaches and those attached to the Marxist view point. I believe this is just what we need to stimulate discussions on the subject on an international basis. Almost every author has a different concept of the intelligentsia, though most of them use the term intelligentsia and intellectuals interchangeably. One of the sharpest points of controversy concerns whether dissidents in the Soviet Union are typical representatives of the intelligentsia, the view assumed by almost any, if not all, western students of the subject, but rejected by the Soviet contributors to this volume. So, while Louis Feuer argues that 'the Soviet intellectuals now known as "dissidents" have taken up the contest against the dictorship of the mediocrats,' Bokarev and Chaplin emphasize that 'all talk about numerous groups of dissidents supposedly existing in the USSR among the intelligentsia are absolutely unfounded.'

I have divided this book into three parts. The first six chapters deal with theoretical and methodological matters. The second part consists of two chapters presenting the revolutionary mood of the intelligentsia, both in politics and in academic life. Part three presents studies in national intelligentsias.

My own chapter includes what I said in my opening paper for the Round Table in Toronto, plus what needed to be added to properly introduce this volume. It does not focus on any one particular topic but attempts to sketch an outline of the sociology of the intelligentsia in both historical and contemporary perspective.

Aleksander Gella   October 1975
State University of New York at Buffalo

Two sociologists from the USSR were introduced to my panel directly by the General Secretariat of the ISA, causing a moment of confusion but making the exchange and confrontation of opinions particularly interesting and vivid.

My work on this book is respectfully dedicated to my teacher, Professor Edward Lipinski.

1

AN INTRODUCTION TO THE SOCIOLOGY
OF THE INTELLIGENTSIA

Aleksander Gella
State University of New York at Buffalo

Comparative study of the intelligentsia, a social phenomenon of rapidly growing importance in the contemporary world, is attracting the attention of sociologists more and more.[1] It is a study concerned with identifying and exploring a number of social issues of global significance. Sociology of the intelligentsia on a national scale arose mainly in Russia and Poland, where the so-called 'classical intelligentsia' appeared in the nineteenth century. However, in the mass societies of the twentieth century some groups of intellectuals and of people close to them have begun to be referred to as 'intelligentsia' and, in some cases, to acquire certain characteristics of the old East-European intelligentsia. It is in the face of this development that comparative international studies of the various national strata of the intelligentsia have taken on contemporary importance.

The term 'intelligentsia' is used today in almost all industrially developed as well as developing countries to designate groups or strata of educated but unpropertied people. But the social characteristics of these groups vary greatly from country to country. Because of the relative newness of the subject and the considerable ambiguities which have arisen, I shall in this essay take the opportunity to clarify some of the key notions and terminology, as well as propose certain concerns governing the conceptualization of the study as a whole.

I would like to express my appreciation and gratitude to Mr. Michael Anderson for his careful and thoughtful correction of my own paper and to Mrs. Norma Burk for her devotion and superb technical skill in assembling this entire book manuscript with patience and loving attention to detail.

Of all the social strata, the intelligentsia is the most difficult to define. It is my view that most western sociologists have been hampered in their attempts to define it by failing to adhere to a strict view of stratum.[2] In one way or another they describe the intelligentsia in terms of its function of creation, administration, and consumption of cultural goods. For instance, Theodore Geiger (1949) reduced the problem to the rather simplified view that the intelligentsia consist of (1) creators of cultural goods, (2) their consumers, and (3) all others with diplomas of higher education. My approach, on the other hand, has been to understand how and why the intelligentsia is appearing and disappearing with a hierarchical structure of society composed of various other classes and strata. In other words, it is an attempt to set down the outlines of the intelligentsia neither in terms of the raw material with which it is dealing (ideas, values, cultural goods) nor in terms of its standard of education, but according to its position and function within the socio-political structure of society. This approach produces a quite different definition of the intelligentsia than has previously been advanced. But we will come to this later.

Confusions and ambiguities concerning the term 'intelligentsia' have arisen for sociologists in part through their adoption of various popular and ill-defined uses of the term[3] and in part through the fact that different schools of sociology have emphasized different aspects of the concept. Historically minded scholars tend to insist upon understanding the intelligentsia as a specific *social stratum* which existed in Russia and Poland during the latter half of the nineteenth and the beginning of the twentieth century. These have, of course, a special claim to accuracy since it was in fact to name this stratum that the term was originally coined.

One difficulty for western scholars has been that, while all other classes and strata of Eastern Europe have had their counterparts in the West, the intelligentsia, strictly speaking, did not.[4] (This will be elucidated below.) This has led to a rather loose application of the term (loose from an historical point of view) among those western sociologists who, in identifying social and cultural characteristics shared among individuals of various societies, have failed to note contrasts defined by affiliation with class or stratum. So long as the term 'intelligentsia' is applied to social strata, we can expect confusions to arise from the failure to distinguish individuals taken in isolation from individuals understood as members of a class or social stratum. Individuals from different cultures may have the same educational background, the same economic and social position, standard of life, interests and hobbies, sharing the common characteristics and attitudes—but they could not make a Westerner a member of the intelligentsia. For no such social *stratum* existed in the West.

Another challenge to the historian's strict application of the term is the premise of sociological formalism that a social phenomenon which we meet in one time and place can repeat itself, though under different names, in other times and places. This has led to applying the term 'intelligentsia' to all groups of intellectuals or, more generally, to all well-educated social strata which have appeared in various times and countries. But, as I will try to show, by drawing a rather more careful distinction between 'intellectuals' and 'intelligentsia', a constructive reconciliation of the historian and the formalist can be produced.

An additional source of confusion follows from the reapplication of term 'intelligentsia' in the Soviet Union and the other countries of the Soviet bloc. I refer to the phrase 'working' or 'toiling intelligentsia', officially used to designate all more or less educated people, ranging from the academician to the clerk of lowest rank. Those who inherited the name also inherited, doubtless, some of the prestige of the classical intelligentsia—but from a sociological point of view the affinities are merely superficial.

Whereas the historical approach is maintained mainly by some sociologists and historians of Eastern Europe[5] the formalistic approach is quite typical of sociologists of Western Europe and America, who are inclined simply to identify the intelligentsia with intellectuals. This is Seton-Watson's characterization of the prevailing formalist definition: 'In Western societies the word is used mainly to denote a *small inner elite or self-styled elite of writers and cultural dignitaries.*' (Seton-Watson 1965: 340) Thus, whereas sociologists of the historical persuasion see the intelligentsia as a unique and particular historical phenomenon, the formalists tend in the opposite direction, divesting the concept of all particular temporal and spacial determinants. The formalists have correctly observed that groups of individuals dealing professionally with ideas, and fulfilling a social role similar to that of the so-called intellectuals of today, have existed in all civilized societies, and that these groups have, from time to time, been specifically united, against the rest of society, by a common set of ideas and attitudes. Thus, the adherents of this approach compare the Philosophers of Nature and Sophists of ancient Greece, the humanists of the Renaissance, and the French 'Philosophes' and Encyclopedists. This transhistorical approach found its best-known expression in Mannheim's concept of the intelligentsia as a 'thoroughly organized stratum of intellectuals' (Mannheim, 1940:11).

Sociologists of the historical persuasion used to begin the study of the intelligentsia with the question of the origins of the name of this stratum. The origin of the term 'intelligentsia' has been attributed to the three nations: Russia, Germany and Poland. Some historians assume that it was coined by Peter Boborykin, a Russian author, in 1860. This is, however, a misconception, as was noted by Waclaw Lednicki, who showed that the term was used in Russian literature by V. G. Belinsky in 1846. But he also knew that the term was used approximately at the same time in Poland and wrote that 'Russia and Poland were the birthplace of this class, and their languages created the term "intelligentsia" . . .' (Lednicki 1967:40). Alan Pollard also questioned the opinion that Boborykin was the inventor of this term (Pollard 1964). Richard Pipes has noted that 'the German word "Intelligenz" was used as early as 1849 to describe the same phenomenon as "intelligentsia", namely a group distinguished from the rest of society by its education and "progressive" attitude' (Pipes 1971). The same year, but six months earlier, I pointed out that the term 'was first used in Polish literature by Karol Libelt in 1844 . . .' (Gella 1971:4).

I still maintain my claim that this term was born first in Poland—persuaded in part by linguistic considerations: (1) the term was taken into modern languages from Latin, which had an incomparably stronger influence on the Poles than on the Russians; (2) the suffic 'cja' in the Polish word 'inteligencja' is closer to the Latin 'intelligentia' than Russian 'tsia'; (3) the suffic 'cja' (tsia in English spelling) is common in Polish but much less frequently encountered in Russian.

For sociologists, however, the question of the emergence of the term is of less concern than the appearance of the intelligentsia itself. It is generally agreed that, in Poland and Russia during the 1860's, a social stratum emerged, constituted of the better educated segment of society but distinct from other educated people of the upper and middle classes.[6] In fact, the intelligentsia developed into culturally homo-genious social stratum only in Poland and Russia.[7] In both countries the intelligentsia was set apart from other educated elements of Euro-pean society by a specific combination of psychological characteristics, manners, style of life, social status and, above all, value system.[8] The historical process by which a portion of the educated people came to form a separate stratum in Russia and Poland never took place in western societies. The appearance of the intelligentsia was determined by the deterioration of the feudal system in the Russian empire (Raeff 1961, Berdyaev 1960) and by legal discrimination and pauperization of the nobility in partitioned Poland.[9] In both countries members of the 'declassé' fraction of the landed nobility, seeking to maintain in an urban environment their traditional style of life, had to separate them-selves from the 'bourgeois' middle class. This entailed selecting only certain occupations and at the same time acquiring an education which would allow them to sustain their societal contacts with those whom history had not yet deprived of their idle forms of existence: the landed nobility and aristocracy. But, basically, the old intelligentsia was united neither by an economic standard of life and income nor by occupa-tional vested interests, but mainly by sharing certain attitudes and accepting a cultural heritage larger than the national one.

The values of this stratum were verbalized by a relatively small group of moral and intellectual leaders. The beliefs, the moral attitudes, and the political behavior of these leaders were not fully duplicated by all members of the intelligentsia. But on the whole, an average member of the intelligentsia maintained his affiliation by imitating the manners and accepting, at least verbally, the basic mores and value-goals typical for the leading moral authorities of that stratum; otherwise, he risked being ostracized. People of lower class origin who through their educa-tional achievements became members of this stratum, in order to be fully accepted into the circles of the intelligentsia, had to behave according to the manners of this stratum, and show by deeds that they embraced the value-goals of the intelligentsia.

The single most important institution for inculcating this set of values and attitudes—and thus for creating the very identity of the stratum—was the educational system. The cultural homogeneity of the Polish intelligentsia (more than the Russian) was fostered and preserved by the gymnasium, through which all members of the stratum passed. This high school was characterized not only by a level of education which was incomparably higher than that of today's American high schools, but also by the manner in which the gymnasium specifically aimed to mould the personality of its pupils. The task of the gymnasium was not only to 'educate' but also to structure and to uplift the character of young men.

The same type of gymnasium existed in the German and Austrian empires, but it produced the intelligentsia only in the cities of partitioned Poland which belonged to these states. This is to say that it was not only the education which determined the rise of this stratum. Excellent German as well as French and English secondary educational institutions of the nineteenth century—wealthier, better equipped and more numerous than in Poland and Russia—delivered educated people to the bourgeoisie, nobility, professional and intellectual circles, but did not cause the rise of a separate stratum. But in Poland and Russia, the particular socio-political conditions meant that the gymnasium's pupils were expected to fill the ranks of a charismatic stratum whose members' fundamental social role was to lead the nation to its destiny. Thus, education, both in Poland and Russia meant something else for the member of the old intelligentsia than for the educated man in the West. Alexander Hertz has observed that education for members of this stratum 'is not a means to achieve personal success but rather *a permanent asset* which sets the individual apart and gives him access to a higher social sphere. The diploma from an institution of higher learning not only entitles a person to follow a particular profession. It gives more than that: *it bestows a title, a dignity that will remain forever associated with its bearer.'* (Hertz 1951).

Members of the intelligentsia, without respect to their occupations and economic status, were united by one common calling: 'serve your nation'. Individuals could find a number of different ways to fulfill this expectation. In general, however, there was in each of the two countries, a single basic attitude characterizing the intelligentsia's devotion to its national cause, though the difference between the Russian attitude and the Polish attitude was significant. In the Russia the motivation was to abolish Tsarism, to destroy the old state by peaceful or revolutionary means, whereas in Poland the motivation was twofold, to abolish the empires of the oppressors but at the same time to rebuild the independent Polish state. (This difference in calling of the Russian and Polish intelligentsias is related to the more predominant tendencies toward nihilism among the Russians; there were many other interesting differences which, however, would demand a separate analysis.)

The old intelligentsia wanted to be free of any class burdens, and members of the old intelligentsia very often insisted that their economic or formal position could not determine their attitudes toward national problems. Even though so lofty an ideal was beyond the reach of some parts of the intelligentsia, it was sufficient for the unity of the stratum that this ideal was realized by those who conferred their ethos upon the whole intelligentsia. The spiritual leaders of the intelligentsia never fought for their own group interest and never formulated an ideology of their stratum.[10] At the same time they produced leaders for all other class movements, parties and ideologies. However, it should be emphasized that those who symbolized the most essential characteristics of the intelligentsias of Russia and Poland were to be found principally on the left, in the service of social progress, revolution or national independence.

The earliest discussion and polemic undertaken concerning the intelligentsia by its own members took place in Poland and Russia at the beginning of the twentieth century. In Russia it was the 1905 Revolution which turned the attention of authors toward this stratum; a number of works written by Russians as well as by Westerners on the Russian intelligentsia appeared before World War I. The Polish intelligentsia similarly began to evaluate themselves in a crucial moment of their existence: the restoration of the Polish state (Gella 1971:3).

It was an irony of history that these two national strata which had contributed so greatly to the cause of revolution in Russia and to the restoration of the state in Poland were mortally affected by their achievements. In Russia, the communist party could not tolerate the intelligentsia as a coherent social stratum. The groups of the creative revolutionary intelligentsia had a period of flourishing during the first years following the October Revolution; it is enough to mention some of internationally known writers and artists of this period: Mayakowsky, Yesienin, Blok, Eisenstein, Malewicz, Chagall, Kandynsky, Babel, Mandelsstam and hundreds of others. But this development was interrupted by the firing squads and concentration camps of Stalin. Sociological studies on this flourishing period of the old Russian intelligentsia have never been undertaken.

Meanwhile, in the Polish Republic between the years 1918 and 1939, the intelligentsia was, to all appearances, enjoying its golden period. Nobody, of course, could realize then that the embodiment of the greatest dream of the intelligentsia, the rebuilding of an independent Poland, unavoidably marked the beginning of the decline of the stratum. Although virtually the entire government was in the hands of the intelligentsia, the stratum itself was involved in a slow process of corrosion. This was temporarily reversed by the events of World War II, which in threatening the very existence of the Polish nation and of the intelligentsia in particular, once again united the stratum in its traditional role of collective hero. But while serving its nation with leadership, it paid a disproportionately heavy tribute of blood, since both Hitler and Stalin understood the significance of the intelligentsia in Poland and shared in common the goal of liquidating the stratum.[11]

Thus, the old 'classical' intelligentsia has ceased to exist in Eastern Europe.[12] Those members of the intelligentsia who survived all the calamities no longer formed a separate stratum. In the new social system, there was no longer a place for the intelligentsia, which for a century had dominated the spiritual and political developments of those nations. The charismatic leadership of the intelligentsia was unneeded and unwanted in the countries where the communist parties took the responsibility for the present and future.

However, the name and the myth of the intelligentsia survived.[13] It has been applied to a new emerging social phenomenon: the shapeless and ambivalent new middle classes of the socialist societies, which are officially called the 'working intelligentsia'.[14] The working intelligentsia is highly stratified into several subgroups: clerical workers, technical intelligentsia, professionals, higher executives, and intellectuals. The core of the last subgroup consisting of writers, artists and leading scholars and scientists is called 'the creative intelligentsia'. On the transformation of the upper ranks of the intelligentsia in a socialist country, a leading Polish sociologist has written: 'the creative intelligentsia has begun to change itself into salaried specialists and certain groups of them are becoming officials' (Szczepanski 1959:31).

The working intelligentsia inherited the occupations and professional positions of the old intelligentsia, but it lacks the social cohesion created by those few fundamental socio-cultural attitudes and values which were a source of the informal power for the old intelligentsia as a stratum. The 'working intelligentsia', in all communist countries, consists of many unrelated groups of educated people. It has become many times larger than the old intelligentsia and socially much more heterogeneous.[15] In regard to cultural characteristics and social function it is similar to those elements of the western middle classes which possess a general or professional education.

After World War II the term intelligentsia spread beyond Europe. Undoubtedly, there are good reasons to designate as intelligentsia certain educated strata which have tended to undertake national leadership in the new nations of Africa and Asia. Although historical conditions for the development of the intelligentsia in the Third World have been very far from those in nineteenth century Eastern Europe, there is one basic formal similarity, namely, the appearance of a generation educated and influenced by an imported body of ideas and knowledge. Such a generation tends to accelerate the modernization of its own country. 'Nobody questions the opinion'—wrote an European researcher of the Black Continent's problems—'that the future of Senegal as well as of Africa as a whole will be dependent to a larger degree upon this small group of young people, than will the future of France upon the crowds from the Quartier Latin' (Komorowski 1969:170).

For the last two decades in the affluent societies of the West, a part of the young, educated generation has come to feel that not only their education and profession, but also their engagement in value-creation processes and devotion to social problems determines their role in modern society. Such groups possessing certain characteristics of the 'classical' East European intelligentsia, can be called incipient manifestations of a western intelligentsia. It is a new stratum 'in statu nascendi'. Their education has exposed them to systems of ideas as contrary to the value structure of capitalism as was nineteenth century liberalism to the prevailing Eastern European feudal system. Consequently manifold feelings of alienation characterize the emergent intelligentsia of the West.

The members of the incipient groups of the intelligentsia in affluent capitalist society, like the members of the old Russian intelligentsia, have been 'infected' by streams of thoughts from foreign civilizations which are deeply incompatible with the foundation of their own society. The acquaintance with the views of Comte, Darwin, Spencer and, finally, Marx made the old intelligentsia the 'critics and rebels' of their semi-feudal societies. Now, 'lux fiat ex oriente': one west European system of thought, fruitfully transplanted into the East, is returning now to the West in such divergent forms as Marxism-Leninism, Stalinism, Trotskism, Maoism, etc., stimulating both the criticism and the social aspirations of the new social stratum. Of course, the various Marxist traditions now being revitalized in the West are only a part of the stimuli pushing educated, unpropertied and alienated persons to challenge the outdated social philosophies of their own countries.

For some time, one was compelled to suppose that the intelligentsia, as a stratum of particular social calling in Russia and Eastern Europe, had vanished forever. However, the last decade of social development has unveiled both in Russia and Poland a reappearance of small groups of independently minded people whose attitude as well as social role is nothing but a continuation of the best traditions of the 'classical' intelligentsia—despite profoundly different historical circumstances. These, the only groups which resemble the old intelligentsia in Eastern Europe, are known today under the term 'dissidents'.[16]

At the present time the development of modern civilization, whatever the country or political system, demands a permanent increase of highly educated and academically trained people. Their social role is becoming as crucial for the shape of modern civilization as was the social role of the industrial proletariat for the development of revolutionary ideology in the nineteenth century.[17]

It is interesting for how long a time western sociologists did not even notice the difference between intellectuals in the West and that unique social formation which, under the name intelligentsia, began to develop in Russia and Poland during the middle of the nineteenth century. Interest in the role of intellectuals was vivid in western sociology at least since Saint-Simon. But the intelligentsia did not receive a separate item either in the *Encyclopaedia of the Social Sciences* or in the *International Encyclopedia of the Social Sciences*. Robert Michels (1932) in the former as well as Edward Shils in the latter (1968) did not differentiate between those two social phenomena. It should be mentioned, however, that Michels used these terms interchangeably, whereas, Shils was more consistent and wrote exclusively about intellectuals, omitting nearly all reference to their East-European counterparts.

The term *intellectuals* was coined by Clemenceau in 1898 to describe the group of prominant defenders of Dreyfus (Nettl 1970:25). In the West the interest in the intellectuals interchangeably called 'intelligentsia' appeared mainly in the works of German sociologists of the first decades of our century. However, the first author who touched the essential problems of the western intellectual community was Julien Benda, a Frenchman. His *La Trahison des clercs* (1927) was a great denunciation of intellectuals for their service of political or social ends and betrayal of what he saw as the very calling of the intellectual: disinterested love and search for truth and justice. This work, written by a philosopher, was not a sociological treatise; nonetheless, it was a milestone in the process of the development of group self-consciousness among western intellectuals.

Alfred Weber's expression, *die freischwebende Intelligenz* [socially unattached intelligentsia], has been widely used though variously interpreted. The major conscious effort to define the intelligentsia belongs to Karl Mannheim. He wrote: 'In every society there are social groups whose special task it is to provide an interpretation of the world for that society. We call these the intelligentsia' (Mannheim 1936:10). This definition as well as his further characterization of the 'organized stratum, a free intelligentsia' (Mannheim 1936:11), show that he is speaking about intellectuals who in Germany more than anywhere else formed a cohesive group. They monopolized the 'right to preach, teach and interpret the world' (Mannheim 1936:10). His analysis fits perfectly to the German case, but it would be wrong to extend it even into many other western societies. English intellectuals never felt they belonged to a separate stratum. In most modern societies the *class* consciousness of highly educated persons has been stronger than the attachment to the agglomerate of people who 'preach, teach, and interpret the world.' They might eventually create small circles (like, for instance, the French *philosophes*) but never a social stratum. 'Neither in the United States nor in England does it [education] provide social distinction in the same degree as do personal success, fortune or even birth . . . in both countries a college graduate may be a member of an "intellectual" group—a faculty, a learned society, a professional association, the bar, etc.—but by no means does his education make him regard himself as a member of a separate social class or caste bound to lead the nation to its destiny. In most cases he defines his social status as that of the middle classes.' (Hertz 1951:13).

Western intellectuals have never formed a social stratum in this sense in which we are using the term for the intelligentsia; they have always appeared as a socially complex group attached to the middle or upper classes. They are usually defined as those members of society who are devoted to the development of ideas, (Lipset, Dobsom 1972) or to the process of creating, distributing and applying culture. (Theodorson, Theodorson 1969:210). Groups of people who have fulfilled these social functions can be found in all, even the most primitive societies; in the civilized ones such persons might be rightly called 'the intellectuals', regardless of the historical period. To become an intellectual has never meant to change one's class attachment or class consciousness. Everywhere in the modern world a person becomes an intellectual by means of the merit of his intellectual interest, activity, training and achievement, but by these he and his wife do not enter a separate social stratum.

In contrast to groups of intellectuals, the intelligentsia appeared from its beginning as a social stratum. This fact basically distinguishes the phenomenon of the old intelligentsia from all other groups of educated people. Because it was a social stratum the mere fact of being born into the family of a member of the intelligentsia usually determined one's membership in this stratum.

The historical revolution which allowed groups of educated people in nineteenth-century Russia and Poland to form a separate stratum, were, as I have argued, unique in comparison with other European countries, and therefore the appearance of a social stratum unknown elsewhere was possible. But of course, one can assert that intellectuals of other countries have often played a role more or less similar to that of the classical intelligentsia. One can, for instance, point to the role of the French Encyclopedists in the social structure of France before the Great Revolution. However, the Encyclopedists (as well as all other agglomarates of intellectuals) consisted only of a small number of outstanding intellectuals who, even together with all other men of letters and science of their time and place, did not form a social stratum. For a social stratum is much more than a group of people united by certain intellectual interests and political goals.

The classical intelligentsia, on the other hand, was a social stratum, because it not only consisted of men and women of a wide range of occupations and various intellectual and educational levels, who shared certain beliefs, attitudes and manners, but it formed a broad segment of society with a relatively homogeneous spiritual culture. As in all other strata and classes the social position of an individual was defined and assigned a value not only by his or her personal achievement but also by family background. Social snobbery divided this stratum into the 'good intelligentsia' and the "masses" of the intelligentsia. However, despite the fact that family background, political ideologies, and educational and personal experience divided the members of the intelligentsia into many substrata, a simple clerk in a patent office was culturally closer to the greatest scholar of his nation than was a wealthy *bourgeois* in the West to his country's outstanding intellectual.

In the last quarter of the twentieth century it is becoming increasingly important for sociologists to draw a clear distinction between intellectuals and the intelligentsia. There are several reasons. In Eastern Europe where the old intelligentsia was replaced by the so-called 'working intelligentsia', the intellectuals have separated themselves into groups of their own.

At the same time a profound change is taking place within the old middle classes of the western society. The increase of 'white-collar workers' accompanied by the overproduction of university graduates has caused the rise of educated but unpropertied and non-business oriented generations. Their place in the social structure of western countries like the United States or England reminds one of the 'university proletariat', as the unemployed part of the old Polish intelligentsia called themselves between the wars. These people are not strictly intellectuals (though often with Ph.D. diplomas in their pockets) but their world-view and social attitudes link them more with the circles of intellectuals than any other social class or strata. Their place in the economic structure of society plus their education make them, as a stratum, similar to the educated part of the 'working intelligentsia' of socialist states.

Within this stratum, groups of dissidents are appearing whose views, political attitudes, feelings of alienation, and non-conformism make them highly similar to the revolutionary wing of the Russian intelligentsia of the turn of the century. We may call them the *incipient groups of the intelligentsia* in the affluent West.

We are emphasizing a distinction between the intellectuals and the intelligentsia because the 'intellectuals are indespensible to society, not just to industrial society . . .' (Shils 1970:51), whereas the intelligentsia appeared only during the processes of industrialization of feudal societies (Gella 1971); while on the one hand it is true that 'an effective collaboration between intellectuals and the authorities which govern society is a requirement for order and continuity of public life . . .' (Shils 1970:51), on the other hand the old intelligentsia as well as those incipient groups of the dissident and revolutionary intelligentsia of affluent societies have formed a stratum of active or potential opposition to the establishment.

After the above presentation of my views on the intelligentsia as an historical social stratum, I should strongly emphasize that it is not my intention to argue that the term be reserved only for socio-historical studies of the old intelligentsia. The use of this term as synonymous with intellectuals is today so common not only because of a lack of understanding of the differences between these two terms, but also because no more proper term has been found to designate two new social phenomena: the 'working intelligentsia' in Russia and Eastern Europe as well as their counterparts in western societies, the well educated but unpropertied segment of the middle class.

Rather than swim against the current, let us accept the various contemporary usages of the term, but without becoming blind in sociological studies to the divergent characteristics of the various groups to which the term intelligentsia is applied. One can differentiate at least seven basic groups of the intelligentsia for comparative studies:

1. The historical 'classical' intelligentsia of Russia and Poland which developed during the nineteenth century and survived in Russia until the Bolshevik Revolution and in Poland until the communist upheavals of 1945.

2. The social groups during the interwar period in Hungary and Czechoslovakia which were called or treated themselves as the intelligentsia.

3. A part of the better-educated and humanistically oriented middle class of the West which together with professional intellectuals have been termed by some sociologists 'the intelligentsia'.

4. The amorphous agglomerate of social groups in the socialist countries which gained the name of the 'working intelligentsia'.

5. The educated strata in new African and Asian nations which compete with the native bourgeoisie for national leadership.

6. The incipient groups of dissident and in part revolutionary intelligentsia which, during approximately the last 20 years, have begun to appear within the affluent societies.

7. The small groups of dissidents in the Soviet Union, and only certain morally and intellectually independent groups in Poland and Czechoslovakia whose social role and place in the social structure resemble very closely the old 'classical' intelligentsia of the nineteenth century.

All these social groups or strata possess certain common characteristics. Today we have separate criteria for defining each of them, but only through an international comparative study can we arrive at a general definition of the new intelligentsia as an actually or potentially influential and powerful component of modern societies.

The seven groups mentioned above can be divided into two types of intelligentsia. The first type could be described as a social stratum, alienated from its own society and having feelings of responsibility for at least the moral leadership of its nation (groups 1, 5, 6 and 7). To the second type belong all those social groups and strata which, as a matter of fact, adopted for themselves the name 'intelligentsia' during the twentieth century but which have little in common with the old East European intelligentsia other than some external characteristics like education and occupation (groups 2, 3 and 4). The intelligentsias of the second type, appearing today in all industrial societies, are incomparably larger than the 'classical' intelligentsia, more heterogeneous, and do not lay claim to national leadership. However, it should be pointed that the intelligentsia in the narrow sense of the term (smaller groups of individuals whose social attitude resembles the classical intelligentsia of the nineteenth century) is, in many cases, appearing within the intelligentsia in this second, the larger sense of the term.

The dissidents of Russia and Eastern Europe as well as dissidents of the affluent societies share basic characteristics reminiscent of the old intelligentsia. They may have divergent political views and ideologies, but their involvement with the socio-cultural and political problems of their nations on the one hand, and their capacity to see these problems from a standpoint larger than that of national interests on the other, make them historical counterparts of the old intelligentsia. Rebelling students and condemned writers in Russia, Poland, Czechoslovakia, Hungary, and Yugoslavia can be considered as the new 'classical' intelligentsia, in status nascendi of modern socialist societies.

After all this has been said, we are in a position to propose a new definition of the intelligentsia as an historical phenomenon which came into existence in Eastern Europe but may appear anywhere else in similar historical conditions. It will be a structural definition.

By comparing the socio-historical conditions in which the old 'classical' intelligentsia developed with the contemporary conditions fostering the emergence of incipient groups of intelligentsia in affluent, democratic societies, as well as groups of dissidents in Soviet Russia and similar groups of Eastern European non-comformists, we are led to the formulation of a new definition of the phenomenon of the intelligentsia—one which goes beyond the simplified but quite common definition of the intelligentsia as a product of backward societies in the period of their socio-economic development.

The intelligentsia stratum develops in a given nation when the educated members of the establishment are unable to face and solve the nation's growing problems. In response, the intelligentsia appears as a new element of the social structure, as a stratum placed between the 'power establishment' on the one hand, and all other classes on the other. And, it is characterized by an objective form of alienation which results both in a negative or revolutionary attitude toward the ruling establishment and in the rejection of the traditionally conservative way of life and roles of the middle and the lower classes. The spiritual case for the formation of this stratum is the accepted calling: *struggle for fundamental socio-political change and help to liberate the lower classes of your nation from their economic and cultural poverty and/or socio-political oppression.*

Beyond the problem of the intelligentsia in the 'classical' sense and the intelligentsia in the larger, western sense of the word, there is for the first time in human history a social phenomenon which can be rightly described as 'world intelligentsia'.

We are living today in an historical moment in which a slow but most essential transformation is taking place—a transformation from national cultures and the civilizations of continents to a more multicultural coexistence and the global civilization. This transformation is not a result of one or other ideology but the consequence of several independent factors in world development. Great danger as well as great promise are the propelling forces of this transformation. The 'classical' intelligentsias appeared, as we pointed out above, in historical periods characterized by the accumulation of social problems which could not be overcome with the help of the intellectuals in the service of a given power establishment. Today in our 'small world' there is a tremendous accumulation of socio-economic problems which not only particular nations but all mankind is facing and must overcome for its own survival. On the one hand, there are the threats of atomic annihilation, global overpopulation, industrial pollution, severe shortages of water and food, and the impending exhaustion of a number of raw materials essential to maintaining the present standard of industrial production. On the other hand, the development of modern economy makes all nations highly dependent on each other; the system of telecommunications creates a platform for mutual understanding; air transportation facilitates personal contacts, and the conquest of the cosmos unites the energy of the nations and stirs hope for unpredictable discoveries. For these reasons we are witnessing a rapid increase in the number of international organizations, associations, commissions, committees, centers, etc. At the same time, an unprecedented growth of scientific communities of a cosmopolitan character is taking place. The fact that scientists have considered themselves as a group above and beyond national boundaries is well known. Edward Shils wrote about them: 'They believe that they belong to a common group because they perform and are committed to the performance of certain types of action and to the maintenance of certain states of mind. . . . They accept in common the discipline of scientific procedure, the unconditional value of truth, and the worthwhileness of striving for it. From this mutuality grows an attachment to one another, not as a person, but as bearers of an outlook.' (Shils 1972:474). Today, however, not only members of scientific communities feel this mutuality, but also thousands of highly educated members of international organizations and associations who employ scientific methods to achieve their world objectives. Members of all these groups have several common characteristics. They are all searching for solutions benefitting all nations; multinational membership of these groups exposes members to the influence of an international or cosmopolitan ethos; their actions aim at more objective goals; if they are true scientists they are advancing the search for truths in their particular fields, and are deeply united by this endeavor. Thus, in our more optimistic moments, we observe the growth of people cooperating with one another in order to secure common goals above and beyond the color of skin, religious dogma, more narrowly defined national interests, or the traditions of their respective countries. (Hay 1962, Gardner 1969, Langrod 1963).

There is of course a more pessimistic prospect as well. In a mass society, the groups of leading intellectuals, especially those of the new and advanced branches of applied sciences and technology, are beginning to live like a caste separated from the rest of the society. Given favorable political conditions, such groups could change a democracy into an oligarchy of intellectuals. Even if modern democracy is, from another viewpoint, more threatened by the emerging ochlocracy, even then the victorious ochlocracy could easily be manipulated by the informally existing and—in such a situation—even more united cast of intellectuals.

To face and overcome the threats as well as to make the best use of modern science and technology, mankind needs not only intellectuals, i.e., groups of academically highly qualified experts, technicians, scientists, scholars and managers; mankind also needs a culturally united *stratum* of educated people communicating and cooperating with one another, oriented toward shared universal goals, and motivated by a set of fundamental values common to all the great moral systems of the world. We could name this the 'world intelligentsia'. The international cooperation of intellectuals, although fragmentary, has lasted for at least three centuries, but as we know it has not been strong enough to deal creatively with the myriad problems which modern society has produced. But if in our own time the pragmatic cooperation of intellectuals will be backed by a large stratum of people educated in the best humanistic tradition to be not only professionals but also carriers of those universal values which mankind needs for survival, then we may be able to look to the future with a reasonable hopefulness.

NOTES

1. In this respect, my position is close to that of Frank Parkin who believes that if Marx were alive today, he would recognize in the intelligentsia of socialist

societies an ascending class capable of formulating, introducing, and carrying out the changes necessary for the modern world. (Parkin 1971).

2. The notion of 'social stratum' is vague, and almost every author gives it a slightly different meaning. In general one can say this term is used in at least three basic ways: (1) to distinguish groups determined by such natural factors as age, sex, health, stature, etc.; (2) to point out divisions according to income, prestige and power; or (3) to name these objectively existing segments of society which are not social classes in the strict Marxist sense, i.e., which do not directly determine the economic structure of society.

Oskar Lange utilized the Marxism concept of 'superstructure' to define social strata; he saw them as consisting of groups basically characterized by serving and maintaining a given 'superstructure', like civil servants, soldiers, police, and clergy. (Lange 1967).

In the present work I am not attempting to advance a general theory of social strata, but I should at least explain my use of the term. I follow a modified Marxist position. I understand by social stratum not a mere statistical or description category imposed upon the phenomena by sociologists, but rather an objectively existing social entity which can be actually discerned in societies and which can be described as coming into objective existence and ceasing to exist, and as having discoverable objective properties.

3. Thus, for example, *Webster's New International Dictionary* defines intelligentsia as: 'Informed intellectual people collectively; the educated or professional group, class or party—often derisive.' (Webster 1939).

4. All the other classes and strata which have existed in Eastern Europe have had their counterparts in the West. Even if the Russian or Rumanian *boyar* or the polish *szlachcic* were not always similar to the French or British nobleman, it was possible to compare the role and position of their classes. Similarly comparable are all the factions of the middle class, the peasantry and the workers from the various countries of the world.

5. In my research on the social stratification in Eastern Europe during the last four years, I have noticed that the only country in which extensive study of the intelligentsia as a social stratum has been undertaken is Poland. There were many publications concerning the Polish intelligentsia between the wars (Gella 1971:3). But after the war a vigorous discussion arose in the fresh ruins of Warsaw, inspired by J. Chalasinski's monograph on the genealogy of the Polish intelligentsia (Chalasinski 1946). For years J. Szczepanski edited a series of monographs on the working class and the intelligentsia (Szczepanski 1961-70's). This mortally wounded social stratum, which, having lost 35 percent of its members during the war (Olszewicz 1947), was passing through its deepest structural change, vigorously discussed its own nature, functions, duties, goals and fate. The national dispute about the intelligentsia in the late 1940's and 1950's attracted the participation of Poland's outstanding intellectuals.

6. Those who study the history of the Russian intelligentsia cannot achieve a mature understanding of this stratum if they overlook the historical relations between the Russian and Polish strata of those two Slavic nations. Dozens of articles and many books entirely or partially devoted to the Russian intelligentsia are available in English. Well known are the following: Masaryk (1919), Fisher (1924), Trotsky (1925), Freeman (1930), Nomad (1932), Berdyaev (1948 and 1960), Land (1959), Pipes (1961), Raeff (1966), Black (1967), Pomper (1970), Lipset and Dobson (1972), Skilling, Griffiths (1971), Parkin (1971), Churchward (1973). Also, a large number of the works by representatives of the Russian revolutionary intelligentsia are available in English, as well as many works of the contemporary Soviet dissidents which in a direct or indirect way present the problems of their own social environment. Although from a sociological view-point the Polish intelligentsia and its history are no less interesting than the Russian one, very much less attention has been paid to it because its development took place in the time when Poland was erased from the map of Europe, when opinions about Poles and Poland were propagated by the governments and diplomacy of her oppressors, and since the Russian empire—one fascinating to western readers—has thrown a shadow of obscurity on its defeated neighbour. Therefore, there are only a few articles on the Polish intelligentsia available in English: Hertz (1951), Borucki (1962), Szczepanski (1961, 1962), Matejko (1966), Gella (1971). The only author who has written a book on the narrow circle of the creative intelligentsia in communist Poland is Cz. Milosz (1953).

7. An essential difference in the origin of these two intelligentsias was that the Russian stratum, developing in its own state where all important governmental positions were occupied by the aristocracy, consisted, to a vastly larger extent than in Poland, of people of the lower classes. These people became alienated from their society in part by the western ideas with which their education had made them familiar. But in contrast, the Polish intelligentsia did not need to be westernized. The term 'westernization' does not exist in Polish because Poland was for a thousand years a frontier of western civilization.

8. An interesting document of the intelligentsia's separation from other members of middle and lower classes was its code of honor (Wladyslaw Boziewicz 1939). One of the rules of this code said that the right and privilege to challenge or accept a duel was possessed only by a man who had a *gimnazium* diploma (this diploma allowed its bearer to enter this stratum without regard to his family background). This code was an interesting formalization of the mediaeval idea of honor; imposed under penalty of ostracism, it was part of the cultural tradition of the old upper classes, which the Polish intelligentsia adopted.

9. The main historical works dealing with the problem of the origin and development of the Polish intelligentsia were published not at the time when this stratum occupied a privileged position in national life, but in communist Poland: Janusz Zarnowski (1964), Tadeusz Lepkowski (1967), Jerzy Jedlicki (1968),

M. Dobrzanska, A. Wallis, (1971) and Bohdan Cywinski (1971). The last of these authors, although his work deals with the development of the Polish intelligentsia in the second half of the 19th century (title: *Genealogy of the Non-Submissive*) was one of three Polish literary works of early 1970's which caused an intervention of the Soviet ambassador in Warsaw (the two other works dealt also with the history of Poland).

10. The old intelligentsia acquired group self-consciousness very late. For example, Ludwik Gumplowicz, himself a member of the Polish intelligentsia which at his time has begun to dominate the social and intellectual life of partitioned Poland, did not notice this development as a social phenomenon. His case seems to be especially revealing, because in the countries of semifeudal social structure the upward mobility and participation in national and intellectual life for persons of Jewish origin (such as Gumplowicz) became possible only with the appearance of the intelligentsia (Gella 1966).

11. Hitler and his chief lieutenants openly expressed the significance of the liquidation of the Polish intelligentsia. Hitler explained to his nation: 'Poles should have only one master, and this master should be German. There cannot exist two masters side by side, and, therefore, the representatives of the Polish intelligentsia ought to be murdered, I repeat, murdered.' Stalin murdered (in Katyn Forest and in many other unknown places of martyrdom) 42 percent of the officer corps of the Polish army, his prisoners of war (about 15,000 people), among them many scholars, scientists and professionals who were mobilized into the army in 1939. Beside this, tens of thousands of the Polish intelligentsia died of hunger and starvation in the concentration camps and areas of settlement in the east Soviet republics where during the period 1939-1941 about 1.5 million Poles were deported. See: Fitz-Gibbon (1971), Zawodny (1962).

12. The term 'intelligentsia' began being used in Hungary after the Trianon Treaty, when, as before in partitioned Poland, a number of expropriated landowners and administrators from the former provinces of the Hungarian kingdom had to settle in the cities. Also in the new Republic of Czechoslovakia (1918-38) the term was in use to designate those educated members of the middle class who did not exactly fit the category of 'bourgeoisie' and had secured high intellectual aspirations and/or achievements.

Discussing the problem of the 'proletarizations of the intelligentsia', Karl Mannheim (basing his views on Walter M. Kotsching's *Unemployment in the Learned Professions*), described this situation in the countries of the former Austrian empire: 'After the War Rumania, Hungary, Yugoslavia, Czechoslovakia, and others built up new bureauocracies out of their own stock, and offered the indigenous middle classes, the peasantry, and urban bourgeoisie new chances of social advancement, and of assimilation with the educated class. They encouraged them to speak their native language, to foster a literature of their own, to build up a national press and so on.' (Mannheim 1940:99).

13. In Poland until 1945 the form for addressing one person to another was different among the intelligentsia (and upper classes as well) than among the lower classes. The former used a courtly form: the third person singular plus 'pan' (sir). It is the form which in English is used only in conversation with a king or queen. The lower classes, on the other hand, used the second person plural 'wy' (English 'you' or French 'vous'). After 1945 this form was administratively imposed on all classes. However, despite 30 years of communist party rule, it is the 'wy' which has disappeared, while everybody has become 'pan'.

14. The term 'working intelligentsia' entails a redundancy, since the intelligentsia were working people by definition. The communist parties wanted, however, to distinguish the 'working intelligentsia' from the petit bourgeoisie, which in those countries survived in the segment of economic life called 'private initiative' and lived on the cultural level similar to the masses of the new 'intelligentsia'. However, the term was also in use by some non-Marxist authors in Poland even before World War II.

15. Whereas the old stratum was often accused by Marxists of being a 'prostitute' among the social classes and strata, the communist governments have taken pride from the fact that the new one, the 'working intelligentsia', the merit of which is service and obedience to the party, has been rapidly increasing. In 1936, 80-90 percent of the entire soviet intelligentsia originated from the peasantry and working class (Rozental, Judin 1954). 'Over 200,000 "intellectual workers" join the Soviet party annually;' in 1970 it included '5.5 million specialists in various fields of knowledge,' (*World Strength of the Communist Party Organization,* 23rd Annual Report, Washington 1971, p. 78 and 80).

16. The most fascinating phenomenon of the rebirth of the intelligentsia is the group of Soviet citizens associated with the Moscow Human Rights Committee (founded in November 1970). Although the founding members of the committee were three physicists, Andrei D. Saharov, Andrei N. Tverdokhlebov and Valery N. Chalidze, its supporters and followers are drawn from all kinds of professions and callings and include many different philosophical orientations and social backgrounds. Alexander Solsenitsyn became a model not only for the Human Rights Movement but for the newly appearing 'classical' intelligentsia as well.

17. In the present work I have been treating the intelligentsia as a social stratum as Marxists do. It is my expectation, however, that, because of present growth, and its increasing significance for modern techno-economic development, as well as because of its informal subdivisions and the influence of its higher substrata on the decision-making process, sociologists will very soon be inclined to consider the intelligentsia (in the larger sense of the term) as a 'new class'. I should make it clear that M. Djilas concept of the 'new class' concerns above all the people of the party apparatus; he calls them 'bureaucrats' (Djilas 1957:38), whereas I would argue that the entire body of the new intelligentsia will soon

go beyond the stage of an amorphous agglomerate into the position of a dominating class. This tendency exists in both socialist and capitalist societies.

REFERENCES

Beerman, Friedrich (1972), Declaration attached to the official record of plenary session of Bundestag, May 17, (*Na Antenie*, X, no. 112-113, p. 5).

Benda, Julian (1927), *La Trahison des clercs*. Paris.

Berdyaev, Nicholas (1960), *The Origin of Russian Communism*. Ann Arbor.

——— (1948), *The Russian Idea*. New York.

Black, Cyril E. (ed.) (1967), *The Transformation of Russian Society: Aspects of Social Change Since 1861*. Cambridge.

Borucki, Andrzej (1962), 'Study of the Socio-Occupational Position of the Pre-War Intelligentsia in People's Poland', *Polish Sociological Bulletin*, 1-2, pp. 131-140.

Boziewicz, Wladyslaw (1939), *Polski kodeks honorowy*. Warszawa (8th edition).

Carlston, Kennth S. (1962) *Law and Organization in World Society*. Urbana.

Chalasinski, Josef (1946), *Spoleczna genealogia inteligencji polskiej*. Warszawa

Churchward, L. G. (1973), *The Soviet Intelligentsia: an essay on the social structure and roles of Soviet Intellectuals during the 1960's*. London.

Cywinski, Bogdan (1971), *Rodowody niepokornych*. Warszawa.

Djilas, Milovan (1954), *The New Class: An analysis of the communist system*. New York.

Dobrzanska, M. and A. Wallis (1971), *Inteligencja polaka XIX i XX wieku*. Wroclaw.

Fisher, Louis (1924), 'Soviet Recognition of the Intellectual', *Current History*, **XXXVI**.

Fitz-Gibbon, Louis (1971), *Katyn a Crime without Parallel*. London.

Freeman, Joseph et al. (1930), *Voices of October, Art and Literature in Russia*. New York.

Gardner, Richard N. (1964), *In Pursuit of World Order, US Foreign Policy and ·International Organizations*. New York.

Geiger, Theodor (1949), *Die Stellung der Intelligenz in der Gesellschaft*. Stuttgart.

Gella, Aleksander (1966), *Ewolucjonizm a poczatki socjologii: L. Gumplowicz— L. F. Ward*. Wroclaw.

——— (1971) 'The Life and Death of the Polish Intelligentsia,' *Slavic Review*. **30**, (1).

Hay, Peter (1966), *Federalism and Supranational Organizations: Patterns for New Legal Structures.* Urbana.

Hertz, Alexander (1951), 'The Case of an Eastern European Intelligentsia', *Journal of Central European Affairs.* 11, (1).

Jedlicki, Jerzy (1968), *Klejnot i bariery spoleczne.* Warszawa.

Komorowski, Zygmunt (1969), 'Studenci-przyszlosc Afryki', *Kultura i Spoleczenstwo,* XIII, (3).

Kulczycki, Ludwick (1910-1914), *Geschichte der russischen Revolution* 103, Gotha.

Lang, David M. (1959), *The First Russian Radical: Alexander Radishchev 1979-1802.* London.

Lange, Oskar (1967), *Ekonomia polityczna.* I, Zagadnienia ogolne (4th edition). Warszawa.

Langrod, Georges (1963), *The International Civil Service, its origins, its nature, its evolution.* Leyden.

Lepkowski, Tadeusz (1967), *Polska-narodziny nowoczesnego narodu 1764-1870.* Warszawa.

Lipset, Seymour M. and Richard B. Dobson (1972), 'The Intellectual as Critic and Rebel', *Daedalus* (Summer).

Mannheim, Karl (1936), *Ideology and Utopia,* New York (quoted from Harvest Books pbk. edition).

——— (1940), *Man and Society in the Age of Reconstruction.* New York: Harcourt (1st edition in German, Leiden. Holland.

Masaryk, T. G. (1919), *The Spirit of Russia.* London.

Matejko, Alexander (1966), 'Status Inconsequence in the Polish Intelligentsia,' *Social Research,* No. 4.

Matthwes, Mervyn (1972), *Class and Society in Soviet Russia.* New York.

Michels, Robert (1932), 'Intellectuals', *Encyclopedia of the Social Sciences.*

Milosz, Czeslaw (1953), *The Captive Mind.* New York.

Nettl, J. P. (1970), 'Ideas, Intellectuals and Structures of Dissent' in Philip Rieff (ed.) *On Intellectuals.* Garden City.

Nomad, Max (1932), *Rebels and Renegades.* New York.

Olszewicz, Boleslaw (1947), *Lista strat kultury polskiej.* Wroclaw.

Parkin, Frank (1971), *Class Inequality and Political Order: Social stratification in capitalist and communist societies.* London.

Pipes, Richard (ed.) (1961), *The Russian Intelligentsia.* New York.

Pollard, Allan (1964), 'The Russian Intelligentsia: The mind of Russia', *California Slavic Studies,* No. 3.

Pomper, Philip (1970), *The Russian Revolutionary Intelligentsia,* New York.

Raeff, Marc (1966), *Origins of the Russian Intelligentsia: The Eighteenth-Century Nobility.* New York.

Rozental, M. and P. Judin (1954), *Karotkey Filozofitskey Slovar.* Moscow.

Rutgers, S. J. (1921), 'The Intellectuals and the Russian Revolution', In Lenin, N.

et al. *The New Policies of Soviet Russia.* Chicago.

Seton-Watson, G. H. N. (1965), 'Intelligentsia' in Julius Gould and William L. Kolb, *A Dictionary of Social Sciences;* completed under UNESCO auspices, New York.

Shils, Edward (1968), 'Intellectuals', *International Encyclopedia of the Social Sciences.*

––– (1970), 'The Intellectuals and the Powers: Some Perspectives for Comparative Analysis', in Philip Rieff (ed.) *On Intellectuals.* New York.

––– (1972), 'Color, the University Intellectual Community and Afro-Asian Intellectual' in his *The Intellectual and the Powers and other Essays.* Chicago, London.

Skilling, H. Gordon and Franklin Griffiths (eds.) (1971), *Interest Groups in Soviet Politics.* Princeton.

Szczepanski, Jan (1959), 'Inteligencja a pracownicy umyslowi', *Przeglad Socjologiczny,* **13,** (2).

––– (1961), 'Problems of Sociological Research on the Polish Intelligentsia', *Polish Sociological Bulletin,* No. 1.

––– (1962), 'The Polish Intelligentsia. Past and Present', *World Politics,* **14** (3).

––– (1961-1970's), *Z Badan klasy robotniczej i inteligencji,* Wroclaw.

Theodorson, G. A. and Theodorson, A. G. (1969), *Modern Dictionary of Sociology.* New York.

Trotsky, Leon (1925), *Literature and Revolution.* New York.

Webster's New International Dictionary of the English Language (1939), Second edition, **II,** 1291, Springfield.

Zarnowski, Janusz (1964), *Struktuna Spoleczna inteligencji w latach 1918-1939,* Warszawa.

Zawodny, Janusz (1962), *Death in Forest: The Story of the Katyn Forest Massacre.* Notre Dame.

I

THEORETICAL AND METHODOLOGICAL PROBLEMS IN STUDIES OF THE INTELLIGENTSIA AND THE INTELLECTUALS

METHODOLOGICAL PROBLEMS IN COMPARATIVE STUDIES OF THE INTELLIGENTSIA

Peter C Ludz
University of Munich
and *New School for Social Research, New York*

THE LEVEL OF THEORY

Comparative studies of the intelligentsia cover a broad range of research work. Thus, from the methodological perspective, restriction to a limited and well-defined point of view is an indispensable requirement. In conveying the methodological problems such studies confront, some preliminary specifications are necessary.

Our concern is the 'intelligentsia', not *the* elite or specific elites. The term intelligentsia indicates a larger and more diffuse stratum than that of elite. Cultural, political, bureaucratic and other elites can be conceived as composing parts of a whole called the intelligentsia. However, the link between elites and the stratum of intelligentsia is not automatic, but rather consists in the degrees to which the particular elite or individual displays that sense of 'critical-utopian' outlook which characterizes the intelligentsia. This then allows for the logical possibility that, as illustrated in the present day, members of different elite groups need not necessarily belong to the intelligentsia. In addition, members of the intelligentsia can conceivably be either engaged in the institutional structure of the society or disengaged from it.

The place of the critical-utopian intelligentsia within the social structure is extremely difficult to determine, since these groups and individuals constantly change their professional positions. This holds for the present as well as for the past. Concerning the past, we need refer here only to one example from German history: Karl Gutzkow, who was one of the most prominent heads of the intelligentsia movement called the German *Vormärz* (1830-48), developed from a freelance political and literary writer to a financially successful and established dramatist.

The foregoing remarks lead to an historical observation regarding the intelligentsia: as conceived here, it exists in only one historico-sociological culture, that of the Euro-American civilization in the time span of the bourgeois-industrial era in the early nineteenth century to the present day.

The methodological problems discussed here range within these specified conceptual and socio-cultural dimensions. (Clearly, in such a discussion we are not directing our interest to the narrower or technical sense of the word 'methodology'.)

In the history of our dicipline methodological reflection on the intelligentsia, goes back to the early *Wissenssoziologie* (sociology of knowledge) and, particularly, to Karl Mannheim. On the other hand, contemporary study of the intelligentsia is rooted in the early twentieth century German sociology of religion (Max Weber, Ernst Troeltsch, Joachim Wach).

Karl Mannheim developed the concept of the 'free-floating intelligentsia' *(freischwebende Intelligenz)*, taking the terminology over from Alfred Weber. His achievement resides in that he manages to relate, at an intrinsic level, modes of thought *(Denkweisen)* to group acting. Here also lies the main characteristic of his methodology.

In his *Ideology and Utopia,*[1] Mannheim defines and describes the intelligentsia as follows: 'In every society there are social groups whose special task is to provide an interpretation of the world for that society. We call these the "intelligentsia".' The medieval clergy performed this task. In the modern industrial societies this intelligentsia has been replaced by a 'free intelligentsia', whose 'chief characteristic is that it is increasingly recruited from constantly varying social strata and life-situations, and that its mode of thought is no longer subject to regulation by a caste-like organization.' The free social status of this intelligentsia is determined by its tasks and vice versa: the intelligentsia's 'experimental outlook, unceasingly sensitive to the dynamic nature of society and to its wholeness, is not likely to be developed by a class occupying a middle position but only by a relatively classless stratum which is not too firmly situated in the social order.'

Such definition and description of the intelligentsia result from Mannheim's generalization of those sociological characteristics which can be observed in the literary societies of the eighteenth and nineteenth centuries. For France, the *écrivains* and their role in the *salons* serve as an example. For Germany, we refer to those groups whose members were termed, by their opponents, 'ideologues and philosophizers', i.e., to the Young Hegelians, the Young Germans and the early romantic poets. Concerning the representatives of these differing social groups, Mannheim extracted a general tendency: all of them intended to explain and evaluate their own social position and, using this as a starting-point, to locate other social groups and strata in society. Thus, this intelligentsia bases its (self-appointed) mission on its consciousness of its own social position.

In general, the sociology of knowledge supplies us with at least two prerequisites of all questioning concerning the intelligentsia: (a) The problems of the intelligentsia have to be put into a specific, historical, political, and sociological context. This means that in dealing with the intelligentsia, we must include the early bourgeois or the 'civil' society in our frame of reference. (b) Research on the intelligentsia cannot be severed from its connections with *Geistesgeschichte,* since in one way or another the intelligentsia is always representative of the 'spirit of the age' *(Zeitgeist).*

Our considerations now are meant to follow up some of the questions put by the early sociology of knowledge as well as the sociology of religion. From the methodological point of view there are three major problems to be discussed: First, who belongs to the intelligentsia?; second, what functions does the intelligentsia perform in society?; third, how is the intelligentsia organized?

As to the first question, the hard core of the intelligentsia consists generally of writers, philosophers, journalists etc. Regarding the second question, the answer given by the sociology of knowledge has continuously been: within society the intelligentsia is the 'carrier' or representative of ideology or ideologies.

Such an answer provokes an additional set of questions concerning 'ideology'. In a sociological understanding, what is ideology? In the context at hand we can answer this broad question only by pointing out that, in contemporary social science research, ideology has often been described as performing specific functions, such as: an activating and directive function; a function of articulating a self-image and a world-view; a critical function; an apologetic function etc. In discerning the functions of ideology on a descriptive level, sociologists are able to conduct comparative studies of the intelligentsia. They can compare these differing functions and relate them to differing social groups in different societies.

In the preliminary steps of such an approach, recourse must be made to the concept of ideology created by Karl Marx. That concept must, though, be immediately qualified since Marx designed it to serve a multitude of functions. Besides providing criteria for a descriptive approach, Marx's concept of ideology was mainly conceived as a 'weapon' to fight the early bourgeoisie. It served to unmask the bourgeois politico-social order and to charge the bourgeoisie with 'false consciousness'.

This militant function of the Marxian concept is clearly of little service to modern sociology. Ideology must rather be regarded as a relational concept that links together specific forms of consciousness and specific historical situations; that is, a concept which permits us to conceive of a specific social group (and this means a specific social organization) as being representative of a specific consciousness.

The third problem asked: how is the intelligentsia organized? Or put otherwise, what forms of organization do certain groups of the intelligentsia choose within society? Are such organizational settings as secret societies, or sects, or the *Bund,* preferred? Or are loose groupings of the type of professional organizations favored? We can find typical characteristics of secret societies, for example, in Germany and France in the late eighteenth and the early nineteenth centuries as well as, in this century, in the protest groups of the sixties. Thus, studies on the intelligentsia have not only to make reference to specific social groups;

but they also should investigate the organization and the ideology/
utopia of these groups.

With this in mind, we arrive at a sociologically defined concept of
ideology. Ideology/utopia can be distinguished according to its degree
of intensity, and such distinctions may be arranged on a continuum.
Likewise the degree of social integration can be arranged on a continuum of socially-engaged/socially-disengaged. The continua can be
related: Full (intense) ideology/utopia would correspond to full social
disengagement of the 'carrier(s)' of ideology, and would define the
intelligentsia as holders of a marginal social position. Full social integration of the carrier(s) of ideology, on the other hand, would correspond
to a less intense, a broken, impoverished ideology/utopia. In other
words, through correlating these continua we would connect ideas with
social structures, that is, interrelate ideology, intelligentsia, and
organization.

If conceptualized in this way, comparative studies of the European-
American intelligentsia are free of the burden of fundamental methodological problems. Within the limits of the given cultural frame, this
statement covers comparative studies of historical and present day, of
Eastern and Western national strata. The major problems of such
research thus shift from the level of theory to that of the substantive.
In a given historical, social, and political situation of one or several
nations we thus ask: what ideology is represented by what group with
what form of organization?

ONE CASE HISTORY[2]

The *Bund der freien Männer* (Brotherhood of Free Men, 1794-99)
provides a heuristically useful—and, in terms of the existing literature,
original—case for the substantiation of the approach outlined above.
The Bund, a group of intellectuals, came into being during that period
in which Johann Gottlieb Fichte, the renown German idealist philosopher, was teaching at the university of Jena. This coincidence of events

is not accidental: it rather indicates how decisively Fichte, who was himself a member of the Bund for some years, influenced both in his person and through his thinking the members of that organization. In addition, it is not accidental that the Bund was established in Jena. Jena, at that time, was a major intellectual center in Germany. Here the lines of republicanism and national pathos crossed and the classical culture of nearby Weimar met with early romanticism, represented by the groups of thinkers who coalesced around Friedrich and August Wilhelm von Schlegel. Moreover, at the university, in addition to Fichte, Schelling, Schiller, Hufeland, Paulus, de Wette, and Thibaut were teaching.

The Bund is a predecessor of the philosophical conventicles and marginal secret societies which began to appear a few years later. At its peak, the Bund had 34 members, all of them students and most coming from bourgeois and petit-bourgeois backgrounds. Some studied theology, philosophy, or literature, others law or medicine. A few were later to become famous in their own right.

The Bund was organized like a reading and educational society. Its statutes were taken from the 'laws' of a 'Society of Free Men', which had existed in Jena before and had been dissolved in 1793. The 'laws' had been published in the *Neuer Teutscher Merkur,* attached to a comment demanding the institution of small elitist circles that would reform the 'social life'. This demand, which the Bund endorsed and which also dominated Schleiermacher's work *Versuch einer Theorie des geselligen Betragens* (attempt at a theory of social conduct, 1799), is characteristic of a transitional period in German history represented among others by the Bund. The Bund found itself attached to both the feudal society as well as to the early bourgeois society. Contrary to later comparable organizations, such as the Brotherhood of the Just *(Bund der Gerechten)* or the Brotherhood of the Outlaws *(Bund der Geächteten),* the *Bund der freien Männer* did not intend to overthrow the established order, but to reform it.

The Bund had statutes to regulate the proceedings of its meetings. It also used a 'protocol book', in which the proceedings of each meeting were put down. However, there existed no detailed statutes designed to bind the members in their personal lives. Furthermore, the Bund lacked both an hierarchical organization and a marked, stereotyped language of procedure. But the organizational characteristics of the Bund included: exclusive admission rites and the limitation of number of members. Thus the Bund is distinguished by some organizational features typical of the radical craftsmen and intelligentsia groups which one generation later would help to spread political and social ideologies.

The Bund discussions focused almost exclusively on problems of mankind, on man as a morally acting person in his society and state. Radical republicanism of the French Enlightenment and the romantic totality oriented philosophy of Goethe's times, admittedly reduced in scope, had been subjected to synthesizing efforts by the members of the Bund. In later years, in the ideologies of the secret societies and also in Marx's thought, such synthesizing was developed in more radical form and gained an explosive power.

In some programmatic pamphlets of the Bund the social life of the feudal society is characterized as 'empty'. The 'few' (i.e., those who are striving for more meaningful social contacts) are told that it is their moral duty to gather in small social groups in order to free themselves from social prejudices and to worship a lifestyle based on reason. Thus the 'few' are distinguished from the 'masses'. The masses are to be enlightened by the few. This elitist and isolationist social character of the Bund is also evident in various discussions on the social position of its members. As can be gathered from two lectures given by an influential member of the Bund by the name of Moeller, one on 'Secret Societies' and the other on 'The Universal History of Despotism', these discussions went so far as to apply the concept of 'secrecy', of a 'secret society' to the *Bund der freien Männer*.

The elitist view can also be found in Fichte's thinking. Fichte, on his part, distinguished between two principal social strata, the populace and the learned: 'For the populace only that action which is immediately caused is perceived; foresight is the prerogative of the learned.' More generally speaking, this view expresses a basic and latent conflict of the bourgeois and industrial societies—a conflict which only in later years becomes manifest. Its ideological supersession and objectification as well as the insecure social status of the members of the Bund, and of the members of comparable later organizations, lead to a building tension.

A further characteristic of the Bund is the quality of awareness of common tasks, a quality manifest in the friendship cult. In the case of the Bund, the cult of friendship mitigated its social isolation and outside position—that situation personified, in the extreme, in the case of Hölderlin. The emphasis on the value of friendship furthered the experience of commonness and of the totality of the Bund; also the structure of the Bund provided support and shelter. The commitment between the members within the Bund reflected each individual's overriding commitment to the brotherhood. A total engagement on the part of each member corresponded to the totality of his vision and to the fully introverted attitude which characterizes his social outlook.

Historically, the romantic-Jacobin organization of friendship, as we may call it, was the first step of self-centered, marginal groups—the intellectual emancipation being an expression of their political and social emancipation. One generation later the stress on politics can be seen as an outgrowth of that earlier social emancipation. In both cases, the earlier and the later, however, the social realm provided the proper criterion and medium of emancipation. In both cases, furthermore, reflections on man and his destiny were linked to utopian visions of a better social order and to a critique of the existing social system. This indicates that all intellectual orientation was preshaped by pro-and-con views concerning the existing social order. Thus, the social dimension entered even the most abstract discussions of the Bund. In both cases, finally, the critics themselves, being members of marginal or semi-marginal ideological groups, believed that through critique they would be able to assess their own social position. Their self-image was tied in with their critique of the existing society, with their wish to introduce new social values and criteria of prestige.

The rather mild utopian critique of the existing feudal society was linked to an utopian volition. The strong adherence to the esoteric-aesthetic and the worship of the artist's genius—which to the members of the Bund were the only possibility of a non-alienated and productive attitude towards life—corresponded to their partial intellectual and social integration into the existing society.

CONCLUDING REMARKS

The interrelation of ideological and organizational manifestations typical of intelligentsia groups have been illustrated by the example of the *Bund der freien Männer*. The methodological concept allows investigation of any number of other groups, past or present. The investigative methodology which we have described and applied can serve a multidimensional descriptive approach and thus can facilitate the conceptualization of cross-national and cross-historical studies.

NOTES

1. Karl Mannheim, *Ideology and Utopia: An Introduction to the Sociology of Knowledge* (Transl. from the German by Louis Wirth and Edward Shils, New York: Harcourt, Brace and World, n.d.; German edition, 1929).

2. For references cf. Peter C. Ludz, 'Ideologie, Intelligenz und Organisation', *Jahrbuch fur Sozialwissenschaft*, XV (no. 1, 1964), 82-114, reprinted in: Peter C. Ludz: *Ideologiebegriff und marxistische Theorie. Ansätze zu einer immanenten Kritik*. Opladen: Westdeutscher Verlag, 1976, pp. 123-153.

3

WHAT IS AN INTELLECTUAL?

Lewis S Feuer
University of Virginia

What is an 'intellectual'? Weber tells us that by 'intellectuals' he understands 'a group of men who by virtue of their peculiarity have special access to certain achievements considered to be "culture values", and who, therefore, usurp the leadership of a culture community.' (Gerth & Mills 1946:17). Parsons in this vein regards the 'intellectual' as a 'cultural specialist', as one who places cultural considerations above social ones in defining his primary role. (Rieff, 1969: 4,7). These definitions arouse misgivings. Let us consider, for instance, such whole classes of educated persons as mathematicians and musicians. They are exponents of cultural values, and may regard themselves as leaders of a cultural community. Their outlook on social existence may be altogether in terms of their cultural values; they may be indifferent to everything except their mathematics and music. Yet such persons are often not regarded as intellectuals. The fact of the matter is that for many years of its usage, it was not necessarily enough for a person to be involved in a cultural occupation or profession to be classified as an 'intellectual'.

Moreover, there is a further ambiguity about the phrase 'cultural considerations'. At any given historical interval, educated persons fall into two classes, those at home with the cultural life of their times, and others that are discontented. The discontented, or the malcontents, often condemn their contemporary culture. In doing so, they may invoke the values of a past era, or the values of primitive peoples or foreign civilizations, or some presumably transcendental values; it is not that they place cultural considerations above the social, but rather that they are at odds with their contemporary cultural setting. Generally speaking, to call a person an 'intellectual' is to suggest that in some basic way he stands against or apart from the contemporary dominant culture. The cultural standpoint, the cultural frame of reference, in terms of which he evaluates his society and its culture, are chosen from Other Worlds, other times in the past or presumable future, or other societies. The intellectual is one, in this sense, who chooses to estrange himself from the cultural superstructure. Consequently, the intellectual at the outset has been regarded as one who for individual psychological reasons stands outside the equilibrium of social structure and culture.

Thus the American usage of 'intellectual' from its first appearance in 1898 until 1930 tended to be a pejorative one; in the overwhelming majority of the cases in which it was used it was encased with warning quotation-marks or the admonitory 'so-called'. In Europe, however, to be among *die Intelligenz* in Germany, or the *Intelligenty* in Russia, or *les intellectuels* in France generally signified that the persons in question were of the educated, professional middle class as opposed to the commercial or industrial one. The term was honorific rather than pejorative.

In defining intellectuals, we must, therefore, bear in mind two sets of considerations, structural and historical. On the structural side, we must deal with three coordinates: to define intellectuals, we must, first, specify their occupations and social situations, second, explicate their emotional-psychological standpoint which may indeed differentiate them from their fellow 'cultural specialists', and third, indicate in what way their mode of thinking differs from that of other educated persons. On the historical side, we must take note that the social meaning of 'intellectuals' has shifted basically during the last 70 years, and both the divergence and continuity of meaning should be defined.

The term 'les intellectuels' first acquired widespread usage in France in 1898 as a consequence of the 'manifeste des intellectuels' evoked by the Dreyfus Case. Its meaning was then clearly indicated by Brunětière, the first also to use it derisively. It signified persons of high scholarly or scientific standing, distinguished writers or professors or artists, who presumed to represent the nation's conscience on basic political questions. To Brunetière it was outlandish that a person who had spent his life studying Sanskrit, for instance, or astronomy, should, therefore, presume to represent the community's conscience. Certainly they were 'cultural specialists' but their philological or astronomical culture was scarcely relevant to or made them more qualified to judge moral and political questions than any other persons. The old priesthood had claimed to be exclusively devoted to moral values. But the scientists and scholars themselves proclaimed that science was neutral, that it had nothing to say on the truth or falsehood of values. How could they claim, therefore, that their scientific or cultural specialties made them in any way the keeper of the communal conscience?

A new definition of 'intellectuals' thus began to emerge: the intellectuals were that section of the educated class which had aspirations to political power either directly by seeking to be society's political rulers or indirectly by directing its conscience and decisions.

An educated or professional class which had no aspiration to political power was simply not regarded as composed of intellectuals. In Great Britain, for instance, until 1950, the graduates of universities had the special privilege of electing 12 members of Parliament. Of the more than 100 of such members who were elected from 1918 to 1950 not a single one belonged to the socialist Labour Party. The elected members were persons who in no way challenged the values of the community, or claimed to constitute its conscience. Thus an English philosopher said as late as 1956 that his country did not have an intelligentsia; its educated stratum, in his view, devoted its energies to its professional activity, and had little time for 'dangerous speculation'. (Hampshire, 1956: 457). There were no cafés where footloose intellectuals congregated restlessly. The educated Englishman, according to the *Times Literary Supplement,* prided himself that 'Oxford and Cambridge are more in touch with reality than the Ecole Normale Supérieure', and that the existence of an 'intelligentsia' was an 'abnormal' phenomenon, an aberration in countries which took the political views of their novelists seriously. (*Times Literary Supplement,* 1955: 533). There was not a sense of alienation, as it is called, among the British educated as well as among most of the American educated until 1930. And when a sense of alienation does arise it is hard to attribute it to the alleged cultural values that they have safeguarded, and to which they give a priority over their social interests. For what are the cultural values transmitted in universities? A student in his courses on philosophy will read Plato, Aristotle, Hobbes, Hegel, Hume and Nietzsche; perhaps the only classical philosopher who was a liberal democrat was Spinoza; most of the others were authoritarians and anti-democrats. In Britain, many graduates nurtured on Plato and Aristotle went out to work in the colonial service, to rule an empire as philosopher-kings. But they were scarcely to be regarded nor did they regard themselves as 'intellectuals'. Not, however, the cultural tradition was significant but rather the sense imbibed that the cultured were ideally the political elite.

The exemplar for the use of 'intellectual' came in the United States in the early nineteen-hundreds. Sociologically, it embraced two kinds of persons, those from the working class, especially in New York's East Side, who were filled with cultural longings, for the boldly questioning modern literature and science, and with the political vision of a socialist world in which people like themselves would be the guiding elite. The second group was composed of well-to-do young men of the middle and upper classes, moved to identify themselves with the lowly in a back-to-the-people spirit, and proposing too to provide the latter with its guiding elite. The intellectual, as it was used first, had an element of the déclassé; he was a workingman who read more than a university undergraduate; he was a man from the upper classes who rejected his origins.

Always the intellectual regarded himself as somehow the chosen; he had a mission conferred upon him as a modern Moses by history. And this sense of mission is intrinsic to the consciousness of the intellectual. It goes together with his sense of alienation. He can accept the social scheme of things no more than could the prophets Amos and Hosea. There is a significant difference, however, between the intellectuals and the ancient prophets. The prophet Amos nourished no direct political ambitions; he thundered warnings against the king and his entourage, but then presumably returned to his herds at Tekoah. Not so the

intellectuals; they write tracts of denunciation, but they also see themselves as the forerunners or future leaders of a political movement. The
intellectual is an amalgam of the prophet and the philosopher-king.
That is why the conception of Lenin that the role of the intellectual
was to bring socialist consciousness to the workers found a ready
acceptance, but Lenin shared a view which had already been pro-
pounded by the Fabian Socialists and the German Socialist, Karl
Kautsky.

The mode of thought characteristic of intellectuals is neither science
nor religion; it is ideology. An ideology expresses both their alienation
and elitist aspiration; every ideology incorporates some version of a
political myth which assigns to the intellectuals a leadership role with
respect to some social group, class, nation, people, or race, and which is
explicated in terms of those philosophical and scientific notions which
are currently fashionable. No scientist or scholar is regarded as an
intellectual unless he adheres to or seems to be searching for an
ideology. In America from 1900 to 1930 adherence to an ideology was
regarded as indicating some psychological imbalance. An intellectual
was regarded as essentially a misfit; he was not unlike the disciples of
the philosophes who fashioned the ideological furniture of the French
Revolution; as Taine said, the briefless lawyer, the unfrocked priest, the
teacher with no pupils, the hanger-on journalists, such were the ex-
pounders of revolutionary ideology. To call a person an 'intellectual'
was to suggest that this was an educated person who had failed to
complete his work, who lacked discipline, who had intellect but not
character; he was neither a scientist nor a scholar. The intellectuals at
this time were not found in the colleges and universities, but flourished
rather in the winding streets of Greenwich Village, in the offices of such
magazines as *The Masses,* in new theatre groups; their chiefs were such
people as Max Eastman and Randolph Bourne. They were unattached,
free-floating intellectuals very different from the institutional intellectuals of the sixties.

A shift in the emotive connotation of the word 'intellectual' began
to take place in the thirties in the United States. It was coeval with the
Great Depression. The business elite was bewildered, confused, and
unable to suggest proposals beyond a patient attendance on economic

forces for self-regulative adjustment. The labor elite wanted jobs but was still suspicious of such schemes as unemployment insurance. At this juncture what was called the 'Brain Trust' emerged. It included such figures as Rexford Tugwell, a professor of economics, an editor of *The New Republic* and above all, a believer in economic planning. The word 'planning' became central for the group which grew in Washington, known as the 'Phi Beta Kappa Revolutionaries'. (Childs, 1942: 61-63). Roosevelt himself had little respect for ideologists such as John Dewey and later Harold Laski who, he thought, had lost their sense of reality. But the economists seemed to him a relatively hard-headed group of scientists, and the notion spread that social science, particularly economics, could guide society out of its morass. What we might call the 'intellectual as advisor' superseded the intellectual as estranged prophet. In the aftermath, however, of the Second World War, the intellectual as adviser fell into some disrepute; a Rexford Tugwell was replaced in the popular imagination by Alger Hiss, that is, the intellectual advisor who was so committed to the notion of a socialized society guided by an intellectual elite that he was prepared to engage in treason. It was during this period that intellectuals were denominated with such epithets as 'eggheads', 'double-domes', 'long-haired', 'bleeding hearts', and *Time* magazine after the election of 1956 wrote of the great separation between the intellectuals and the American people.

Until the sixties, the intellectuals had conceived of themselves primarily as an advisory elite; their numbers had been too few for them to regard themselves as a class; as ideologists within their respective professions, they were a handful, though an influential one, above all as the setters of intellectual fashion. By and during the sixties, however, the unprecedented expansion of the universities created a new mass constituency, which moreover, was exceedingly volatile and mobilizable. While the working classes, having become prosperous, lapsed back into their traditional mistrust of intellectuals as a would-be authoritarian elite, the standpoint of universities was still characterized by an ideological invariant; its members regarded themselves as the wisest and fittest to rule. Whatever the place or time, the unchanging trait of the university ethos has been that its members bore the mantle of philosopher-kings. The socialist agitators who found themselves ignored in lean years of prosperity always could find welcomes among university groups. Meanwhile, too, the universities acquired a further importance as the base for institutional intellectuals. The old intellectuals had been lawyers, doctors, writers, teachers. Now the universities provided the consultants, research teams, library and laboratory facilities, for a variety of projects from atomic research to African tribalism to Vietnamese culture and the Soviet Communist Party. It was part of an evolution from Little Brains to Big Brains, from Little Ideology to Big Ideology. The election of 1972 was a landmark in the history of the American intellectual class because for the first time they were able to dominate a national convention of a major political party. During the sixties, as the political power of the intellectual class grew, the term acquired such prestige that even such persons as Richard M. Nixon and Henry Luce, the publisher of *Time,* both of whom had been unfriendly toward intellectuals came to wish to be regarded among them. (Mazlish, 1972: 40). A coalescing of the staffs of popular magazines, journals and television operations with the university intellectuals likewise took place. The reviewers in the *New York Times Book Review,* for instance, came to be predominantly professors, and the books reviewed very largely the works of academic authors; this had not been the case in the twenties. A considerable amount of writing during the sixties on the responsibility of the intellectuals reinforced the notion that they were most fitted to be society's guiding elite, but now for the first time, a majority of the universities' social scientists seemed willing to enroll themselves among the intellectuals. From Kautsky to Stalin, Marxists had said that the intellectuals were a stratum, not a class; now based on the mass universities, on the cultural and communications industries, on institutions whose policies they themselves largely controlled, they had become a class.

There are signs, however, that a great fission is in the making among the world's intellectual class. It arises from the distinction we might make betwen the middle intellectuals, the lower intellectuals, and the high intellectuals, or put in political terms, the contrast between the superiocrats, the mediocrats, and the inferiocrats. These distinctions began to emerge first in the Soviet Union. A small group of intellectuals such as Lenin, Trotsky, Bukharin, had led a revolution in which the armed power was provided by soldiers, sailors, workers, and peasants. The bulk, however, of what was called the *intelligentsia,* the civil servants, the teachers, the commercial and banking employees, the doctors, and lawyers had opposed the Bolshevik Revolution. Their spirit was broken during the terror. In the next decade, a new intelligentsia began to emerge whose culture was technical, and which was conditioned to abstain from philosophical and moral questioning. The last distinguished Communist sociologist, Nikolai Bukharin, described it in his essay *Culture in Two Worlds:* 'the vast majority of all the new intellectuals (our new proletarian intelligentsia) consists of technicians, engineers and agro-technicians. The "humanities" are far in the background ... We now often meet people who are perfectly at home in technology ... but who do not have the least idea of ancient Greek tragedy ... or even of Pisarev, Dobrolyubov, and Chernyshevsky. They are often ignorant of the most elementary historical facts ... This is the "cultural style" of the period ...—the clearly expressed technical ideology of the day." Trotsky complained that the medocrities were taking over, but trusted this was a passing phase, due to psychological weariness. The sociological truth gradually emerged that though a socialist revolution might be first guided by high intellectuals, the society which emerged was one dominated intellectually by mediocrats. In one field after another some mediocrity took advantage of his party position to humiliate, subdue, or destroy some scientific or literary genius. In genetics, an envious laboratory deputy conducted the secret police investigation of the famed scientist Nikolai Vavilov. (Medvedev, 1969: 262, 56, 71). In physics, Lev Landau and George Gamow were penalized by an ignorant party officialdom for accepting the theory of relativity. The fates of the novelists Babel and Pilnyak and the poet Mandelsstam are well-known. In more recent years, the best of the Soviet poets have been disciplined by literary bureaucrats: the editor-in-chief of *Pravda* threatened Andrei Voznesenky that 'he would be ground to dust' if he didn't connive at official lies. (*Problems of Communism,* 1968: 48). The minutes of the Moscow Writers' Union have a remarkable record of the confrontation between the literary bureaucrats and Alexander Solzhenitsyn. The Soviet intellectuals have learned in experience certain sociological truths: in a planned socialist order, the mediocrats enjoy their high status on state committees, and take a certain pleasure in lording it over writers and scientists of genius. The first generation revolutionary intellectuals may have thought they were working both for their power and the cause of intellectual liberty; 50 years afterward it is clear that the power went to the mediocrats, whereas the superior men lost their liberty. Under these conditions, a new type of intellectual has emerged in the Soviet Union; he repudiates all ideologies, regards them as myths and slogans which irrationalize people, and prevent the different countries from meeting their planetary problems wisely; he rejects all historic missions and conceptions of historically elect classes; he has rediscovered eternal, universalistic values as opposed to the 'dialectical' ones; he has scrapped Marxism which for almost 100 years provided the intellectuals with most of their varieties of ideas. In the Soviet Union, the regime endeavors to set the middle intellectuals against the high, much as 50 years ago it tried to set the rural poor and middle peasantry against the kulaks; the high intellectuals are those who struggle against (what we might call) 'the collectivization of the mind'.

Solzhenitsyn indeed has traced the stages of this process of the collectivization of the mind. From the beginnings of the Bolshevik Revolution there were a series of trials designed to break the independent spirit of the intellectuals. Lenin had an enormous contempt for them (pp. 31, 328) which he early expressed in his pamphlet *One Step Forward, Two Steps Back*. There were, of course, intellectuals in the leading ranks and the older membership of the party; these were destroyed. As Solzhenitsyn notes: the arrests that were carried out were 'predominantly among Party members who had joined before 1924' (Solzhenitsyn 1974: 69). 'This mockery of the intelligentsia, this contempt for the intelligentsia, was subsequently adopted with enthusiasm by the publicists and newspapers of the twenties and was absorbed into the current of day-to-day life' (Solzhenitsyn 1974: 328). The engineers were deprived of the most elementary freedoms, and forced to accept 'the dictatorship of their subordinates in industry, so little skilled or trained and comprehending neither the physical nor the economic laws of production, but now occupying the top positions from which they supervised the engineers' (Solzhenitsyn 1974: 390). By 1930, especially after the trial of the fictitious Industrial Party, 'the word "intelligentsia" got established here in Russia as a term of "abuse" ' (Solzhenitsyn 1974: 399). It was especially the higher talents who were rendered suspect. In every village, 'this was the perfect time to settle accounts with them of jealousy, envy, insult' (Solzhenitsyn 1974: 56). And the collectivization of the mind in this respect was not different from the collectivization of agriculture. If a student denounced a lecturer for not citing Stalin but only Lenin and Marx that was 'all that was needed for the lecturer not to show up for lectures any more' (Solzhenitsyn 1974: 73). The definition of an intellectual under these conditions was the following: any educated person, with outstanding abilities, and who is likely, therefore, to prize independence of mind. An intellectual was a person who refused to accept the dominant Bolshevik-Populist culture of the creativity of the masses, and refused to act masochistically with reference to his own intellect, to deny what he thought and saw. The Moscow trials from this standpoint were the most symbolic collective rite of the self-immolation of intellectuals' freedom; the mediocrats had humiliated the superiocrats. In the seventies the Soviet intellectuals now known as the "dissidents" have taken up the contest against the dictatorship of the mediocrats.

Throughout the history of the intellectual class, there has been this tension between the superiocrats and the mediocrats. This was the issue essentially in the famous Rolland-Barbusse debate in France in 1922 when the novelist Romain Rolland proclaimed that he would never join a party: 'My mission is to be a heretic, to break fetishes.' (Fisher, 1974: 134). The prophet, in words, refused to become a priest; he refused to sacrifice his independence of mind to the dictates of a party bureaucrat. For this reason, the notion of a 'fellow-traveller' was invented, that is, an intellectual who invokes universal values to justify what party bureaucrats do for their own power-motivated reasons, and who thus presumes that he has preserved his intellectual independence while acting as an apologist for the party mediocrats. This stance, however, becomes increasingly difficult to maintain during the long rule of the party mediocrats. The 'fellow-traveller' is a species of intellectual found in the Western countries rather than in European Communist societies.

Meanwhile, the emergence of Soviet dissidents is creating a schism in the international intellectual community. We might say that a phenomenon is taking place that arises from the 'uneven development' of the world's intellectual class. In the United States and Western Europe, intellectuals still tend to be advocates of socialism as their avenue to power and the overcoming of 'alienation'; their animus is sometimes called 'anti-American'. In the Soviet Union and European communist countries, on the other hand, the intellectuals having experienced socialism realize that this is not a society in which they rule, and that far from overcoming 'alienation', they must watch their art, literature, and humanities languish under political controls. If it were not for the competition with the United States, the same would be the case in the sciences. All of John Stuart Mill's fears that a centralized, socialist bureaucratic society would entail a mediocracy and a 'liberticide' seem to have been realized. The intellectuals in the European Communist countries, therefore, tend to be pro-American. The standpoint of an Alexander Solzhenitsyn is not that of *The New York Review of Books*. In ancient Hebraic times, there was once a conflict between wisdom and prophecy; the schism now may well be between the ideologists and the scientist-philosophers. The ideologists will disown the latter from the ranks of the intellectuals.

REFERENCES

Childs, Marquis W. (1942), *I Write from Washington,* New York.
Fisher, David James (1974), 'The Rolland-Barbusse Debate', *Survey,* **20** (Spring): 121-159.
Gerth, H. H. & Mills, C. Wright, eds. (1946), *From Max Weber,* New York.
Hampshire, Stuart (1956), 'An English Intellectual', *New Statesman and Nation,* LI, (April 28): 457-458.
Mazlish, Bruce (1972), *In Search of Nixon,* New York, Penguin.

Medvedev, Zhores A. (1969), *The Rise and Fall of T. D. Lysenko,* (translated I. Michael Lerner) New York, Doubleday.

Problems of Communism (1968), **XVII.**

Rieff, Philip (editor) (1969), *On Intellectuals,* New York, Doubleday.

Solzhenitsyn, Alexander I. (1974), *The Gulag Archipelago,* (translated by Thomas P. Whitney) **I-II,** New York, Harper & Row.

Times Literary Supplement (1955), 'The Role of the Intellectuals' (16 September): 533-534.

4

MEMBERS OF THE INTELLIGENTSIA AS DEVELOPERS AND DISSEMINATORS OF COSMOPOLITAN CULTURE

Helena Z Lopata
Loyola University of Chicago

The development of a cosmopolitan culture, freed from restrictions imposed by, or growing out of identification with, the social units into which the world is divided such as religious societies, political states, influence regions, or nations has been a gradual and not an even-flowing process. Of recent years the development of such culture along several lines of specialization has been assisted through the purposeful activity of individuals and groups. In the past, it has been dependent upon cultural expansion enforced on social units through limited interest groups such as armies or religious societies, or upon the diffusion of selected cultural items from a variety of sources of their original development or repository to peoples of other territorial, associational or ideational location. Cultural items and complexes have been carried across local tribal, national, religious or other social boundaries through primary person-to-person contact of individuals or groups, or through established secondary means of communication ranging from the telephone or telegraph to official reports, books, films, newspapers and inter-group journals. In some cases, this diffusion has been unplanned, an incidental or accidental consequence of contact initiated for different purposes. In other cases, it has been the focal point of interest, the raison d'etre for the contact itself. In spite of the ebb and flow of expansive and constrictive trends of human grouping in world history, there has been a gradual expansion of cosmopolitan culture both through independent diffusion and through purposeful, cooperative action in the creation of new, and the diffusion of existing, cultural items into the common fund.[1] This overriding trend toward a world culture has been particularly evident in the past two to three centuries. It is the purpose of this paper to analyze the contributions of the intelligentsia to this cosmopolitan culture, and the contravening tendencies which have resulted in relational and role strains for this social stratum.[2]

These contributions can be organized in terms of source and direction of flow: the dissemination of one's own culture to other groups, the adoption of cultural items of other groups by one's own group, the mutual though not necessarily symmetrical exchange, and the cooperative development of culture by transgroup sets of representatives who then return to their own group and disseminate the invention or discovery within it. Finally, cosmopolitan culture has been built up by individuals and groups who identify with the world as their main reference group and contribute directly to its common pool.

THE DISSEMINATION OF CULTURE

Without going too extensively into human history prior to the development of national culture societies (Znaniecki, 1952), we can acknowledge the contributions to the dissemination of culture across group boundaries of individuals such as troubadors, missionaries, salesmen, scientists or doctors and by groups functioning in governmental, educational, economic, religious, scientific or technological spheres of life (Znaniecki, 1940; Field, 1971; Crane, 1971).[3] The items selected for diffusion varied, however, by the cultural familiarity and identification of the diffuser and by the goals which the diffusion was expected to accomplish. The Holy Roman Empire was mainly concerned with imposing its system of laws upon the conquered populations, being uninterested in converting the 'barbaric' Gauls into cultural Romans;

the Roman Catholic Church, on the other hand, was determined to convert anyone defined as eligible to membership. There is a basic difference in the concept of Empire as 'An extensive territory (esp. an aggregate of many states)' (*Oxford Universal Dictionary*, 1955: 602) and the ecumenical or 'belonging to or representing the whole (Christian) world, or the universal church' (*Oxford Universal Dictionary*, 1955: 1359) which the Roman Catholic defined as its province.[4]

The diffusion of cultural items and complexes in the early history of mankind but after it had already formed itself into large and organized units, was usually accomplished through force or through conversion, with the help of some economic exchanges. By the seventeenth century in Europe and the territories under its influence the opportunities for such diffusion expanded dramatically and they were accompanied by the expansion of creative efforts designed to add new cultural complexes to the various divisions of mankind, local group or sphere of life. The development and diffusion of culture took place under the influence, and sometimes in spite of the hinderance of another trend, the restructuring of human units into national culture societies in most cases organized into political states.[5] The national states arose from the break-up of political empires and the supression of the religious society and its value system, converting Roman Catholics into Polish Roman Catholics, French Roman Catholics, etc. as well as from the unification of small principalities and kingdoms through wars of centralization. The reorganization of social units of interaction, organization and identification was accompanied by an intensive building of national cultures, and the dissemination of each of these to persons deemed candidates for membership in the society. National cultures were transmitted to people living within political state jurisdiction through mass education of the young and various attempts to 'detribalize', or convert from other identification, the adults. This move to develop and unify the national culture was assisted by those members of each national society who by training and life style were able to create and disseminate. A major part of their function was the selection of already existant cultural items out of folk or other location, while developing new items which could symbolize the national spirit (see Znaniecki's *Modern Nationalities*, 1952 for a detailed analysis of the processes and content of newly emerging national cultures). This very powerful trend had two effects upon cosmopolitan culture: it expanded the cultural base, particularily of secular and ideationally transmitted items of arts, literature, and, increasingly, science and technology, while simultaneously it created an ethos of national possession of the products of its own nationals.

The inwardly oriented nationalism could not stem the tide of cosmopolitan culture, although it did place its stamp on everything by converting the cosmos into an international arena. Evidence of the pervasiveness of this concept is contained in the special issue of a current journal which is devoted to 'Transnational Relations and World Politics' (Kochane and Nye, 1971); the journal itself is called *International Organization*. Within the world now converted into national states many trends served as facilitators of the rapid expansion of cultural creation and diffusion. Field (1971) pinpoints one of these in his *Transnationalism and the New Tribe* as: modernity 'compounded of the thrust toward freedom, self-determination, liberalism and nationalism, the rapid advance of science and technology, and the rush toward industrialization and urbanization' (355). Transnational development is also attributed by him to the 'process of discovery and exploration', expansion of capital and large-scale banking, the creation of large industrial complexes and corporations with branches in many nations, the building of transnational railroads and shipping lines, the importation of technical advisers across national borders, governmental treaties and the actions of foreign representatives such as diplomats, merchants and educators. In addition, there has been a growth in the twentieth century of non-governmental organizations. Skjelsback (1971: 425) documents the existence of 1,899 of these in 1968, explaining their expansion not only in number, but in the number of countries with representatives, the scope and intensity of their activity, the interconnections and cooperative action they involve, the breadth of their specialties and their distribution around the world.

The special issue of *International Organization* devoted to transnational relations documents these in many areas of cultural activity, economic, religious, political, revolutionary, scientific, etc. Each of these is supported by an ethos or ideology which justifies such international activity through a set of values understandible not only to those who engage in it, but also to those who 'allow' such behavior in spite of the importance of national welfare and the presence of international competition and even conflict. Some of these ideological arguments point to the interdependence of peoples on what is symbolized as 'spaceship earth', (deSeynes, 1972) others to capitalistic needs for raw material and cheap labor, still others to the need to free the exploited masses in all nations. A very powerful ethos justifying international cooperation has gradually grown among members of the different societies concerned with the development and the diffusion of 'high culture', of science and technology or with humanitarian wishes to benefit humanity through new knowledge in fields such as medicine.[6] In order to understand the intelligentsia's contribution to cosmopolitan culture, which is the task of this paper, we must examine the content of the ethos, the value systems stated or implied in its various sub-divisions and the interweave between the ethos, the behavior of individuals and groups committed to it and the relations of these peoples to local communities within which they function.

THE INTELLIGENTSIA AS DEVELOPERS
AND DISSEMINATORS OF CULTURE

In order to be able to discuss the intelligentsia as the developers and disseminators of selected aspects of human culture I am using the concept in the traditional Polish sense of 'cultured' men and women of knowledge (Znaniecki, 1940) of not only the history and literature but also of 'the arts and good manners' (Szczepanski, 1962: 408), able and willing to take an active part in the social structure (Chalasinski, 1945: 15). This concept of intelligentsia thus refers to a group, more or less loosely integrated, sharing knowledge of a complex literate, artistic, and interactional culture which is not limited to secularism, scientism and many of the aspects of the ethos which American and modern technological experts assign to the more limited concept of 'intellectual' (Merton, 1968). The Polish view of the intelligentsia is similar to the

Lipset and Dobson (1972) idea of 'creative intellectuals' in its stress upon creativity and the obligation to contribute to culture, but it encompasses a much broader view of the areas of culture which fall into the province of this stratum of society (Szczepanski, 1961: 330-335; 1970). The intelligentsia is seen in this framework as a stratum of a national culture society (Mannheim, 1936) but it is more likely to be identified in the socio-economically higher rungs of the social structure than the lower because of the time and cost of developing a person into the cultural wo-man, knowledgeable in a whole variety of subjects which cut across speciality and national culture boundaries and who internalizes the value system shared by this stratum (Chalasinski, 1945: 15).

The intelligentsia as so defined may be a vanishing stratum in some societies. As Szczepanski (1962) points out in 'The Polish *Intelligentsia: Past and Present'* there has been a recent change in this stratum in Poland with the decimation of former members by World War II, the development into intellectual roles of more narrowly trained technicians, and the exigencies of life under Stalinist communism. Aleksander Gella (1971) finds the change to be so strong as to entitle his analysis 'The Life and Death of the Old Polish Intelligentsia'. Simultaneously, commentators on the intellectual life of other societies point to a shift away from the 'Renaissance Man' training of the broadly cultured and cosmopolitan members of society arising from the current stress upon science, narrowly and instrumentally defined, and technology unconcerned with the cultural consequences or implications of useful techniques. Daniel Bell (1973) makes this point very clearly and at length in his *The Coming of Post-Industrial Society.*[7]

In spite of dire predictions of its demise or conversion into more limited interest groups, an analysis of the intelligentsia's contribution to world culture in the past might shed some insights over the controversies now emerging or expanding over the function of intellectuals in modern societies. Whether belonging to a 'culturally homogeneous social stratum of educated people united by charismatic feelings and a certain set of values' (Gella, 1971: 1), because of early socialization into the gentry or other upper classes, or after being drawn from all social strata (Mannheim, 1936), members of the intelligentsia, or 'intel-

lectuals are people for whom ideas, concepts, literature, music, painting, the dance have intrinsic meaning—are a part of the socio-
psychological atmosphere which one breathes (Gordon, 1964: 224).'
Milton Gordon limits his comments to this group in the United States
alone in his *Assimilation in American Life* but there is nothing in his
definition which restricts it nationally. In fact, 'the geographical disper-
sion of intellectuals by no means argues against the existence of an
intellectual community. Furthermore, the abundant reading which
intellectuals engage in, either as part of their occupational role or their
avocational interests, tends to create a common framework of leadership, reference groups, and conventions of discourse (226).'

To the extent that the intelligentsia is cosmopolitan, it is a diffused,
unorganized aggregate with loose ties binding some persons and groups
to others. Even on local levels, membership is not usually formally
established, except in sub-groups of the stratum and contact, direct or
indirect, is influenced by interests and activities. As among the Russian,
Polish, or similar intelligentsia, the person need not be engaged in
'intellectual' or 'artistic' pursuits as a vocation and did not have to be
an active contributor to all spheres of culture with which s-he was
familiar. The separation of occupation from membership in the intelligentsia is evident in the interaction of political refugees to a foreign
country who are able to win acceptance among other refugees or other
members of the cosmopolitan invisible college (Crane, 1971) even if
they earn their livelihood by non-intellectual and even status-demeaning
ways. All that is needed to belong to the intelligentsia is knowledge of
'high culture', a certain manner of deference and demeanor (Goffman,
1956) and interaction through the world-wide norms of 'polite compan-
ionship' (Znaniecki, 1965) adjusted to local sub-norms. Of course, the
ideal member of the intelligentsia not only has the cultural background
and manner, but also is able to combine these with life circumstances
facilitating the creation and diffusion of high culture. In some societies,
the ideal is further enhanced by official membership in groups deemed
representative of this culture, including groups providing livelihood in
order to free the creative person from common maintenance concerns.[8]
A final feature of the life of the intelligentsia as a social stratum is its
location vis-a-vis the other elements of social structure. There is no

inevitable relation of the intelligentsia to other powers (Shils, 1972) or strata in society since there is no universal function to which the intelligentsia is inevitably relegated. For example, as Szczepanski (1961, 1962, 1970) and Gella (1971) point out, the function of the intelligentsia and its position in the national culture society was very different in Russia, where it was 'alienated' and external to the political powers (see also Lipset and Dobson's 1972 comparison of the Russian and American intellectuals and comments on this article by Conway and Malia) and in Poland where it was at the centre of a society developing and maintaining its national culture in the absence of a political state and in face of de-nationalization efforts of two of three occupying powers. The intelligentsia, or segments of it, can be co-opted by political, religious, economic or any other groups in or out of power in larger social units, may be independently revolutionary, can be unconcerned with the local scene in its concentration of attention on the world society and cosmopolitan culture.[9] This concentration, interestingly enough, is often defined as 'alienation' but such a definition implies a local perspective and reference group (Merton, 1958; Gouldner, 1957). This concentration can lead, however, to attempts to impose external standards and values upon local populations and leaders. It is this use of external criteria of judgment rather than the function of critic within the local cultural matrix which often concerns the non-intelligentsia power elite (Shils, 1973).

CONDITIONS FACILITATING INTELLIGENTSIA'S CONTRIBUTIONS TO THE DEVELOPMENT AND DISSEMINATION OF COSMOPOLITAN CULTURE

A major factor facilitating socialization into, and participation in, whatever levels and divisions of cosmopolitan culture exist at any time by the intelligentsia has been the development of the ethos of the universality of certain aspects of culture. The belief that 'truth', 'beauty', and similar values are best contained in artistic and literary products is very old, obviously preceding Socrates and Plato. The rationale or justification presented by the scientific community to the rest of the society at different levels of its organization is contained in many pronouncements and public statements, the following, dating from 1937, being typical. The ethos is contained in a speech by the new president of the Rockerfeller Foundation, a group devoted to international cooperation in medicine and other scientific fields:

> For, in the last analysis, knowledge cannot be nationalized. No successful embargoes can be maintained against export or import of ideas. Whether new conceptions in atomic physics come from Copenhagen or from Cambridge, England; whether the cure for cancer is developed in New Haven or Berlin; whether it is a Russian or Italian or an American who takes the next step forward in mankind's struggle with virus disease—we are all of us, under whatever flag, the joint beneficiaries of the intellectual property of the race. In all the clash of competing nationality, the single aim and language of science is the discovery of truth. It is this principle which challenges the twentieth century with the conception of civilization as a cooperative achievement and with the ideal of intellectual capital as an international possession [quoted by Lopata, 1946].

This argument has a dual thrust, focusing on the inevitability of the cosmopolitanism or cultural diffusion of knowledge, and on the assumed benefits to be derived from cosmopolitan ownership of the products of science. It is limited to 'scientific' works entirely, leaving aside any question as to the ownership of artistic or other cultural innovations.

However broad the area of culture which is subject to the cosmopolitan ethos sharing, the ethos and the content of that which is being developed and transmitted has, in Gordon's (1964) terms, contributed to a universe of discourse and a common 'air which is breathed' even by people in different locations on the globe. In order for this to be true the intelligentsia has had to develop some means of obtaining and understanding cultures other than those into which they had been socialized in lifetime years prior to aspiration to this world-wide stratum. It has developed, over centuries, several facilitating means of such sharing. A basic one has been the creation of common symbols, particularily language. Until very recent years there has been a failure to create, or diffuse an existing language to the whole world, the universes of discource and reference falling into several major areas of influence excluding isolated social groups. Over time, the Western European and American intelligentsias have shared Greek, Latin, then French, and literary German and of recent years, English. Countries culturally or politically dominated by peoples speaking these languages have had an advantage over those totally unfamiliar with them, although translators have served as the gatekeepers of knowledge.

There are many interactional opportunities through which the intelligentsia, located throughout the world or in one of its sub-regions have been able to come to direct or indirect contact for the sharing of cultural experience or development. In the first place, becoming a member of this stratum has required familiarity with the cultural products of not only the group into which the person is initially socialized and educated, but of other groups whose specified items are generally deemed worthy of cosmopolitan renown. The early years of European growth witnessed the popularity of widely known charismatic cultural leaders to whom were drawn people anxious to share their religious or secular knowledge or art. Plato's Academy, the Roman schools of law, Florence's studios, replaced individual prophets with more organized sources of apprenticeship or education. Universities such as Padua or, later, Paris drew young men, and in some cases young women from a variety of cultures. Kingdom's and duchies imported artists or scholars to form part of the culture-developing circle around the power centers (Znaniecki, 1940; Field, 1972). Gradually, as Mannheim (1937) and others have documented, the intelligentsia developed into an independent stratum free from dependence on wealthy patrons and free to interact with each other independently of organized groups. The invention of printing simplified this contact as people were able to read each other's work, or describe, for broader audiences, artistic products so that the dissemination of ideas was not limited to personal contact. Throughout the history of the intelligentsia personal communication, particularily through written correspondence, has facilitated the exchange of ideas as men and women outside of easy face-to-face contact would educate each other or cooperatively test ideas. Many of the famous debates of members of the cosmopolitan intelligentsia have taken both this private or the semi-public form of correspondence, frequently published in periodicals and the public and secondary form through books and articles obviously directed at refuting or contributing to the dissemination of a school of thought (Znaniecki, 1940). The autobiographies or even the prefaces to other works by famous thinkers or artists often contain acknowledgements of influence, direct or indirect of men and women in a variety of settings.[10]

The use of secondary means of learning or disseminating the products of the intelligentsia has been facilitated by the expansion of opportunities for personal contact. These contacts tend to follow the reference group lines of shared interests. Thus, a scholar working on an idea, invention or new artistic medium may find out that his/her counterpart in another part of the world is also working on the same problem and may arrange to visit the other. The history of international cooperation in medicine is replete with such incidents (see Lopata, 1946).

The desire to exchange knowledge or just to meet indirectly known colleagues or other members of the world intelligentsia have resulted in two international developments of growing popularity. One is permanent international organizations, such as the World Health Organization or the Association for Asian Studies, the second is the regular or special congress or conference. Many of these occasions for contact are sponsored by governmental groups because of the costs and concerns for security, and some of those developed by professional or scientific groups are limited to representatives of national states who can not interact independently. However, many groups, such as the International Sociological Association and its congresses involve individuals directly interested in cosmopolitan knowledge, within a specified field of intellectual or scientific endeavor.

STRAINS ARISING FROM INTELLIGENTSIA'S FUNCTION AS DEVELOPERS AND DISSEMINATORS OF COSMOPOLITAN CULTURE

There are certain self-oriented, relational and role strains created by the intelligentsia's attempt to contribute to the development and diffusion of cosmopolitan culture. O'Dea (1972: 163) refers to what he calls the 'Socratic tension' which leads the intellectual into internal conflict and strains in relations with the society: 'Three antinomies are involved: (1) traditionalism versus rationality, (2) stability and continuity versus innovation and creativity, and (3) institutional legitimation versus critical evaluation.' Most commentators on the roles of men and women of knowledge or on the relations between them and other segments of the societies in which they exist have been stressing the problems created by the intellectual innovative function. There is in much of this commentary an assumption that societies inevitably wish to conserve the status quo of all of their culture, to cling to tradition which the intelligentsia, and particularily the scientists, are trying to strip away. Actually, many societies are consistently encouraging their intelligentsia to write, paint, compose, build, etc., in order to expand their cultural 'treasurers' and as sources of prestige in international competition. It is not innovation or creation per se which is the subject of strain between the intelligentsia and other segments of societies, but the content of the product or idea. It becomes strainful when it threatens either important values or the distribution of power. Thus, the intelligentsia is more threatening in certain societies than in others, especially if the area of its activity cannot be controlled, and it is more threatening in certain activities than in others. These facts can not be generalized into an assumption that there is inevitable strain between the intelligentsia and the remaining parts of society.

Whenever the role of the intelligentsia has been narrowed to that of critic of any segment of society, the power groups, other classes or each other, the very act of criticism has, not surprisingly, led to strain. This strain has been particularily severe in cases in which the criticism uses cosmopolitan or other values not acceptable to the local group, because such criteria of failure undermine the total structure. Of less strain have been the 'reforming' activities of the intelligentsia, designed to work within the value framework and the 'advising' function which has helped the existing local group achieve its own goals with the help of cosmopolitan knowledge (Merton, 1968; Gouldner, 1957). Thus, Japan imported intelligentsia to help it modernize and carefully nurtured such relations (Field, 1971), while the Soviet Union finally deported Solzhenitsyn, not for being a contributor to intellectual culture but because his creation contained criticism of the system.

Strain can arise from mutually negative feelings between the intelligentsia and the rest of the society, as documented by Hofstadter (1966). The intelligentsia tends to treat members of other strata as inferior, which does not endear it to people experiencing or suspecting such judgment. Differences in universes of discourse, even language used for interaction, in manners and interests inevitably create gaps in identification. Very frequently the society at large does not even understand what the intelligentsia does, or its value system; confusing, for example, science and technology as Handlin (1965) noted, or wiretapping for personal use with sociological surveys.

NON-COSMOPOLITAN FEATURES OF THE INTELLIGENTSIA'S EFFORTS

Another source of strain for the intelligentsia bent on contributing to or diffusing cosmopolitan culture comes from relations with colleagues. In spite of the idealized one-world, one-community image of the world intelligentsia there are numerous problems due to the ethno-centrism of its members, evidenced by the content of the cosmopolitan culture. The ethno-centrism is of areas of cultural specialization deemed worthy of diffusion or of national culture or of segments of national culture which are most apt to be stressed or used as vehicles for dissemination. Each member of the intelligentsia, each intellectual, each scientist or technocrat, each artist is socialized initially, into a currently specific national culture, with its language and sets of values. However is this socialization augmented by formal education, obtained in the form of instruction by others or by self-education, the underlying value system tends to remain a set of blinkers preventing ventures into other cultures. Besides, no one has the time during a life span to learn everything about all the cultures of the world in order to then formulate his or her package of cultural items judged worthy of dissemination. Few people able to contribute to diffusion really seek out 'worthwhile' cultural items or complexes in 'foreign' cultures in order to present them to the common fund of cosmopolitan culture. In fact, non-rational or universal value judgments, fads and all forms of elitism operate in the selection of items judged worthy of learning in ones own culture, as forming 'high culture'. Also, in the competition for scarce resources of human potential and developed ability among fields of cultural endeavor each arena of cosmopolitan cooperation feels justified in demanding more time, more money, 'better brains', etc. than it considers as necessary for competing fields.

As it has developed, cosmopolitan culture had been contributed to unevenly by a few groups from a very limited number of cultures. Artists, scholars, scientists and others who identify themselves as part of the intelligentsia or the intellectual elite tend to push their own religious, national or political or specialization groups more than those of the others. Elitism and ethno-centrism have resulted in many products never even being considered for adoption on a world-wide basis.[12] The monopolization of cosmopolitan culture by a few intelligentsia sub-elites is apparent at any international congress, including sociological congresses, or in the advice intellectuals give their students as to which products or persons are worth knowing about. Thus, even the 'old intelligentsia' has a 'long way to go' before it develops and diffuses a truly cosmopolitan culture and creates a community to which the intelligentsias of all geographic and ideological areas of the world have free access and open hearing. Complaints over the transformation of the intelligentsia into the more limited intellectuals, scientists or technocrats still do not remove the fact that even the 'cultured' men and women of the past had very limited ideas concerning whose culture formed the 'high' culture. The strains produced by conflicting demands on the intelligentsia in its relations on the local scene with the power elite or other segments of national, ecclesiastical and other types of societies, should not blind this stratum to the very serious strains created in its own world community by the same tendencies toward ethno-centrism and imperialism which it criticizes in others.

NOTES

1. The Useems (1965, 1963, 1967, 1971a, 1971b) have been studying the presence in the modern world of what they call 'the third culture . . . the behavior patterns created, shared, and learned by men of different societies who are in the process of relating their societies, or sections therefore, to each other (1963: 1).' They are particularily interested in the communities of American scientists who live in foreign countries as part of cross-cultural programs. The first culture which they must 'take into account' is that of the host culture, the second being the American culture. The Useems focus on the consequences of these combined efforts of binational contact in producing new cultural items, which they term third culture. This research, like that of the United Nations or of International Cooperation in Medicine (Lopata, 1946) provide basic data on the content and the method of development of the various aspects of cosmopolitan culture.

2. Ever since Mannheim's *Ideology and Utopia* (1936) the intelligentsia, or the more limited intellectuals, have been seen as forming a stratum, rather than an estate or social class, partly because members can originate anywhere along the class ladder and partly because they can 'attach themselves to different classes in different societies and at different periods of history. 'This unanchored, relatively classless stratum is, to use Alfred Weber's terminology, the "socially unattached intelligentsia" (155).'

3. Znaniecki (1952) defined the national culture society in *Modern Nationalities* as one 'which has a common and distinct secular, literary culture and an independent organization functioning for the preservation, growth and expansion of this culture'. (21) He also saw the potential of a world society or 'cosmopolis' as growing out of world culture (174-184).

4. See O'Dea's (1972) discussion of how the Roman Catholic Church lost its intellectual leadership in the creation of world culture in Europe by the late Middle Ages, with the help of the Reformation, laicization and secularization of knowledge. 'The lay intelligentsia of the eighteenth century supported the middle classes in their struggle against the church, the monarchy, and tradition, but their own aspirations went far beyond those of their allies (175). These aspirations were to change history with the help of reason and science.

5. Znaniecki (1952) makes an important distinction between a national culture society and a political society or state 'which has a common legal system and an organized, independent government controlling all the people who inhabit territory.' (21) An example of a real-life situation in which these two social units were separated occurred when the Polish state was dismantled and the territory partitioned by three political states, Russia, Prussia and the Austrio-Hungarian

Empire, but the national culture society survived for over 125 years until and after the state was finally restored; see Jan Szczepanski, *Polish Society* (1970) and Helena Znaniecki Lopata, *Polish-Americans: Status Competition in an Ethnic Community,* (1976).

6. Znaniecki, (1952) points to the ethos of 'appreciation and preservation of the common cultural heritage of mankind (176) as a foundation for world culture, even in opposition to the purely nationalistic goal of destroying the enemy's possessions. *International Cooperation in Medicine* (Lopata, 1946) has been extensive and based on both humanitarian and the 'science-as-the-possession-of-mankind' ethos.

7. See also Hofstadter's discussion of the 'Decline of the Gentleman' as the intellectual in politics in his *Anti-Intellectualism in American Life* and Oscar Handlin's (1965) discussion of the hostility toward science in the American popular mind because of its confusion with technoligy in 'Science and Technology in Popular Culture'.

8. The Polish intelligentsia's ethos contains a distinction between workers who are paid to produce a specified number of a specified product with a market value and the intelligentsia whose members are given a salary simply in order to free them from economic concerns so that they can devote their time and energy to appropriate pursuits of scholarship, artistic meditation, or active creation of valuable cultural contributions which are 'priceless'.

9. George B. de Huszar's (1960), *The Intellectuals: A Controversial Portrait* contains many different portraits of traditional and 'modern' intellectuals and their location in different societies as well as the roles they have chosen to carry forth vis-a-vis the powers or other segments of their own systems. Such articles run throughout this edited book, not only in the section devoted to 'Intellectuals in Various Countries'. Interest by intellectuals in the wide range of locations and roles of intellectuals has been strong in recent years, as evidenced by special issues of major periodicals aimed for this audience. In reference to these periodicals we may note that Milton Gordon (1964) defines membership in the intellectual stata by the newspapers and magazines they read while Kadushin (1972) defines the 'elite intellectuals' by publication. 'A leading intellectual is simply any person who writes regularly for leading intellectual journals and/or has his book reviews in them (110).'

10. I was able to re-construct much of the influences upon Znaniecki and the evolution of his sociological thought from a chronological reading of his prefaces to the various books written in Polish and English (see Lopata, 1972)

11. The concept of 'high culture', or 'high-brow' culture is a popular one in American society and, among non-sociologists the very word 'culture' is limited to artistic, literary, philosophical, and even other humanistic works which are to be 'enjoyed for their own sake' or which are the province of the higher classes. Marcuse's (1965) 'Remarks on a Redefinition of Culture', in the special edition of *Daedalus* devoted to 'Science and Culture' are dependent upon such a limited

definition of culture. Discussions of high culture are contained in Shils' book of essays (Ch. 5 'The High Culture of the Age'.)

12. In recent experiences of discussing Polish culture in the process of writing a book on the Polish Americans with American intellectuals, or at least university faculty, I have been appalled by their ignorance of even cosmopolitan contributions from that national culture society. By contrast, the 1354 page *Nauka w Wielkopolsce* (science, very broadly defined to really include philosophy, logic, philology, etc., in a province of Poland in which Poznan is the central city) contains 43 pages of a 'person index', many of 'foreign' identity with special reference to the influence of these persons or of their works upon the Polish intelligentsia's thought and writing.

REFERENCES

Bell, Daniel, 1973, *The Coming of Post-Industrial Society: A Venture in Social Forecasting.* New York: Basic Books, Inc.

Bell, J. Bowyer, 1971, 'Contemporary Revolutionary Organizations', special issue of *International Organization,* **VXXV**, 3 (Summer): 503-518.

Bell, Peter D., 1971, 'The Ford Foundation as a Transnational Actor', special issue of *International Organization,* **VXXV**, 3 (Summer): 465-78.

Chalasinski, Josef, 1946, *Spoleczna Genealogia Intelligencji Polskiej.* Poland: Spoldzielnia Wydawnicza 'Czytelnik'.

Confino, Michael, 1972, 'On Intellectuals and Intellectual Traditions in Eighteenth and Nineteenth-Century Russia'. *Daedalus* (Intellectuals and Tradition). (Spring): 117-149.

Conway, Jill, 1972, 'Intellectuals in America: Varieties of Accommodation and Conflict'. *Daedalus* (Intellectuals and Change). (Summer): 199-205.

Crane, Diana, 1971 'Transnational Networks in Basic Science', *International Organization,* **XXV** (Summer): 585-601.

Field, James A. Jr. (1971) Transnationalism and the New Tribe, International Organization **XXV** (Summer): 353-72.

Gella, Aleksander, 1971, 'The Life and Death of the Old Polish Intelligentsia', *The Slavic Review,* **30**, N.1 (March): 1-27.

Goffman, Erving, 1956 'The Nature of Deference and Demeanor', *American Anthropoligist,* **58** (June): 473-502.

Gouldner, Alvin, 1957, 'Cosmopolitans and Locals', *Administrative Science Quarterly*. (December): 281-306.

Gordon, Milton, 1964, *Assimilation in American Life*. New York: Oxford University Press.

Handlin, Oscar, 1965, 'Science and Technology in Popular Culture'. *Daedalus*, 94, 1 (Winter): 156-170.

Hoffman, Stanley, 1959, 'The National Attitudes and International Order: The National Studies on International Organization'. *International Organization*, XIII, 2 (Spring): 189-203.

Hofstadter, Richard, 1966, *Anti-Intellectualism in American Life*. New York: Random House, Vintage Books.

Huszar, George B. de, 1960, *The Intellectuals*. New York: The Free Press of Glencoe.

Kadushin, Charles, 1972, 'Who Are The Elite Intellectuals?' *The Public Interest*, 29 (Fall): 109-125.

Kaohane, Robert O. and Joseph Nye (eds.) 1971, *Transnational Relations and World Politics*, special issue of *International Organization* VXXV, 3 (Summer).

Kent, Donald Peterson, 1953, *The Refugee Intellectual*. New York: Columbia U. Press.

Kolakowski, Leszek, 1972, 'Intellectuals Against Intellect'. *Daedalus* (Intellectuals and Change), (Summer): 1-15.

Labudy, Gerard (ed.), 1973, *Nauka w Wielkopolsce*. Posman, Wydawnictwo Poznaniecki.

Laqueur, Walter, 1962, 'The Role of the Intelligentsia in the Weimar Republic'. *Social Research*, 39, 2 (Summer): 213-227.

Lipset, Seymour and Richard B. Dobson, 1972, 'The Intellectual as Critic and Rebel: With Special Reference to the United States and the Soviet Union'. *Daedalus* (Intellectuals and Change), (Summer): 109-168.

Lopata, Helena Znaniecki, 1946, *International Cooperation in Medicine: A Sociological Study*. M. A. Thesis, Department of Sociology, University of Illinois, Urbana, Illinois.

——— 1972, 'Florian Znaniecki: The Creative Evolution of a Sociologist', Paper given at the conference on 'Florian Znaniecki and his Role in Sociology' organized by the Sociological Institute of the Adam Michiewicz University and the Poznan branch of the Polish Sociological Society, December, 1972, Poznan, Poland.

——— 1976, *Polish-Americans: Status Competition in an Ethnic Community*. Englewood Cliffs, N.J., Prentice-Hall Publishing Co.

Malia, Martin E., 1972, 'The Intellectuals: Adversaries or Clerisy'. *Daedalus* (Intellectuals and Change). (Summer): 106-216.

Mannheim, Karl, 1936, *Ideology and Utopia*. New York: A Harvest Book, Harcourt, Brace and Company, translated from the German by Louis Wirth and Edward Shils.

Merton, Robert, 1968, *Social Theory and Social Structure.* New York: The Free Press, enlarged edition.

Milson, Menahem, 1972, 'Medieval and Modern Intellectual Traditions in the Arab World'. *Daedalus* (Intellectuals and Change), (Summer): 17-37.

Morse, Edward, 1971, 'Transnational Economic Processes'. *Transnational Relations and World Politics,* special issue of *International Organization,* VXXV, 3 (Summer): 329-349.

O'Dea, Thomas F., 1972, 'The Role of the Intellectual in the Catholic Tradition'. *Daedalus* (Intellectuals and Tradition), (Spring): 151-189.

The Oxford Universal Dictionary, Oxford: At the Clarendon Press, 1955: 602, 1359.

Pachter, Henry M., 1972, 'The Intellectuals and the State of Weimar'. *Social Research,* 39, 2 (Summer): 228-253.

Seynes, Philippe de, 1972, 'Prospects for a Future Whole World'. *International Organization,* 26, 1 (Winter): 1-17.

Shils, Edward, 1972a, *The Intellectuals and the Powers & Other Essays.* Chicago, University of Chicago Press, 1972.

――― 1972b, 'Intellectuals, Tradition, and the Traditions of Intellectuals: Some Preliminary Considerations'. *Daedalus: Intellectuals and Tradition,* (Spring): 21-34.

Skjelsback, Kjell, 1971, 'The Growth of International Non-Governmental Organizations in the Twentieth Century'. *Transnational Relations and World Politics,* special issue of *International Organization,* VXXV, 3 (Summer): 420-426.

Szczepanski, Jan, 1961, 'Problems of Sociological Research on the Polish Intelligentsia', *The Polish Sociological Bulletin,* 1-2 (June-December): 33-41.

――― 1962, 'The Polish Intelligentsia, Past and Present'. *World Politics,* XIV, 3 (April): 406-420.

――― 1970, *Polish Society.* New York: Random House.

Useem, John and Ruth Hill Useem, *Studies of Third Cultures,* Michigan State University Institute for International Studies in Education including:

――― 1963, with John Donoghue, 'Men in the Middle of the Third Culture: The Roles of American and Non-Western People in Cross-Cultural Administration', (No. 5, originally published in 1963).

――― 1967, 'The Interfaces of a Binational Third Culture: A Study of the American Community in India'. (No. 4, originally published in 1967).

――― 1971, John Useem only. 'The Study of Cultures', (No. 6, originally published in 1971).

Useem, Ruth Hill, 1973 'Third Culture Factors in Educational Change'. in Cole S. Bremback and Walter H. Hill (eds.) *Cultural Challenges to Education,* Lexington Books, D. C. Heath and Company.

Useem, John and Ruth Hill Useem, 1955, *The Western Educated Man in India.* Copyright by John and Ruth Hill Useem.

Vallier, Ivan, 1971, 'The Roman Catholic Church: A Transnational Actor'. *Trans-*

national Relations and World Politics, special issue of *International Organization,* **VXXXV,** 3 (Summer): 479-502.

Znaniecki, Florian, 1940, *The Social Role of the Man of Knowledge.* New York: Columbia U. Press.

––– 1952, *Modern Nationalities,* Urbana, Ill.: University of Illinois Press.

––– 1965, *Social Relations and Social Roles.* San Francisco: Chandler Publishing Company.

5

CHANGES IN THE CONCEPT OF INTELLECTUALS*

Tibor Huszar
Eotvos Lorand University, Budapest

If I go no further than to place the opinions maintained by the
bourgeois essayists of the past half century alongside one another, it
will be only too obvious that there are quite a few ideas and approaches
and, accordingly, different definitions of the intellectuals to be found
in the sociological literature of our age.

The concept of the intelligentsia, however, is of a comparatively
recent origin. Before the nineteenth century there are references to
scribes, learned people travelling from place to place and earning a
living from their knowledge or reading and writing, philosophers, poets
or lawyers—but they consistently described one another as philosopher,
lawyer or poet, never using the term 'intellectual'.

In the last century, however, terms used to denote collectively
groups or individuals engaged in a certain mental activity appeared one
after another at a fantastic pace, sometimes contradicting, at other
times confirming one another. In some languages the variations are of
such a broad range that a number of terms appear to be untranslatable.
There are also several related terms in the Hungarian language, which
are the equivalents of mental workers, cultured strata, intellectuals,
people with a free profession, and so on.

The language acts like a highly sensitive precision instrument indicating the rapid changes that have taken place in the last century along

with the complexity of mental activity and its diversity. At the same time it also reflects the large number of patterns used to denote the social stratum described as mental workers or the intellectuals.

While the stream, only too rich in epithets and adjectives that either run parallel or counter to one another, continues to flow on, it is the duty of science to take the terms that act as a common denominator and separate the different implications and generalizations from one another. A reader of sociological literature, however, finds that a number of studies fail not only to distinguish the philosophical, psychological and sociological elements that are present in the words or phrases qualifying the human properties and in the references denoting the content of values and expressing the essence of the social status of the different strata—but to make matters worse, at times they also increase the confusion by attempting to unify the different references, introducing arbitrary and definite thoretical constructions in order to verify them.

One of the most widespread variations of the bourgeois theory of the intellectual, the traces of which are discernable in everyday thinking, is to make the ideal type of the intelligentsia 'timeless'. This is not simply characteristic of an isolated trend, but it is a tendency that can be identified on different levels and with different outward manifestations in the most diverse trends. The related assumption may be derived from a mosaic of one's memories from reading, of cocktail-party conversations, even of family traditions. It does not always emerge as a fixed theory, but it can give the opinion an identifiable direction.

As I mentioned, the concept of the intelligentsia is of a relatively recent origin. In spite of this, however, a number of theoreticians write in a most natural manner about the intellectuals as reaching back thousands of years, leaving their indelible mark on the documents of every age.

It is beyond any doubt that there were many outstanding creative people in past societies. Virtually all of them including Socrates, Plato, and Aristotle were concerned with the responsibilities borne by the thinking man. As a matter of fact their activity as a whole is summarized in the endeavour to understand and to make others understand the 'essence of the world', to find out the secrets of Nature, to give a reply to what the meaning of life is, to create new ideas, and to recognize and make others aware of the driving forces of action. All this can be applied to the outstanding creative individuals of the Renaissance and the Enlightenment.

But to make a direct identification of the history of philosophy with that of the intelligentsia is highly problematic and gives rise to several sorts of misunderstanding. The major thinkers did not use the term 'intelligentsia' before the middle of the nineteenth century; they were in the habit of writing about the responsibilities of the thinker and scholar and then of the philosopher, writer, physician or judge. If the Latin word 'intelligentsia' occurs in their writings after the Roman period, it was used merely as a philosophical or psychological term to denote the level of cognition and the degree of comprehension. The thinkers were neither interested in the status of the intellectuals, nor were they concerned with the intelligentsia as an independent group.

Thus an opportunity is offered to the representatives of the above trends to explore the existing parallels in the thinkers of the different ages, in their attitudes, styles and ways of life. But observations which were otherwise quite justified went astray at this particular point. For the abstract analogies served as a basis for an arbitrary theoretical construction leading to the creation of an 'eternal' 'type' of the intellectual—made out to be 'timeless' from these related features and parallel properties.

In a book that triggered heated debates and has left its mark even on the most general thought of Hungarian intellectuals, Julien Benda (1927) characterizes the eternal intellectuals as follows: in essence they are not guided by practical objectives in their activities, they find pleasure in cultivating arts and sciences or in metaphysical thinking, and not in possessing privileges or advantages of a material nature and so they have the right, to a certain extent, to say, 'My kingdom is not of this world'. Then Benda goes on to say that throughout history to the present day, we can find an endless line of philosophers, founders of religions, men of letters, artists, scholars and scientists whose influence has been directly opposed to the realism of the masses. To turn to political passion specifically, 'learned people' have been opposed to it in two ways: either they have been completely indifferent to the passions of this kind, as with Leonardo da Vinci, Malebranche or Goethe, pursuing their spiritual activities completely free of any political interests, and lending weight to a belief in the superiority of this way of existence; or like Erasmus, Kant, or Renan, they have observed the conflict of human selfishness from the viewpoint of moralists and, speaking in the name of humanity or justice, have called for the acceptance of an abstract principle which is positioned above and runs counter to the passions mentioned.

There are several definitions available similar to that of Benda. All classify the intellectual, the scientist and the artist in the same category. The theme of all these definitions is that irrespective of the historical period, intellectuals have always been characterized by a passionate desire for knowledge and for the expression of truth, by a readiness to innovate, by the need for creative work, by inspiration and intuition, by indifference towards inferior political passions, by service to spiritual objectives free from any interest, by moral purity, and by independence of personality.

The various definitions have their fundamental differences. From the point of view of this study, however, their common theoretical and methodological basis is of greater importance including either the way they transpose into the past the roles, properties, attitudes, and even ideologies of the intellectuals of our times, or the way in which they unnaturally modernize the features of a previous period, placing the actual historical implications in brackets. In this way the sophists emerge as the forerunners of the non-conformist intellectuals of today, and Diogenes is identified as an intellectual model of the hippies.

For the time being let us ignore the number of roles, positions and actual meanings the picture of the intellectuals thus interpreted combines apart from and partly as a consequence of this contraction of time. The question of whom to consider as the type of the 'eternal intellectual' will remain the greatest problem for readers of Julien Benda, Ortega or Huizinga. Is this intellectual the representative of the idea or the bearer on this earth of transcendent values? Or is he, as Aristotle suggests, the one concerned with creating order out of chaos? Is the intelligentsia the spiritual elite that guards quality against the threat of the 'revolt of the masses'? In any case can a sense of 'calling', or human properties, or a way of thinking, or a value-orientation independent of professional qualifications be regarded as the characteristics of the intelligentsia? Or must it be assumed that vocation and these factors coincide and that these properties act as conditions and, at the same time, as symptoms of having an intellectual profession?

It is most convenient, for the time being, to disregard these possible but, for the moment, unarticulated implications of the roles of the intelligentsia which are 'stratified on top of one another'. Let us for now emphasize the references Benda made to the sciences and arts. For both Julien Benda and the representatives of the intellectual tendencies who have much in common with him base the myth of the eternal intellectual on the continuity of the sciences and arts. As Antonio Gramsci (1949) put it: since the different traditional intellectual fields tend to feel their uninterrupted historical continuity and qualification in a way as is befitting the 'spirit of a body' they think that they are autonomous and independent of the ruling social group. This kind of 'self-styling' has had its consequences in both the ideological and political fields, and they are far-reaching. The idealist philosophy as a whole can easily be associated with this position taken up by the social ensemble of the intelligentsia, as well as the social utopia in the spirit of which the intellectuals think of themselves as independent and possessing characteristics of their own.

The key to the very complex and diverse problems of the intelligentsia is historical. That necessitates a detour, though it follows from the nature of this study that it cannot be more than an outline and must be centered around its principle theme.

The history of the arts and sciences over thousands of years is in fact the history of the continual creation and preservation of values, of truths and beauty. Neither the sciences nor the arts would have developed if the internal compulsion to something new, the awareness of a critical approach, will-power, inspiration and the ability to create had been absent from their most outstanding representatives.[1] The dividing lines have never been drawn between the 'society' and the 'sciences' or between 'society' and the 'arts', but between the progressive and conservative forces within the society, sciences and arts, even if they have not always run parallel and have not been easy to recognize.

The fact is that certain virtues are exppropriated exclusively by the intelligentsia and that they cannot see the negative underside of their timeless image: the meditative and reluctant intellectual who is unable to act and is alien to life and easy to mould (a counter image of reliability). In respect to the subject being considered in this essay the most problematic point is that the characteristics of science and knowledge and those of the arts and the artist are identified on the basis of abstract analogies, and since both the arts and sciences are considered to be worlds in which their own laws apply, both the scientist and the artist are considered to be independent of their society.

It would go beyond the scope of this study to dwell on individual examples to this effect. It would be no difficult task to prove that Leonardo da Vinci who designed forts, war machines, and submarines was by no means the type of the artist-intellectual who turns his back to the outside world or the people of 'practice'. Again, it is a hopeless venture to attempt to find the key to Kant and Erasmus in an approach other than the one made from the direction of their own age and looking at their activity as a whole. I am not going to list here arbitrary examples to prove the contrary. It does not prove anything if we can find vain and mean scientists or artists even in the ranks of the most prominent, or show that those holding office in the government have often turned out to be more cunning or merciless than princes and 'professional' politicians.[2]

The diversity of the philosophers of the ancient polis and the speculative nature of their meditations engaged with Nature are faithful reflections of very poorly developed forces of production and division of labour and an unarticulated stage of spiritual activity. It is the structural characteristics of the ancient society that explains how philosophy was standard as a form of public life for the free citizens of Athens as was the theatre and the ancient mystery plays. The 'agora' provided an open forum for a wide scope of activities ranging from the council sessions meting out justice, philosophical criticism of the moral standards of the community, meditations on the meaning of life and death, and drama which introduced new ways of honoring the ancient gods.

The history of the Roman Empire is essentially the history of a 'detour'. Julius Caesar induced 'men of spirit'—orators, doctors, teachers of the free arts to settle in Rome. Suetonius wrote that Caesar had granted citizenship to every doctor and master of the free arts in order to get them to remain in the city, thus making settlement in the capital attractive for others as well. That idea was aimed at building up a constant 'cultural organization'. According to Gramsci's hypothesis this marked the beginnings in Rome of the category of intellectuals of the empire that was succeeded by the Roman Catholic clergy and which left innumerable marks on the history of the Italian and, for that matter, European intellectuals up to the eighteenth century when it assumed a 'cosmopolitan' character. The substantial social, national and racial gap that existed between the considerable masses of intellectuals and the ruling class of the Roman Empire reappeared after the fall of the Empire between the German warriors and the original Romanized intellectuals of the class of freemen. Those were the phenomena with which the birth of Catholicism was associated, the Church that virtually absorbed the overwhelming majority of intellectual activities for several centuries to come, monopolized cultural leadership, and brought sanctions against all of those courageous enough to come out in opposition to this monopoly. (That is why the word 'clerical' generally meant 'intellectual' or 'expert' in several languages based on, or influenced by, the new latin as is the case with the Hungarian language in the Middle Ages; 'layman' which is its opposite denoted the unitiated.

The Middle Ages has its own heroes, yet the stagnation that lasted almost 1000 years shows Nature from the reverse side of the theorem: once the forms of the society grow rigid and there is stagnation in the development of the forces of production, the process of cognition comes to a standstill. The feudal society that followed not only fixed the different ranks but it also very strictly delimited the areas of activity.

The fact that every kind of spiritual activity became the monopoly of the church brought about the narrowing down of the sphere of spiritual mobility. As a result the forms of communication and publicity that are indispensable for sciences and arts were missing. Church rites such as the liturgy, mass or the procession were the exclusive institutions of publicity.

Changes at a very slow pace took place in that state of affairs only in the period that followed the eleventh and twelfth centuries. The way of life of the courts was gradually established in the castles of rich noblemen. Love songs were played by the minstrels. Builders' guilds which emerged as the workshop of contemporary architecture built the churches. In the meantime universities and other schools were founded in Paris, Bologna, Pisa and in other settlements of Europe well on the way to becoming new cities.

In the Italian city-states princes and citizens engaged in trade and people who had seen the world and had a practical approach, regarded the church builders, sculptors and painters engaged in making and painting the altars as members of the renaissance court. Philosophy, considered to be 'ancilla theologiae', the maidservant of theology, turned again towards discovering the secrets of Nature, in compliance with contemporary requirements. The distance to be covered from the Italian Renaissance to the French Enlightenment was still quite long. In the meantime scientific and artistic activities underwent fundamental changes. Actually it was those intervening centuries in which the institutions serving as a basis of the arts and sciences interpreted in a modern sense were established.

Industry which developed in that period emerged as the major laboratory in which the modern natural sciences carried out their experiments. National markets and then international ones, as the relations based on the exchange of goods became universal, necessitated the establishment of new forms of communication and contacts. The establishment of the network of communication composed of the postal services, roads and later of the railways went hand in hand with the birth of the 'written news', the forerunner of today's daily press. At the same time, this process laid the foundations for the systems of institutions of modern publicity without which the institutions of modern sciences and arts would not have existed.[3]

Conflicting interests of a political character gave birth to the changes in the structure of publicity and then colored it in specific ways. Coffee-houses, salons, and groups gathered around a table emerged as the forms of bourgeois thought in contrast to the court. Views opposed to one another led not only to the birth of new ideologies and tendencies; they also induced changes in the functional properties and structural characteristics of the arts and social thought from which the social sciences subsequently stemmed. The scientist and artist interpreted in a modern sense—whose type and essential features have been arbitrarily reflected back into ancient society[4]—and the feudal world of the Middle Ages[5] appeared in fact during the above discussed process.

The bourgeois society gave birth to a new group of consumers that modified the functions of culture and art and transformed their structure. The 'auditorium' of the arts came to be broadened as a result of the increasingly universal relations based on exchange. Works of art and the products of the mind were turned into goods, though in a different manner than usual. There were personal contacts between the patron and the creative artist in the Renaissance principalities and later in the royal courts and in the noblemen's country houses. Widening bourgeois publicity brought about profound changes in the characteristics of those relations by ending the personal and direct nature of communication between the two parties.

The writer produced his works for a public completely unknown to him. The patron was replaced by the publisher who transmitted the literary work of art to the unknown readers. This institution was in complete harmony with the structure of the bourgeois society in which every form of the exchange and communication is based on a sort of anonymous turnover.

Parallel to this, fundamental changes took place in the structure and functions of the theatre as well. The theatre moved out of the narrow domains of the court and became an open theatre to continue the traditions established by the comedies of fairs and university amateurs. The moulding of the 'audience' or public was, of course, far from a simple process moving along in one direction. The ways in which the people of the stalls and the boxes came to be stratified has its own specific story. The result of the process was that those who acted at court became professional actors and the theatre became an enterprise increasingly independent of patrons.

Perhaps the changes in the relations between music and its audience are even more demonstrative of the structural and functional changes taking place in the arts. Up to the end of the eighteenth century every kind of music had been bound to the function of what can be termed as representative publicity; in other words it was music for an occasion. It was designed to contribute to the devotion and solemnity of the church service or to enhance the atmosphere of a specific site or the parties at a court. Composers were, as a rule, employed as church or town musicians. In this field the establishment of public concert societies marked the beginnings of a profound change. They recruited the audience for the open concerts they held through advertising. The fact that people had to pay to participate transformed the concerts into goods; at the same time, however, something described by Arnold Houser (1953) as music without purpose also came to be established: for the first time in history people assembled to listen to music for its own sake, a group of competent individuals who could be joined by anyone provided he had the appropriate property and culture.

Painters were emancipated in much the same manner from the bondages of the guilds, courts, and the church. Craftsmanship assumed the status of liberal arts ('ars liberalis'). At first the academies founded by the state and later the salons and exhibition halls played a role similar to that of publishers. However, emancipation in this particular line of art also made its representatives components of a new 'invisible' system of dependence. They were no longer placed at the mercy of the taste of the feudal lord who collected works of art; instead, they had to run the risk of producing for the market. It follows from the monolithic character of culture that political and economic power came to be associated with spiritual privileges, or more exactly with the exclusiveness of spiritual power even in the late stages of the feudal society. As was proved perfectly by Habermas (1962), the state and church authorities retained the privilege of interpretation not only on the pulpit but also in philosophy, literature and arts. The work of art was part and parcel of the symbolism of the church and the court; this accounts for their glory or sacramental character. No doubt market relations deprived the arts of this sort of glory and made them profane; at the same time, however, they broadened the field of view and rendered the works of art generally accessible—in principle. To form a judgement of a specific work of art became the subject of a free debate which, in turn, was an integral part of the battle waged by the bourgeoisie for an end to the political and spiritual privileges of the aristocracy.[6] Presence in culture is part of an expression of the process of 'viewing one's own self'. The bourgeoisie, through a phase described by Karl Marx (1844, 1845-46) as the class existing in itself also became a class existing for itself. The modern artist and thinker moulded in the new social institutions were partners of the bourgeoisie in that process. For one of the spiritual catalysts of the process was the secular thinker interested simultaneously in the secrets of mechanics, reflexology, rational law, virtue, cognition and creative activities. Those called the encyclopaedists were not just the editors of the new encyclopedias, but their own knowledge and life-work were also of an encyclopedic nature. Their philosophy was associated with criticism, and the arguments they put forward undermined the very foundations of what was described as the sacred and eternal system of values of the feudal society. Their art, which raised doubts as to whether or not the previous forms of human intercourse had been natural, also involved a critical approach. That is why the philosophers and artists of the period of the Enlightenment stimulated the bourgeoisie in its view of itself; that is why the bourgeois public managed to reach the stage of self-enlightenment and moreover to consider itself as the living process of the enlightenment in processing knowledge of philosophy and an overview of literature and the arts.

These processes also serve to explain how artists and scientists were regarded as organic components of a new bourgeoisie which had just been born—a cultured stratum distinct from the cultured people in the bourgeois societies of Western Europe that were progressing rapidly.

After the bourgeoisie had come to power the functions of bourgeois' arts and sciences came to be modified. The representation of the interests of the bourgeois embodied in the institutions of civil law and the guarantee for free competition provided a satisfactory status quo for the bourgeoisie—at least in the period known as 'classic capitalism'. Parliament, the political parties, and the daily papers became the legalized institutions of political publicity. Politics, art and the sciences appeared to split off from one another, with sciences becoming special sciences, and literature, the fine arts and music becoming the institutions of culture.

This phenomenon of the apparent separation of sciences from one another will be considered later in this study. In any case it is beyond doubt that what was on the surface had its own objective foundations: the social division of labour further differentiated human activities and the spheres of social coexistence in compliance with the changes that had taken place in the economic structure of the society and on the level of its superstructure.

Not only the natural and technical sciences came to be institutionalized and, as a result, separated from one another. The pace of this process accelerated in the case of the social sciences as well: political economy, law and psychology became independent of philosophy and emerged as the means of acquiring knowledge of and influencing reality. Bernal (1957) suggests that the idea of the scientist was introduced into common use in the eighteenth century. The arts and literature also came to be institutionalized and to pursue either of them became an independent vocation. Describing that particular period R. Williams (1960) writes that earlier every human trade had been a sort of art, but later the term art denoted a specific group of trades or crafts: the 'creative' and the 'imaginary' crafts. Artistic activity emerged from the status of a craft to become a kind of institution, the system of certain activities.

Culture was codified as a sphere of human activity possessing comparative autonomy in the decades in question. Education, a function of the family and of church institutions in feudal society, assumed the status of a social and secular duty. At first, culture was identified with education. An indication of this is the origin of the word, for in the early stages the idea it denoted meant—as a parallel of agriculture—the conditions necessary for natural growth, in other words, care and supervision. As a result of the Enlightenment, however, its meaning was gradually extended to cover 'acquired knowledge' and the institutions in which accumulated 'knowledge' is institutionalized and gets richer. At the subsequent stages the meaning of culture underwent further changes. In connection with the separation of the spheres of activity from one another I intend to underline again and from the subject of this study that culture, science and the scientist, as well as arts and the artist—as we know them today—are the children of the age in question.

So far as the changed relations between the arts and sciences and politics are concerned, it must be emphasized that individual examples are not of decisive importance. That Defoe wrote pamphlets in the period of transition and that Swift held political office while editing a journal cannot be regarded as decisive arguments once they are removed from their context. Nor can Flaubert's statement that politics are the poisoning substance of the arts be accepted as being of decisive importance.

The positions taken by the above-mentioned people should be considered as essential symptoms, or if you like, characteristics of the age concerned. From the point of view of the subject of this study which could be described as the changes in the meaning of the concept of the intellectual, or more exactly, the understanding of the real social functions of the learned, it is essential to analyse the points of intersection of the political plane and the intellectual plane. While examining the literary trends of the French society in the nineteenth century, Pierre Bourdieu (1971) arrived at the conclusion that in the period of consolidation the situation of the artist and the writer was characterized by a specific ambiguity: he was a member and a dependent of the group in power simultaneously, that is he belonged to the oppressed faction of the ruling class.

This ambiguous situation serves as an explanation to the emotional dualism which is so characteristic of intellectuals engaged with arts and writing. A feature that is reflected not just in the emotional wavering observable on the surface and is not confined merely to the dislike of or affection for the ruling groups, or to the difference to or profound sympathy with the lot of the oppressed, or to the alternation of demands and contempt for privileges, a quality that often appears to be too irrational. This stratum is also inclined to form an ambiguous image of its own social position and duties. Its members are prisoners of the fetish of the goods, the mechanism that reverses the relations between men and things, the 'market for literature and arts' whose anonymous, incalculable, and very often changing sanctions bring about unprecedented difference between them. However, no one or very few of them are aware of all this. In a tradition going back to Julien Benda, they are unable to consider their position in terms of 'objective' implication, in other words, as the producers of goods, a fact that is obviously related—at least since the romantic period—to their ideas formed in connection with the social mission of the artist and the writer. That is why they are at a loss to understand, among other things, the public at large as a sociological formation which acts simultaneously as the source of their well-founded success and as the impertinent mob deserving nothing but contempt, a large group of people whose ranks are meant, at least in moments of passion, to include both the bourgeois who 'grapples with the inferior cares of commerce' and the 'people rendered stupid by productive labor'.

It goes without saying that reality is much more complex and differentiated than the picture outlined above. The rise in the proportion of cultured people is attributable to a number of social requirements. Judged by the standards of today, the growth was still of a slow pace, but it is beyond any doubt that it resulted already in the expansion of the ranks of the consumers of literature and arts. The fact that the authority of the 'producers of the symbolic goods' increased was one of the consequences of the above process. This is in fact a specific paradox: under the conditions of capitalist society it is the market that determines most 'stubbornly' the dependence of the artist and the writer. At the same time the extent of the artist's and writer's independence or, as Bourdieu (1971) put it, that of the intellectual plane, increases in proportion to the expansion of the market of symbolic goods. The higher the values that circulate within the framework of the market of the symbolic goods, the more important the values that explain the intellectual and artistic characteristics of the 'manufacturers' of the symbolic products. This brings about corresponding changes in the position occupied by the faction of intellectuals in the set-up of the ruling class.

It is a source of several kinds of misunderstanding that sociological writings dealing in particular with the intelligentsia tend to regard the bourgeoisie and the intelligentsia as people of the same brand. Analysis of both the political plane and the intellectual plane supplies evidence to the effect that the bourgeoisie is split up into factions in much the same manner as the intelligentsia.

The separation of the intellectual factions from one another explains the wider room allowed for movement within the limits of the intellectual plane. Three major separate fractions can be distinguished in the 1830's and 1840's, and more or less throughout the whole of the last century. They are: 'bourgeois arts', the 'l'art pour l'art', and the 'social arts'.

Bourdieu does not consider them to be pure literary or artistic groupings. Their inherent contradictions simultaneously reflect those existing among the segments of the ruling classes, the relations between the oppressor and oppressed classes and the ways in which the categories of artists and writers of a different position are related in the market. All this is reflected in a highly contradictory manner. This is due, in fact, to the complex combination of affiliations and exclusions in which the different economic and symbolic emphasis corresponding to the different relations are condensed.

Thus the various segments of the group of intellectuals made up of artists and writers were attached to the different groups of the bourgeoisie or the opposition as their component parts. The increased role they played is expressed, among other things, by the fact that they had become the participants of the struggles waged by the different groupings of the ruling class against one another not because they had been commissioned to do so but on their own initiative.

Of the three principal factions of the intellectuals the situation of the 'bourgeois' writers and artists was the most clear-cut. They were the faithful and conscious representatives of bourgeois society and they were given high income and moral privileges by the well-to-do bourgeoisie for services rendered. Since the representatives of the 'social arts' were excluded both socially and economically, they were made to sympathize with the oppressed who, at the same time, expressed their dislike of the 'dominant factions' of the ruling class or the 'bourgeois' men of letters.

The most puzzling and, in many ways, the most contradictory representatives of the age in question were those in the 'l'art pour l'art' category. Their position was ambiguous even if it is considered within the limits of the intellectual plane: their political and artistic values are determined by their simultaneous opposition to and distaste for both the 'bourgeois' and 'social' arts. This pattern, however, is far from being a simple and clear-cut one, for they thought not only their own situation to be contradictory but also that of the groups that they strongly opposed. Another characteristic feature of their standpoint was that the political element seemed to have been eliminated from their attitudes. They appear to have divided up social reality according to merely aesthetic categories and, as a result, they had as much contempt for the bourgeois who did not understand the arts as the people who had to grapple with everyday survival. This attitude was expressed by Flaubert who said that the term 'bourgeoisie' for him covered not only citizens wearing overalls but also those with a frock coat and added that only people of his brand, the men of letters, were the true representatives of beauty and culture (Bourdieu, 1971).

Dualism was present in the whole of their life work from beginning to end. They deeply sympathized with those excluded from the society by the partialities and prejudices of the 'merciless' bourgeoisie. They included the happy-go-lucky type, the dilettante painter, the rope dancers, the minor nobility, the good hearted servant and, above all, the prostitute, who was considered to be the real symbol of the relations between the artist and the market. Thus the artists of that particular age displayed profound contempt of and hatred for the bourgeois, and on the intellectual plane which acted as the arena of the aesthetic and political conflict among the factions of the artists, this hatred found expression in their feelings for the bourgeois artist. However, in case they were threatened by the happy-go-lucky ones who had come down in the world in terms of both their bourgeois or artistic existence, they tended to favor the bourgeoisie. Since they were people jealous of both their own successes and the arts, they wrote with disdain about the literary proletariat which they often described as a mob.

Refraining from political passions and paying more respect to artistic values than to anything else was, to quote Julien Benda again, the expression of a specific political and artistic attitude. If any analysis is made of their statements and confessions (which are frequently quoted arbitrarily by placing them in their corresponding historical context) it is quite evident that in 1848 their manifestations were characterized by hopes and commitment. After the failure of the 1848 revolution and during the period of the Second Empire, but in particular during the Paris Commune these undisturbed hopes and pure enthusiasms were transformed (by the changes that had taken place in the power relation of the classes and in the relationship between the ruling factions and that of the intellectuals) into political indifference and backwardness.

And since from the point of view of the myth of the 'eternal intellectual' this is of vital importance, it must be underlined that historical reasons are responsible for their turning their backs on history. The only way in which they were able to find a resolution to the inherent contradictions in a way of creation which rejected every sort of open content was by the 'l'art pour l'art' principle. While endeavouring to enforce the absolute privilege of artistic competence—as is stated very wittily by Bourdieu—they wanted to reverse the objective relations prevailing between the ruling class and intellectuals composed of artists on a symbolic level. The cult of style for its own sake as practised on the aesthetic level was the expression of political indifference directed against those writers and artists who committed themselves socially.

In connection with this, references must also be made to the changes in the functions of the social sciences. In this respect, however, only one point will be underlined because it is important from the viewpoint of this study. The formation and the early stages of the development of capitalism were characterized by the conviction that free enterprise ensures the dynamism of the economy and the balance of productive forces. Economic automatisms have no need whatever of intervention whether on the part of the state or of science, for the hidden hand in the background, in other words the mysterious rules of the game that govern the market and the exchange of goods can guarantee the continuity of progress. The system of liberal thought faithfully reflects this concept. However, contradictions that grew ever sharper undermined the illusion of spontaneous and harmonious development. This occurred first in France and then in other highly developed countries. Saint-Simon was the first to put into words the idea that social processes need to be regulated with the aid of scientific foresight. Following the Revolution of 1848, the tendency to regard the elaboration of reform plans serving the government's policy of stabilization appeared as the sociologist's duty. Sociology, as a science was born in the spirit of this very idea, and later the other social sciences followed.

What is termed the 'Science of Reform' that came into the picture after the 1870s and had order and progress on its banner was completed by two other trends. One was the endeavour to establish 'value free' analysis; thus science seemingly managed to be independent of political struggle. Other groups composed of bourgeois scientists wanted to place the sciences at the service of transcendent, eternal and unchangeable values. To this end they virtually removed the sciences from the social reality because bourgeois reality had become unstable and the everyday life of the bourgeoisie, based on profit and concrete assets, had become a cemetery of spiritual values. This attitude was often combined with a rebellious approach. But the revolt, however passionate and ingenious it might have been, left the foundations of the bourgeois system intact. That was the spiritual medium in which 'culture' and 'civilization' as well as 'the mass', and 'quality' were contrasted for the first time as factors that subsequently emerged as leading spiritual elements of different intellectual movements. This tendency had either a 'soft' or a 'militant' version of anti-Marxism in common which expressed the relations existing among the factions within the bourgeois intelligentsia and the ruling classes similar to the different factions of art. These relations involved their conflicts and identities of interest. All these disputes regarding standards occurred within the limits of the bourgeois intellectual plane. The essential condition for a radical turn of events lay, especially following the Commune of Paris, in the undertaking of sharing the positions of the proletariat, which meant not only the abandonment of an internal standpoint protected by the state power but also doubts as to the philosophical foundations on which the bourgeois society rested. An analysis of intellectual careers, however, reveals that the lines of distinction were too far from being absolutely clear-cut and that the phenomena of the revolution that are very much like tidal movements brought about the most unexpected combination of identifications and separations in the working-class movement of the end of the nineteenth century.

The functions of the natural and technical sciences also underwent certain changes as a result of which theoretical and applied research were separated from one another, with the latter becoming ever more directly an essential element of industrial and military development strategy. The internal logic of industrial production and increasingly sharper competition necessitated the introduction of new production lines; the permanent technological revolution emerged as the symptom of the industry.

The value of fixed capital was reproduced only to the extent to which it was utilized in the production process. It was possible now for capital to replace live labour through the analysis and application of mechanical and chemical laws. This stage of the development of machines was only possible after large-scale industry had reached a certain stage and all the sciences had been placed at the service of capital, and the existing installation could act as a major power source. Invention assumed the character of business and the application of sciences directly in production became a viewpoint determining and stimulating invention.[7]

The modern intellectual vocations like those of the lawyer, physician, engineer and economist are the products of the second thousand years of European history. It is possible to find parallels in the history of China, Japan, and the Moslem countries, but the analogies contain a number of incidental and disputable elements and do not alter the fact that the initial forms of the modern European intellectual vocations were associated with the emergence of the European universities and developed to meet definite social needs. However, there are remarkable shifts in the phases of the formation of the vocations in question. In the feudal society what might be termed as the 'aristocracy of the robe', a group of people with specific privileges was established parallel with the foundation of the central state power and side by side with several other strata including that of the clerks of public and local administrations, secular scientists, theoreticians, philosophers, and so on. As Gramsci put it, the capitalist enterpreneur established the technical expert, the scholar of political economy, the organizer of the new culture and law, and so on in his own image.

The history of the vocations mentioned above supplies unchallengeable evidence to the effect that all the spiritual vocations and special activities in question sprang up from social practice and became independent professions in accordance with the demands of the given economic system, social organization of labor and power relations.

That is why the type of the ideal of the eternal intellectual can only be built up from the characteristics of the 'artist' and 'scientist' that have been rendered timeless. Here we are more likely to lose track of the beginnings, while the analogies are more convincing and more misleading. Plato's *Republic* or Sophocles' *Antigone* have an appeal to the man of today, and most of the problems they grapple with are as current as they were in the time of the two great figures.

So far as their sociological criteria are concerned both the sciences and the arts are as much the products of history as the industry or the state. This means not only that the above institutions are also the products of social practice and that the sciences and arts have their own history but also that parallel with the social changes, social awareness and the planes of the superstructure are also rearranged; changes take place in the structure of scientific and artistic activity in accordance with this process of rearrangement.

It is the history of the sciences and arts, specifically that of scientific and artistic activity that can supply evidence that the figure of the eternal intellectual is nothing but the child of legend. The historical processes quoted above prove that the differentiation of scientific and artistic activities, their spread to the broader strata of the people and their becoming independent vocations are the functions of the structural changes.

At this point we must go back to the theoretical and methodological question we began before the detour, the tendency of bourgeois sociology to identify—by different standards and with different convincing power—the concept of the intelligentsia as such with the intellectuals of a specific historical period or with only one of their numerous functions.

The type of the ideal of the scientist, artist, jurist, or physician cannot be described by just one pattern. This applies, to an even greater extent, to the intellectual who is the generalized figure embodying the artist, scientist, jurist and physician on the basis of one or more functional features of characteristics of the personality that are made independent of both space and time.

Marxist sociology is of the opinion that the political power relations, the administrative requirements of the developing national states, the systems of the institutions of publicity, cultural conditions and the formation of culture all collectively serve to explain the characteristics of the separation of mental work from physical labour, and the privileges or lack of them that coincide with spiritual activity, and the process of the intellectualization of certain types of work that used to be regarded as physical labor. The characteristic techniques of directing and administering society can only be interpreted through a knowledge of the properties of the social organization of labor, of the technical and technological standards of production, and of the class structure of a given socio-economic formation. Thus the actual socio-historical implications can explain not only the activities that call for the sort of handling of ideas that can be generalized, and for the independent and, in some cases, creative application of knowledge and symbols, but they can also explain how those who become intellectuals are positioned in the social hierarchy. Even their functions, way of life and characteristics of the personality can only be interpreted in harmony with the systems of social relations.

While facing the myth of the eternal intellectual our attention is being focused on the ways in which the intellectual activities and their characteristics are established and change in accordance with the prevailing historical conditions. The supposition, or question, of the extent to which the activities concerned can be regarded as characteristics sufficient to lead to the formation of a stratum, or more exactly, whether or not the representatives as a whole of the related professions can constitute an independent social stratum remains open. For quite a few authors are in the habit of treating the intelligentsia and the intellectual identically or at least of placing the two ideas next to each other. The question raised appears to be a simple and final one: once there are intellectuals active in a certain society, there is good reason to speak of the intellectuals as being part and parcel of this specific society. Parallel to this train of thought, the lawyer, judge, and the prosecutor collectively make up the group or section of jurists, while the section of artists is composed of the sculptor, actor and writer and the intellectual vocations put together constitute the stratum of the intelligentsia, or if you like, the professional class. The logical approach alone, however, cannot bring us nearer to a solution, for the historical situations have brought about such a rich variety of points of linkage that concrete historical analysis cannot be replaced by any logical construction.

A fact that should not be left out of consideration is that the history of the intellectual professions, that is professional and vocational groups, dates from a time centuries earlier and that the word 'intelligentsia' began to be used as a sociological term denoting the intelligentsia as an independent stratum.

The shift in the phrase alone cannot prove anything. However, it is food for thought that the emergence of the awareness of the intelligentsia as a stratum and parallel with this the qualification of intellectuals as an independent social stratum did not come to be commonly used in the countries in which professional groups of a comparatively large number and development were active but in those where progress came to a standstill and the cultural institutions serving as a basis for the intellectual way of life were less developed.

The first examples of the word intelligentsia used as a sociological term dates back to the middle of the nineteenth century. The idea it denotes assumed the status of an independent theoretical system, the work of the Narodniks, above all Michalovsky (1902), Lavrov (1869), and Ivanov-Razumnikov (1908) regarded the intelligentsia as an opposition group displaying an attitude of criticism toward society and whose mission is to carry out the moral renewal of the society. Their Messianic approach was filled with strong and romantic anti-capitalist feeling. They believed that the village community was the image of the society of the future and that their intentions based on the idea of innovation would find support in the ranks of the peasantry. The definition given by Ivanov-Razumnikov is most demonstrative of their image of the intelligentsia. In his view the intelligentsia displayed an anti-bourgeois attitude from an ethical viewpoint, while from a sociological aspect they constitute a group that lies outside the existing order and classes. They accept and transmit cultural heritage. This group is characterized by creative work and ideals and by the endeavour to introduce these ideals into life for the spiritual, physical, social and individual liberation of the personality.

In Poland, Czechoslovakia and Hungary, countries in which the delay in industrialization and urbanization, as well as the integrity of the positions of huge estates, were combined with the partial or complete absence of national independence (structural properties which characterize Eastern Europe) the awareness of the intellectuals' mission also included responsibility for the national existence.

This concept became a term commonly used in West European and, in particular, the Anglo-American sociological literature prior to the turn of the twentieth century. As has already been mentioned briefly this fact is paradoxical because, owing to the delay in bourgeois progress, the development of the modern bourgeois intellectuals in Russia and in the other East European countries took place at a slower pace. In Western Europe, however, the institutions of a modern bourgeois culture were established as early as in the seventeenth and eighteenth centuries parallel with the industrial revolution. Strangely enough, the problems of the intellectuals, the specific part they play, and their awareness of their mission were considered for the first time in countries other than these.

As I have already attempted to show, the development that took place in Britain supplies the most universal example of the combination of the newly born bourgeois intellectuals with the institutions and forms of existence of the bourgeoisie. In Britain, the intellectuals, or professional classes, are the products and men of practice. The sciences were revived as a subsidiary phenomenon accompanying the industrial revolution. 'Science' came to be identified with the idea of sciences (both the natural and technical ones) and the Royal Society (the equivalent of the Academy of Sciences in other countries) rallied primarily the inventors and innovators of industry and technology. The new order of the bourgeois state governed by laws sprang up in the course of practice from the formations of the feudal society. The old type of the bourgeois, made up of shopkeepers and craftsmen, ran lower on the social scale, and at the beginning the enterpreneur, the 'learned' people including the physician, parson, army officer, professor, and the land-owner (the latter being well under way to becoming a member of the grand bourgeoisie) were positioned alongside one another in the 'speculative' community, with the land-owner retaining the functions that the French nobility subsequently lost during the French Revolution. To distinguish the above-listed strata from the illiterate people (it is interesting to note that at the beginning of the 18th century the illiterates were higher in number than in the Elizabethan Age) their contemporaries described them collectively as the cultured classes.

The philosophy that considered experience the paramount source of science and regarded utility as the greatest of all values and principles reflected the special characteristics of the development in Britain. The spirit of the age is reflected by the linguistic fact that the word 'professionals' came to be used to collectively denote those pursuing intellectual professions. (The term specialist which is the Hungarian equivalent of the English word fails to contain the original meaning of the English word.) The term 'intellectual' which can most conveniently be related to the concept of the man of spirit found its way into the language at a later date and in the English-speaking world it has some ironic implications. It is noteworthy that the archaic variation of the word 'intellectualistas' was used fairly early by Bacon and denoted a style of thinking but not a social stratum. It is instructive to quote the term used by Bacon because it suggests the opposite of what was proposed by the very early stages of bourgeois development in Britain. The British regarded the expert, the thinker serving and analysing practice, and not the ideologist as a mental worker. That is one but not the least of the reasons why the line of distinction drawn between the manufacturer and the scientist or philosopher is only of a relative value. Too much respect for and adoration of the human mind and the intellect act as the source of another misunderstanding, that people unnecessarily refrain from observing Nature, considering the experiences gained and stumbled on in the jungle of their own reasoning and ideas. It is quite justified that intellectuals of this kind were condemned and regarded as laughing stock.

While analysing the characteristics of the development taking place in Britain, Gramsci made references, among other things, to the one-sidedness of the practice-centered approach and called attention to the negative consequences of the historical compromise. He says that while the new social grouping that grew up on the basis of industrialization made an unprecedented economic and institutional progress, it more or less groped its way in the spiritual field. The category of the 'organic intellectuals' which was born along with the economic group in the same field was very broad. However, the virtually monopolistic position of the old landed class had been preserved on the highest level. It is true that their economic superiority was gone, but their political and spiritual superiority was retained for a considerable time and the new group that came to power assimilated the leading stratum as the 'traditional intellectuals' (Gramsci, 1949). The links connecting the old landed aristocracy with the factory owners is of a type that unites the traditional intellectuals with the new ruling classes in the other countries.

The French pattern of development is different from the British one in several respects. The path covered by the French aristocracy is not the same; the ways in which the bourgeoisie gained political ground were more dramatic and were filled with greater tension. Again, the French Enlightenment ran a different course. The differences lay not only in the fact that the French salons were not similar to the English coffee-houses; the French style of thinking that made rationalism a European tradition was also different from the English tradition. In connection with this, Gramsci had every reason to underline that France offered a perfect example of the harmonious development of every area of the national force, in particular, of intellectual groupings. When 1789 saw a new social grouping coming to the surface, even in political terms, the system that provided for the practice of the new social functions had already been completely established. That is why at that state the new grouping was engaged in fighting for complete domination of the nation without making any essential compromise with the classes of the old order. It rather subordinated them to its own objectives. The first intellectual 'cells' of a new type were born along with the first economic 'cells' and even the organization of the church came to be influenced by them. This strong intellectual organization was responsible for the remarkable part played by French culture in the eighteenth and nineteenth centuries.

When a comparison is made with what happened in the eastern part of Europe the features that are similar to those of the French and English developments gain importance. During the phase of the upward swing of bourgeois development the engineer, the economist, and the specialist of bourgeois law (that is the groups of intellectuals that were born together with the bourgeoisie and whose existence was attributable to the industrial revolution) regarded themselves as a part of the bourgeoisie. Others, however, denoted by the term 'traditional intellectuals' and having been members of the court in the feudal society or financed by patrons, established their own independent existence both in Britain and in France as the beneficiaries or losers of the relations based on the exchange of goods that became universal following the elimination of feudal ties. In the early stages of capitalism it was a common characteristic of the people active in what might be described as the 'free professions'—irrespective of whether they were physicians, lawyers having their own office or artists—that they were situated outside the social hierarchy; their actual or believed freedom, however, contributed to strengthening their awareness of belonging to the bourgeoisie. The analyses made by Pierre Buordieu and quoted earlier in this study supplies evidence to the effect that both their apparent neutrality towards the social processes and their criticism of society, which often took the form of a solitary revolt, emerged within the political realities of the period of liberalism and were attached to the political and ideological trends of the different factions of the bourgeoisie; few people were ready to display an attitude of radical negation and share the spiritual positions of another class—that of the workers.

In certain German principalities—especially in Prussia where, according to Marx (1844), the feudal ruling order was gone but no classes had as yet come to replace it—the picture was essentially a modified one in the early decades of the nineteenth century. (That is why the origins of the concept 'intelligentsia' introduced by the Russian Narodniks dates back to the period of German enlightenment and Max Stirner, the True Socialist and the other representatives of the German ideology who were the forerunners of the type of the intellectual lying outside the feudal structure and the classes.) The more eastward one proceeds on the map of Europe in the nineteenth century, in other words the more delayed and distorted the bourgeois' development, the more one finds that the sphere of movement of the men of spirit was shifted into the realm of ideals, desires, hopes or illusions. The absence of industry, the small populations of the towns and the low standard of the development of cultural institutions necessarily made the cultured stratum in the countries concerned not only more ideological minded but also rendered them more solitary and more prepared to revolt.

Tensions took a number of forms and launched movements in differing directions. They were expressed in many ways, including literary tendencies fulfilling a political mission, in peaks such as the works of prose of Russian realism or Hungarian poetry, often leading to lonely revolt, decadence, disappointment, doubt that there is any sense in action, and the apology of isolation. There was one thing in common to all of those following the failure of the revolution of 1848: there was no realistic path leading from the 'thought' of revolt to 'action'. Their representatives felt themselves to be 'redundant people' and professed the ideals of the bourgeoisie while having to do without the institutions of bourgeois society. Awareness of this particular crisis became obvious in the picture of the intellectuals drawn by the Russian Narodniks, or more exactly, it became a false one, a system of ideals serving noble objectives and offering the path of suffering. The deeper the crisis, the more painful and hopeless the intellectuals' awareness of their isolation.

Alexander Blok (1909), the outstanding figure of the poetry of Symbolism, asked in 1908 whether the dividing line separating the intellectuals from Russia was in fact impossible to cross, and added that as long as the line existed the intellectuals were confined to within the limits of a magic circle of which they were unable to find their way out, forced, as they were, to move round and round. It was visible every day that the number of intellectuals saved by the positive principles of the sciences, social activity and arts dwindled gradually. As long as it was not available revolt and violence gained the upper hand, ranging from the vulgar revolt against God of the decadents to open self-destruction in a variety of perversities, drunkenness and suicide. The intellectuals came to be increasingly influenced by the desire to die while the people were imbued all the time with the desire to live.

Paradoxically enough, the demand for definition of the intelligentsia, as an independent stratum arises as a necessity in the West European countries at a point of regression in the history of bourgeois society when either seemingly or in fact the path along which the bourgeoisie and the intelligentsia (or, more exactly, certain intellectual groups) wish to proceed came to be separated. In this respect the idea of the intellectual as one lying outside the feudal order and the class system, as 'free-floating' to use a modern phrase—and the theories attached to this idea are also the products of a crisis, the specific precipitates of the crisis of the bourgeois society.

Naturally this process can be characterized in more than one way. First and foremost the reality or its segments that are reflected by the different theories of the intellectuals is contradictory, too, while acting as a framework for the different tendencies. The theoreticians concerned witness a shift from the period when the productive forces of the capitalist society develop and become concentrated, to a period when the dividing up of the world into colonial spheres has practically ended and the struggle for the redistribution of the globe leading to a new world war began. Recurrent economic depressions and the endeavour on the part of the monopolies to gain exclusive rights in a combination of these and other factors have weakened the omnipotence of the belief in free enterprise and liberalism. Intervention by the state in the economic sphere that had previously been qualified as a sovereign domain grew stronger, in parallel with and as a result of the above process. State administration increased substantially extending its influence to a number of new fields. The system of social insurance was established, partly in an attempt to counter-balance the powerful demands of the working class and later to meet the challenge of the October Revolution. An increasing number of social strata came to be covered by compulsory education. The goods produced by the artists were turned into a substantial source of income following the broadening of the international market. What used to be elite intellectual professions assumed a mass character. The undivided power exercised by the huge corporations engaged in publishing, the international news agencies, then the film industry, the private radio and television companies gradually destroyed the hopes and illusions of unlimited freedom for the sciences and arts.

As a result of the above changes the intellectuals who had never before constituted a unified stratum became more and more polarized. Separations and confrontations taking place within the ranks of the intellectuals following the turn of the twentieth century were revealed not only in the differences of income level, rank and social authority, for the political and spiritual division intensified partly under the influence of the increasingly stronger working class movement and as a result of the reaction to it. The processes in question were joined and amplified by the October Revolution. The task of their analysis, however, is left for another study.

NOTES

1. In reviewing the facts of the history of science and art it is too vulgar to state that the values of truth and beauty are not timeless, that the ideas also come to be institutionalized, that innovators have always had to enforce their new principles, ideals, and novel methods of creative activity in the face of conservative trends in the sciences and arts.

2. If we wish to reply to the question as to whether the arts and sciences have ever existed independently of society, we must begin with the structural characteristics of human activity, that is from the relativity of the separation of mental work from physical labour. Like the arts, science was not born and has not developed as a result of the self-generation of ideas. Even the most abstract science or the most esoteric kinds of art grew out of practice and their subsequent 'history' cannot be considered to be independent of the characteristics of the social division of labour and its respective socio-economic formations.

3. One of the most essential elements of this process from our point of view was that private individuals came to be organized into a public. The bourgeois family instilled a need for getting to know and inform our own selves which has been associated by Jurgen Habermas (1962) with the necessity of the systematiza-

tion of the experiences gained by the new sort of private humanity. This interest led not only to the irth of a new science: psychology, but it also revived 'reasoning' in the h   of culture hat became public: in the reading rooms, theatres, museums, and concert halls. Again, it is the 'town' that was the center of attraction for movements of this nature.

4. In the ancient polis the audience of the spectators were identical with the agora; thought and drama, the architecture and decoration were not separated from the other forms of social action.

5. In the early stages of the Middle Ages the Church acted as a framework for all of these relations; at the subsequent stages of the development of the feudal society the 'medium' which commissioned works of art was the court; this was a king of 'consumption' regulated by strict etiquette and described by Sombart (1919) as spectacular consumption.

6. That was the period that saw the establishment of the first public libraries, clubs of readers and reading societies; the different strata of the bourgeoisie developed the habit of reading novels. The circulation figures of the periodicals doubled; analyses containing criticism got separated from the discussions and the systems of reviewing works of art developed separately. The reader was offered the opportunity of making himself familiar with the particular work of art and its review simultaneously. Similar to the theatres and concerts, the museums also institutionalized the secular judgement of the arts. All those were part and parcel of a social class gaining increasing spiritual ground. Even if the institutions of bourgeois publicity adhered—in the early stages of their establishment—to the aristocratic society that gradually grew independent of the court, the 'larger' public that was moulded into an audience in the theatres, museums and concerts was recruited from the bourgeoisie in terms of their social background.

7. However brief and sketchy this review of the highlights of history of the arts and sciences is—for the guiding principle was not to recall their history which is infinitely rich in figures, ideas and tendencies with chronological accuracy—the correlations outlined are sufficient to show that the development of the institutions of sciences and arts—as we know them today—is a very long process which can only be interpreted properly in the context of the changes in the structural and functional characteristics of the forms of social activity.

REFERENCES

Benda, J. (1927), *La trahison des cleres.* Paris.
Bernal, J. (1957), *Science in History.* London.

Blok, A. (1909), *Narod i intelligentsia.* Saint Petersburg.
Bourdieu, P. (1971), *Champ de pouvoir, champ intellectuel et habitus de classe.* Paris.
Gramsci, A. (1949), *Gli Intelectuali e l'Organizaccione della Culture.* Torino.
Habermas, J. (1962), *Strukturwandel der Offentlichkeit.* Neuwid u. Berlin.
Ivanov-Razumnikov (1908), *Sto takoe 'Machovschyna'. K voprosi ob intelligentsii.* St. Petersburg.
Hauser, A. (1953), *Socialgeschichte der Kunst und Literatur,* I-II. München.
Lavrov, P. (1869), *Istoricheskiye Pisma. Kultura i Musl.* Saint Petersburg.
Marx, K. (1844), *Zur Kritik der Hegelschen Rechtsphilosophie.* (Werke Bd. I.)
———(1845-46), *Die deutsche Ideologie.* Werke Bd. III.
Michalovsky, (1902), *Polnoe sobranie sochimeniy,* T.2. Saint Petersburg.
Sombart, W. (1919), *Der moderne Kapitalismus.* München und Leipzig.
Williams, R. (1960), *Culture and Society 1780-1950.* New York.

6

THE ROLES OF THE INTELLECTUAL AND POLITICAL ROLES

Seymour Martin Lipset
Stanford University, USA
and Asoke Basu
California State University at Hayward

Literature on the role of the 'intellectual' consists of a vast body of descriptive 'linguistics' which is not integrated into any coherent theoretical framework. The present analysis, centered on the political role of the intellectual, attempts a limited contribution to that objective, a 'paradigm' based upon independent, but cross-cutting, dichotomies: intellect-intelligence and innovative-integrative. Our intent is to provide a heuristic though still largely descriptive model reflective of the complexity of politically relevant roles performed by the intellectual. Such a model hopefully may aid in future empirical endeavors to understand the intellectual's place in society. A note of caution must, however, be exercised. The term 'paradigm' has formal, logical connotations. It is not our attempt to pigeonhole various roles intellectuals perform into a rigid logical framework. To do so would deny the fluidity of the societal process. Rather, we wish to stress the diverse manifestations of the role of the intellectual.

This essay has been written as part of a comparative study of intellectuals undertaken at the Center for International Affairs of Harvard University under grants from the Ford Foundation and the National Endowment for the Humanities. It is also appearing in Lewis Coser, ed. *The Idea of Social Structure* (New York; The Free Press, 1975). This article is copyrighted by the Free Press © 1975. It is reprinted here by permission of the copyright holder.

Before engaging in an analysis of the role of the intellectual, we present relevant comparative and historical literature documenting the generality of an inherent antipathy between intellectuals and the powers throughout modern history, particularly since the rise of the secular intellectual. Reference to factors inherent in the nature of the role of 'intellectual' which gave rise to such phenomena will be discussed in subsequent sections of this paper.

Much of the analytic literature dealing with the intellectuals has emphasized their seemingly inherent tendency to criticize existing institutions from the vantage point of general conceptions of the desirable, ideal conceptions which are thought to be universally applicable.

These concerns are iterated by the fact that 'intelligentsia' and 'intellectuals', the two words most commonly used to describe those in occupations requiring trained or imaginative intelligence, were used first in the context of describing those engaged in oppositional activities. 'Intelligentsia' first began to be used widely in Russia in the 1860's referring to the opposition by the educated strata to the system. It was generally defined as 'a "class" held together only by the bond of "consciousness", "critical thought", or moral passion' (Malia, 1961:5). 'Intellectual' as a noun first secured wide usage in France during the Dreyfus case in 1898. A protest against Dreyfus' imprisonment signed by a variety of writers and professors was published as the 'Manifesto of the Intellectuals'. The anti-Dreyfusards then tried to satirize their opponents as the self-proclaimed 'intellectuals' (Bodin, 1962: 6-9; Paléologue, 1955: 90-91; Hofstadter, 1963: 38-39).

These generalizations about the characteristic moral and political stance of intellectuals have also been noted with respect to specific historical periods. Robert Waelder concludes that 'since the last days of the Sophists, they have been in the habit of questioning and challenging values and the assumptions that were taken for granted in their societies' (1962:15). Luther's revolt against the church found its initial support from the faculty and students of his University at Wittenberg and elsewhere in Germany (Moller, 1966:238). Hobbes, writing of the causes of the English Revolution in *Behemoth,* concluded that the universities were the principal source of the rebellion.

Tocqueville, in an analysis of the next great European revolutionary wave, made reference to factors which affected the outlook of intellectuals and their influence on the *Body Politik* as major sources of revolutionary ardor. Joseph DeMaistre, an even more conservative analyst of the Revolution, also emphasized that 'many French intellectuals were instrumental in bringing about the Revolution'.

A variety of other analyses of political developments in France, the German states, Italy, and Russia, point to the role of intellectuals and students in undermining the legitimacy of existing regimes. Friedrich Engels credited the growth of social criticism in Germany in the 1840's, in part, to the writings of the literati, who were wont to include 'political allusions' in their writings.

Though the Marxist movements have made the leading role of the working-class in the revolution a matter of dogma, and have frequently treated intellectuals as predominantly members or allies of the dominant strata, they could not avoid recognizing their involvement in the movement. In Russia the various revolutionary movements were intellectual and student based until the Revolution of 1905. That revolt began with a student strike, which subsequently spread to the workers and sections of the peasantry (Benturi, 1960; Pares, 1962: 161-282; Feuer, 1969:88-172). The Chinese movements favoring modernization, which first led to the overthrow of the Manchu dynasty, and later to the massive protests which culminated in the formation of the Communist Party, also were primarily based on the students and intellectuals (Wang, 1966:229-361; Tse-Tung, 1960; Walker, 1963:87-108; Israel, 1966 and 1969:310-333).

Historically, the American intellectual has been seen as a source of unrest. The abolitionist and later editor of the New York *Tribune,* Whitlaw Reid observed:

> Exceptional influence eliminated, the scholar is pretty sure to be opposed to the established. . . . While the prevailing parties in our country were progressive and radical, the temper of our colleges was to the last degree conservative. As our politics settled into the conservative track, a fresh wind began to blow about the college seats, and literary men, at last, furnished inspiration for the splendid movement that swept slavery from the statute book. . . . Wise unrest

will always be their [the scholars] chief trait. We may set down . . . the very foremost function of the scholar in politics, *To oppose the established* (1873:613-614).

Much more recently, Daniel Patrick Moynihan concluded that since about 1840, the cultural (intellectual) elite in large measure have rejected the societal norms (1970).

The reader may get the impression that intellectual and student involvement in protest is confined to left-wing or progressive movements. This is not true, as witnessed, for example, by the intellectuals and students who constituted a core segment of the activist support for the Fascist Party of Mussolini, and of the National Socialist Party of Hitler, before they took power, as well as among fascist and assorted anti-Semitic right-wing extreme groups in France and various countries in eastern Europe up to World War II (Hamilton, 1971).

As Wilhelm Röpke noted, 'In Germany . . . where the university professor has always had exceptional standing . . . it was from the universities that most of the other intellectuals drew the disintegrating poison that they then distributed' (1960:346-347). Fascism, like diverse forms of leftism, had many meanings for diverse groups of supporters. But 'the Fascism of the intellectuals above all, had its origins in sheer rebelliousness, in an anarchistic revolt directed against the established order' (Hamilton, 1971:xx). It was a militant anti-bourgeois movement. The French fascists who took 'the avowed socialism and anti-capitalism of fascist ideology more seriously than others . . . were especially literary intellectuals . . . , men who were violently opposed—emotionally, intellectually and morally—to bourgeois society and bourgeois values' (Soucy, 1966:91).

The complacency of the despised, hard-working bourgeois was accompanied by a threat which struck the intelligentsia as equally distasteful and far more frightening—the threat of anonymity, due to the speed at which industry and mechanization were advancing and the progressive rise of masses who could at last participate in the administration of a world in which they had previously been voiceless. . . .

To this threat of anonymity Fascism seemed to offer a solution, for it reconciled the cult of the hero with a mass movement. It defied social transformation by its deliberate protection of traditional values and attempted to impose a social structure which, though aristocratic in form, was based on individual merit regardless of social origin (Hamilton, 1971:xx-xxi).

There is, of course, no reliable quantitative estimate of the distribution of political sentiments among Italian and German intellectuals before the triumph of fascism. In both countries, particularly in Germany, left-wingers were also prominent. Much of the literature concerning the Germans in the Weimar period deals with the role of various groups of left-wing intellectuals, many of whom were Jewish, who attacked German political, social, and economic institutions in bitter terms, exhibiting total contempt for the culture.

Although as the example of the Weimar intellectuals demonstrates, intellectual criticism may be 'leftist' or 'rightist', intellectuals are rarely defenders of the status quo. As Florian Znaniecki pointed out, radicals or 'novationists', as he called them, require serious 'critical reflection', intellectual analyses, a formal ideology to develop an oppositional force, while those who seek to maintain the established, base their position on traditional standards. Consequently, 'conservatives are less "intellectual" and rationalize their defense of the traditional order mainly in reaction to arguments of their opponents. This does not apply to "reactionaries", that is, to critics of the society from the right who base their position on a belief in the superior worth of a previous social order' (1968:70-71).

The disposition of intellectuals to find the dominant culture and institutions of their society in distress need not take a political or activist form. Indeed, as Max Weber has noted, the tension between intellectualdom and the imperfect, confused, messy social order often may take forms far removed from the political arena. His discussion of alternative reactions has obvious relevance to the contemporary scene.

> The salvation sought by the intellectual is always based on inner need, and hence it is at once more remote from life, more theoretical and more systematic than salvation from external distress, the quest for which is characteristic of nonprivileged classes. . . . It is the intellectual who transforms the concept of the world into the problem of meaning. . . . As a consequence, there is a growing demand that the world and the total pattern of life be subject to an order that is significant and meaningful.

The conflict of this requirement of meaningfulness with the empirical realities of the world and its institutions, and with the possibilities of conducting one's life in the empirical world, are responsible for the intellectual's characteristic flights from the world. This may be an escape into absolute loneliness, or in its more modern form, e.g., in the case of Rousseau, to a nature unspoiled by human institutions. Again, it may be a world-fleeing romanticism like the flight to the people, untouched by social conventions, characteristic of the Russian *Narodnitschestvo*. It may be more contemplative, or more actively ascetic; it may primarily seek individual salvation or collective revolutionary transformation of the world in the direction of a more ethical status. All these doctrines are equally appropriate to apolitical intellectualism and may appear as religious doctrines of salvation, as on occasion they have actually appeared (Weber, 1963: 124-125).

To limit analyses of intellectuals to their roles expressing their alienation, however, would be a clear over-simplification of the complexities involved in the relationship of intellectuals to their society and polity over time, and in different countries. It would ignore their system integration and value elaboration function.

Any attempt to understand the dimensions of the roles of the intellectual in the polity must also include a study of the *sources* of authority in the cultural system. Weber attempted to explain the critical dimension of power within a particular cultural system by delineating three concomitant forces of society—authority, material interest, and value orientation. The greater the monolithic direction of these forces, the greater the concentration of power (Weber 1954:324; Bendix 1960:286-297). Weber identified the intellectuals as the group 'predestined' to propagate the national value system, who form the 'leadership of a "culture community".' He saw a necessary relationship between them and those who 'wield power in the polity', since 'there is a close connection between the prestige of culture and the prestige of power' (Gerth and Mills, 1946:176, 448).

To examine the role of the intellectual in the various systems, it is necessary to account for the nature and the source of the allocation of authority between intellectualdom and polity. A basic structural requisite for the intellectual's positive adaptation to the broader cultural system is mechanisms to integrate these two communities.

A brief review of different historical-cultural systems will serve our point. Weber, in discussing the nature of Brahminical scholarship, noted that 'the concept of legitimacy was rather simply that the single prince was ritualistically correct when and to the extent to which his behavior, especially toward the Brahmins, conformed with the holy tradition . . . but no matter what power an Indian king might yield in matters of ritual he was never at the same time a priest . . . in contrast, the oldest tradition of the Chinese knows nothing of independent priests standing beside a strictly secular prince. Among the Indians the role of the prince has apparently grown out of strictly secular politics . . . whereas in China it grew out of the role of supreme priest' (1958:141). Different configurations of political and theocratic power were equally consequential in the rise first of Christianity, and later of the Protestant sects.

In the Western intellectual tradition, separated increasingly from church and state, intellectual activity has been more disposed to question the very source of authority. Particularly, in the developed democracies of the United States and Europe, the failure to provide '. . . support for a universalistic ethics of merit, of freedom, and of scientific and intellectual creativity and originality' has frequently resulted in tension between the intellectual and the state (Lipset, 1969:15). It is not surprising that Western educated leaders from Asia and Africa were among the first to call for freedom from the same countries in which they had studied.

Inherent in the structural changes which have been described as leading to a 'post-industrial society' since World War II, has been a growing interdependence between political authority and intellectualdom. Such socioeconomic systems are highly dependent on superior research and development resources, which mean better support for universities and research centers and a much larger component of persons who have passed through the higher education system thus creating a mass high-culture market which pays for the institutions and products of the artistic community. Governments are often the main sources of financing for both sectors of intellectualdom. Recognition and financial rewards from the polity conceivably should help to reduce the historic tensions and the intellectual's sense of being an outsider. A further trend pressing in this direction is the fact that the complexities involved in 'running' an advanced industrial or post-industrial society forces laymen, both political and economic leaders, to seek advice in depth, to defer to the scholarly-scientific community. Many, therefore, have seen these trends as fostering the role of the intellectual as participant, as leading to the 'interpenetration' of scholarship and policy (Coser, 1972).

Such 'integrative' trends have been questioned as undermining the capacity of intellectuals to act as social innovators. Thus Nettl has suggested that the very processes which enhance the worth of scholars to the powers, the growth of needed arcane knowledge, has resulted in a variety of highly minute particularistic specialties thus reducing their potential to behave as intellectuals in the political arena, to be concerned with structural rearrangements according to universalistic principles (Nettl, 1969:80-82; Bottomore, 1964: 70-71). And given such developments, a society with the 'much-vaunted freedom of expression' such as the American 'is less conducive to intellectualism' than one like the Soviet Union which by its very demand that intellectuals be totally committed presses them to criticize a more repressive society from the vantage point of universalistic principles.

From a quite different political perspective, Kissinger has raised a comparable query to Nettl's concerning the capacity of the scholar to combine the roles of participant expert and spokesperson for societal values. His cogent question signals a dilemma. Fifteen years ago he remarked that 'the intellectual as expert is rarely given the opportunity to point out that a query delimits a range of possible solutions or that an issue is posed in irrelevant terms. He is asked to solve problems, not to contribute to the definition of goals' (1959:23).

WHAT IS AN INTELLECTUAL?

Many attempts have been made to describe what is meant by the term 'intellectual'. These tend to depict the 'intellectual' as a man of ideas who creates and symbolizes the broader function of the human mind. He harnesses the essential and critical values of the society. Thus he is a creator, evaluator, and applicator of societal expositions on which culture takes form. This problem was elaborated by Knight (1960:45), Coser (1965:viii, x), Barzun (1961:3), Shils (1972:3), Aron (1962:210), Baran (1961:17), and Dahrendorf (1967:268).

Many of the efforts to define the stratum have included almost all those employed in occupations involving higher learning. The most influential contemporary analyst of the behavior of intellectuals, Edward Shils, has offered a comparable comprehensive definition of the category.

> Intellectuals are the aggregate of persons in any society who employ in their communication and expression, and with relatively higher frequency than most other members of their society, symbols of general scope and abstract reference, concerning man, society, nature, and the cosmos. The high frequency of their use of such symbols may be a function of their own subjective propensity or of the obligations of an occupational role, the performance of which entails such use (1968:399).

Given the diffuse character of his definition, it is not surprising that Shils includes among intellectuals, not only those engaged in 'the production (creation) and consumption (reception) of works of science, scholarship, philosophy, theology, literature, and art', but those involved in 'intellectual-executive roles' as well.

To fully grasp the variation in behavior of the broad classes of activities which are perceived as 'intellectual', it is necessary to differentiate among the dichotomies, intellect-intelligence and innovative-integrative.

The distinction between intellect and intelligence in mental activities has been made by a number of writers. As Hofstadter noted:

> . . . intelligence is an excellence of mind that is employed within a fairly narrow, immediate, and predictable range; it is a manipulative, adjustive, unfailingly practical quality—one of the most eminent and endearing of the animal virtues. Intelligence works within the framework of limited, but clearly stated goals, and may be quick to shear away questions of thought that do not seem to help in reaching them. . . .

Intellect, on the other hand, is the critical, creative, and contemplative side of mind. Whereas intelligence seeks to grasp, manipulate, re-order, adjust, intellect examines, ponders, wonders, theorizes, criticizes, imagines. Intelligence will seize the immediate meaning in a situation and evaluate it. Intellect evaluates evaluations, and looks for the meanings of situations as a whole (1963:25).

The link between the application of 'intellect' or 'intelligence' to political orientations has been put well by G. Eric Hansen.

Both intelligence and intellect are involved in all cognition, yet there seems to be a relative ascendance of one or the other not only in individual cognitive acts, but in the total existence and self-affirmation of the individual person. Esthetic, normative and religious judgments are typically marked by the ascendance of intellect: abstracting, synthesizing, judging, wondering, and imagining. More objective, mechanical judgments, those broadly conceived as involving "economics" or "engineering"... tend to be marked by the ascendance of intelligence. While intelligence moves out toward a meeting of the world and reality, to treat with them [extroversion], intellect brings the world to the self, interiorizes it, and makes it part of the ontic processes of the self [introversion]....

The political styles of the two tendencies are thus fundamentally divergent and only marginally related to intelligence or levels of education. Engineers, though requiring high intelligence and superior education, have shown very conservative tendencies in politics. The other extroverted and manipulative professions, dentists, physicians, and lawyers, have also tended toward the right. The more detached, introverted, and abstract professions... have shown very marked liberal/radical tendencies. The more detached and introverted the person [and thus choice of occupation] the more strongly the intellectual component seems to manifest itself in liberal politics. ['As a tendency', these include 'the poet, the artist, and the man of morals and letters...'] ... In the case of the scientist, natural or social, it is especially difficult to make distinctions. The fine blend of both intellect and intelligence needed in these fields reflects the tension between the objective world and the discrete methologies used to explore it (1969: 312-314).

Some of the authors cited earlier have suggested another fruitful dichotomy to account for the variation in political beliefs, the difference between those oriented towards innovation and those primarily concerned with integration, including the transmission of the traditional culture and skills. Prototypically, these may be seen in the variation in activities between the research scholar or creative artist, and the teacher or preacher. It has been argued those engaged in *creative* work in the area of ideas, art, and science are inherently disposed to also reject other aspects of the status quo, including politics. This capacity for criticism, for rejection of the status quo is not simply a matter of preference by some critical intellectuals of this quality of mind. Rather it is built into the very nature of their occupational roles. The distinction between the integrative and innovative roles traditionally implies that those involved in the former use ideas, findings, to carry out their jobs, while the latter's activities involve the creation of *new* knowledge, *new* ideas, *new* art. To a considerable extent, in scholarly and artistic endeavors, one is much more rewarded for being original than for being correct, an important fact, a crucial aspect of the role insofar as we consider the consequences of such intellectuals becoming more significant politically (Mornet, 1967).

This emphasis on creativity is central to many definitions of the intellectual, such as those of Robert Merton and Theodore Geiger, which stress that intellectuality defined as a concern for creativity and a role component, which may be found in varying occupations, is the most useful way to approach the subject.

To stress the innovative aspect of various professional activities as 'intellectual', does not deny that most intellectuals involved in such roles are also engaged in activities which involve reaffirming and transmitting aspects of existing culture. There are inherently relatively few pure innovators, that is, individuals who spend their vocational energies on efforts at creation. However, as one of the authors has noted elsewhere:

> The creative intellectuals are the most dynamic group within the broad intellectual stratum: because they are innovative, they are at the forefront in the development of culture. . . . The characteristic orientation of these 'generalizing intellectuals' is a critically evaluative one, a tendency to appraise in terms of general conceptions of the desirable, ideal conceptions which are taught to be universally applicable (Lipset and Dobson, 1972:138).

Here the creation of knowledge forms the foremost concern. To such innovators, rules and regulations often pose frustration. As guardians of ideas, they wish to search for the timeless origin of 'truths'. Yet, they hopefully seek their final fulfillment in integrating these into the wider domain of the society. Such an effort may not result in a positive acceptance by the laity. Thus alienation may ensue. However, as Shils has noted, all those involved in intellectual activities also serve *integrative* functions. It is clear that their creative skills may be used for the 'presentation of orientations toward general symbols which reaffirm, continue, modify or reject the society's traditional inheritance of beliefs and standards. . . . They fulfill authoritative, power-exercising functions over concrete actions as well.' (1969:32-33; 1968: 3-24).

MATERIALIST INTERPRETATIONS OF INTELLECTUAL PROTEST

The interpretations of the critical orientations of intellectuals which credit them to the inherent concerns of roles involving more emphasis on intellect as distinguished from intelligence or on innovation as distinct from integration are in conflict with those advanced by analysts who would explain the diverse products of the mind, solely or primarily in terms of existential determinants, as responses to interests and affiliations.

Marx and Engels, though denying any dominant thrust to the politics of intellectuals, found it necessary to discuss the factors related to varying forms of political involvements. In line with their emphases on materialist (interests) as distinct from idealist (values) explanations of behavior, the early Marxist fathers indentified intellectual radicals as drawn from the deprived or unsuccessful members of their stratum, suggesting that protest politics reflected discontent with their inferior social position. This assumption produced invidious explanations such as proposed by Engels to account for the critical politics in the German states before 1848. He argued: 'It became more and more the habit, particularly of the inferior sorts of literati, to make up for the want of cleverness in their productions by [anti-governmental] political allusions which were sure to attract attention.' (1967:134).

During the 1960s, the heavy participation of students and intellectuals in the New Left movements clearly necessitated some analysis of
the sources of this 'bourgeois-based' radical movement. Some Marxist
writers have continued to explain intellectual radicalism in 'materialist'
terms. Thus, the Belgian Trotskyist, Ernest Mandel, has argued that the
protest of intellectuals is related to 'profound change in intellectual
employment', that is, to the downgrading in status, opportunity, freedom of work, and reward, inherent in the mass growth and consequent
bureaucratization of the occupations subsumed in the stratum
(1969:47-53). Communist literature on New Left activism often suggests the related thesis that students and intellectuals are a coerced
alienated stratum forced to carry out the tasks which the economy
requires. In seeking to explain why 1968 was a year of widespread
student and intellectual revolt through much of Europe, an article in
the *World Marxist Review,* the organ of international (pro-Russian)
Communism stresses that the years 1967 and 1968 'have been marked
by the rise of mass unemployment', that jobs were not available in
sufficient quantity to keep up with the wave of expansion of universities. The article argued 'These contradictions affect the intellectual
community in the same way as they affect workers. After all, are not
80 to 90 percent of the intellectuals in the big capitalist countries
wage-earners.' (1968; 11:6-7). An analysis by a Chilean Communist of
the prevalence of a radical anti-imperialist outlook among Latin American intellectuals suggests that it reflects their excessive exploitation
inherent in the fact that few intellectuals can earn a living from creative
activity, that 'most of them can devote only their spare time for their
vocation' (Teitelboim, 1968: 73-74).

On the whole, efforts to account for intellectual revolt as reflecting
the narrow self-interests or the resentments of the declassed intellectuals have declined. Rather, the growth in the numbers of revolutionary
intellectuals is perceived by many radical writers as a consequence of
the collapse of bourgeois institutions and values, a breakdown which
intellectuals can see and react to, more clearly than others. Except to
identify intellectuals as a harbinger of radical change, the Marxist
movement, however, still lacks an explanation of intellectual radicalism.
Any real effort to understand the sociology of protest must return to

the concerns of Hobbes, Tocqueville, and others, namely aspects inherent in the role of the intellectual which repeatedly place him in the alienated and revolutionary camp. Crucial to understanding the nature of such aspects is the distinction between intellectual as innovator and the integrative dimension of intellectual activity, and between the emphasis on intellect and intelligence.

THE POLITICAL ROLES OF THE INTELLECTUAL

We have discussed two dichotomies: intellect-intelligence and innovator-integrator as related to varying political roles. These dichotomies are cross-cutting, though independent. While 'intellect' tends to be 'innovative', and 'intelligence' tends to be 'integrative', the correlation is far from unity. This distinction forms the basic focus of our specification of the political roles of the intellectual. Our attempt to circumscribe the activities of intellectuals from early times to the present to interpret their society and culture indicates they fall primarily in four prototypical roles—(a) Gatekeeper; (b) Moralist; (c) Preserver; (d) Caretaker. The first two terms are derived from discussions by Coser (1965:x, and Hofstadter (1963:28-29).

The following paradigm contains the logic of our typology.

	Intellect	Intelligence
Innovator	A (Gatekeeper)	B (Moralist)
Integrator	C (Preserver)	D (Caretaker)

Our discussion of these four types is designed largely to illustrate the typology, rather than to demonstrate its utility as a research tool. The examples point up the complex interrelated aspects of the different roles, and the difficulties involved in any effort to unravel their over-lapping interconnections in the 'real world'. For the most part, we have sought to illustrate the types by discussing variations in behavior among those involved in high cultural institutions, rather than to take the easier path of contrasting the more obvious differences between those clearly involved in cultural and scholarly activities, and those engaged totally in what Shils calls 'intellectual-executive roles'. If this paradigm has any utility, it should ultimately lend itself to an analytical under-standing of the varying political behaviors of those engaged primarily in what may be called the 'cultural-scholarly' roles.

Type A: Gatekeeper

Since his appearance as a recognizable social type, the *creative* intellec-tual has frequently assumed the gatekeeper role, often becoming the innovative spokesman for contending tendencies, opening the gate of ideas. His *essais* concern the 'whole' man (Montaigne, 1948). He is an independent thinker whose Talmudic search is for the universal histor-ical meaning. His concern is with the 'core values' of a given civilization (Coser, 1965). Edward Shils, though stressing that a creative scholar or writer may actually be much more involved in roles which press him in a more conservative (preserver) direction than those involved in being a tradition breaking intellectual, also emphasized the gatekeeper role in suggesting that in

> all societies, even those in which the intellectuals are notable for their conservatism, the diverse paths of creativity, as well as inevitable tendency toward negativism, impel a partial rejection of the prevailing system of cultural values. The very process of elaboration and development involves a measure of rejection (1969:30).

As long as higher education was primarily in the hands of the churches, instruction by the faculty involved revealed traditional truth, and basically sought to socialize new generations in the accepted system of values. Colleges, therefore, were centers of conservatism. The secularization of the university with the associated emphasis on original research and creativity is a major factor associated with the university becoming a major center of social unrest in modern times.

The difference between those who use intellect to create knowledge and those who apply intelligence to carry out the work of society has been used by C. P. Snow to account for the variations in political behavior of engineers and scientists.

> The engineers. . . . the people who made the hardware, who used existing knowledge to make some thing go, were, in nine cases out of ten, conservatives in politics, acceptant of any regime in which they found themselves, interested in making their machine work, indifferent to long-term social guesses.
>
> Whereas the physicists, whose whole life was spent in seeking new truths, found it uncongenial to stop seeking when they had a look at society. They were rebellious, protestant, curious for the future and unable to resist shaping it. The engineers buckled to their jobs and gave no trouble, in America, in Russia, in Germany, it was not from them, but from the scientists, that came heretics, forerunners, martyrs, traitors (1955:176).

Yet if the hypotheses discussed earlier which relate the critical politics of the intellectual to the emphasis on originality and creativity as the key aspect of the role are correct, then it should follow that *the most creative people are also among the most alienated politically*. The few systematic quantitative efforts to test these hypotheses seem to indicate such a relationship (Ladd and Lipset, 1975; Lipset and Dobson, 1972). We should note that these results do not, of course, demonstrate that activities associated with intellectual creativity press men to take a more critical political position. They are congruent with the argument that the kind of mind or background which impels men to question society also makes for success in intellectual activities.

Outside the university, among the 'free' intellectuals, such as the artistic ones, (or scientists before they were absorbed by higher education) stress on originality and innovation, on creativity, on following up the logic of development in a field, has been held responsible through much of the modern history for the conflict between intellectuals and their patrons, the people who pay for what they do. Hence, the greater length of their record as gatekeepers. Conflict is endemic in the intellectuals' need for autonomy and freedom, and the control exercised by those for whom they work, a fact which is magnified in authoritarian societies. In such systems the hostility of the intellectuals toward the dominant authorities of their societies is extremely strong, since in these countries, it is clear that they are under dictation as to what they can and cannot do (O'Brien, 1971: 834-836, Kessler, 1969: 410-431; Kolegar, 1965: 79-90; Onis, 1971: 18; Solzhenitsyn, 1968: 39-43; Voronitsyn, 1968: 19-23; Frankel, 1971: 25; Chun and Hiu, 1969: 5-6; Gittings, 1971: 4; Bouc, 1970: 8; Matejko, 1966: 611-638; Rawin, 1968: 353-377). As politics intrudes on them, they become more oppositionalist. This was strikingly evident in Communist China before the crackdown. As Schwartz notes:

The particular animus of the [Chinese] regime toward the intelligentsia [since 1957] . . . reflects of course the shocking revelations of the 'Hundred Flowers' episode of 1956-57 . . . [T]he official slogan, 'Let the one hundred flowers bloom, let the hundred schools contend', was meant to suggest to the intelligentsia that a certain undefined area of free discussion was now open to them. What emerged was highly revealing. Not only were the literary and cultural politics of the regime attacked; not only did professionals challenge the authority of the Party within their areas of competence; but there were even those who raised the dread question of power itself. The very grounds on which the Communist Party claimed political infallibility were challenged. In raising the question of political power, the 'civism' of the Chinese intelligentsia went beyond anything that has occurred in the Soviet Union since the inauguration of the 'Krushchev era' (1961:180).

In recent years there has been an encroachment on the self-image of the intellectual as a person who can comment on whatever is going on in society. The technical expert increasingly argues that the areas in which he has expertise should not be open to intellectual debate or, for that matter, to popular argument. The growth of, or emphasis on, expertise, or specialization threatens the general intellectual's self-esteem and is, therefore, resented and rejected by many of them. Thus journalists Joseph Kraft and Max Ways have pointed to a steady decline in the influence of 'outsider' intellectuals, including scientists, on US policy from Roosevelt to Kennedy stemming from the fact that the numbers of intellectuals directly involved in full-time high-level government posts increased greatly (Kraft, 1963: 112-17; Ways, 1967: 147-149, 212-216). Kenneth Galbraith in a 1963 talk regretfully noted that the growth in reliance on bureaucratic intellectuals meant that brilliant general intellectuals had much less influence, in part because there is much less 'abrasive controversy within administrations, and much greater emphasis on order, discipline, and conformity.' (Kraft, 1963: 116). Ironically, therefore, the factors making for greater reliance by government on some significant intellectuals as *experts* may have enhanced the sense of separation, of alienation from government, by the much larger number who remain outside, and see themselves as more ignored by power than ever.

In a sense, this process through which an increase in the influence of the intellectual class as a whole may be experienced by many of the politically concerned among them as a decline is paralleled by the way in which the enormous increase in support for all forms of intellectual activity, involving a massive growth in the numbers involved, has also served to heighten the possibilities for frustration and consequent political alienation among them (Geiger, 1949: 118-119; Birnbaum, 1969: 220-232). Intellectual life is characterized by a marked emphasis on a relatively few winning recognition for significant achievements (Hoffer, 1968: 14). Hence, the large majority are 'failures', as well as 'outsiders', a fact they are disposed to blame on the 'patron', the existing society, even though many more intellectuals than ever have great influence on public policy and there is much more support for cultural and scholarly activities, including much higher incomes. Even the 'successful' at any given moment, probably feel much more insecure, and therefore frustrated, about their position, given the constant threat to their eminence from the ever-increasing number of young competitors seeking to dethrone them.

Modern society is in a position of needing the university, needing intellectuals, needing students more than any other society ever has, and thereby has become more dependent on them, more influenced by them. Ironically, the increased status and consequent greater political influence of the intellectuals as a stratum form part of the source of the radical intellectual's rejection of American society.

The university, however, has gained influence over other social elites.

More and more it has become the major source of all elites, who must be certified as competent by their passage through the university. Thus the dominant tendencies, ideas, and moods, of the university infiltrate into the summits of most other key institutions.

This process suggests a reversal of Tocqueville's description of nineteenth century American intellectuals who, finding themselves at variance with the laity, withdrew into private circles, where they supported and consoled each other (1956: II, 375). It is more in line with efforts such as those of Mills and Bottomore to identify intellectuals as a 'class' which seeks to affect society.

The distinction to be emphasized here differentiates 'aristocratic' versus 'democratic' elite linkages rather than 'class' power as such. It is in the West particularly that transformation of intellectuals from aristocratic to democratic elite linkages have occurred.

These shifts have affected many once integrative institutions, including both the Protestant and Catholic churches in recent years. Harvard theologian Harvey Cox in the early 1960s heralded the dawn of the secular era. 'Secularization is the liberation of man from religious and metaphysical tutelage, the turning of his attention away from other worlds toward this one.' (1966:15). The changes in the churches reflect an identify transformation, along with adjustments in theology and ritual. One of the major sources of this shift results from the fact that key theological figures in these churches have taken the leading secular intellectuals as their key reference group, and now include people who consider themselves as intellectuals.

This modernization of the church reflects the extent to which theology has become a part of intellectual life generally. Thus, religion has become an institution pressing for social change, even for radicalization, a fact which has consequences for the general value system of the larger society (Pike and Pyle, 1955; Pike, 1967; Berrigan, 1967, 1970; Preston, 1971).

The mass media is another integrative activity which is showing signs of being affected by ties to the learned world. More and more people who write for the major papers, or are in charge of broadcasting, share similar values and political orientations as the critical intellectuals (Lipset and Dobson, 1972: 180-181).

Type B: Moralist

We begin with Dostoevski's apostolic injunction from *The Brothers Karamazov*—

> Judge Thyself who was right—Thou or he who questioned Thee then? Remember the first question; its meaning, in other words, was this: "Thou wouldst go into the world, and art going with empty hands with some promise of freedom which men in their simplicity and their natural unruliness cannot even understand . . . for nothing has ever been more unsupportable for man and a human society than freedom (1948:28).

In this prototypical role, the intellectual is both the examiner and the evaluator. In pre-industrial society, intellectuals assumed the 'sacred' right to *interpret* their society. The 'monopoly' of the early Mystics of the Middle Ages articulated alternative Christian values (Cohn, 1971). The moralist role in the West, the concern with rooting heresy, often found in high secular places, is linked to the fact that in 'Christian Europe the intellectual class first appeared as clergy, a fact that still conditions the attitudes of intellectuals today—not least those of them who are irreligious. In today's criticism of political policies one can still find the explicit statement that it is the function of intellectuals to be "the conscience of society". Europe's clergy criticized "the world" from the view point of higher spiritual values' (Ways, 1967: 149).

With increasing differentiation in the Western societies, the 'organized stratum' began to dissolve. The 'free' intellectuals began to undertake the task of *inspection*. In Europe this development was linked closely to the emergence of the 'idea' of the Renaissance. As Robert Nisbet has stressed, the humanists of this period closely resemble the morally righteous intellectuals of earlier and later eras. Unlike the 'gatekeepers', however, most of them were 'not scholars, not scientists, not philosophers, and not genuine literary creators or artists.'

> What we do find in rich abundance [among them] is cleverness of thought and brilliance of style. If there is a single word that best describes the mentality of the Sophists, humanists, *philosophes,* and others, it is *brilliance:* manifest in the quick thrust or *riposte,* the use of paradox and of inversion of meaning, the derivation of iridescent qualities, overwhelming verbal, from the already known, and perhaps above all, the polemical style (Nisbet, 1973: 486-487).

This category of brilliant innovative critics who have used intelligence more than intellect has often focused on cultural and educational critique as distinct from a concern with actual institutional change. That is, the moralists hold up the society to scorn for failing to fulfil basic agreed upon values. They challenge those running the society with the crime of heresy. As a group, however, they tend to be fascinated with power, exhibited at times in exaggerated fear of it when seemingly directed against them, and at other times in adoration of the charismatic leader with whom they can identify.

It is difficult to operationalize the distinction between the 'gate-keeper' and the 'moralist', but it may be argued that in the twentieth century United States, politically involved intellectuals have been more prone to resemble the latter than the former, beginning with the pre-World War I intellectuals who backed the egalitarian seemingly anti-business objectives of the Progressives and Socialists. The proto-typical examples of this group were the 'Young Intellectuals', drawn heavily from Ivy League backgrounds and 'from secure upper-middle class families' (May 1964). Their characteristic locale was Greenwich Village in salons maintained by wealthy precursors of the Manhattan-based radical chic of more recent times (Coser, 1965: 111-119; Lipset, 1972: 153-155). But this 'movement' of radical cultural critics, who held fund-raising parties for poor Wobbly strikers and marched in women's suffrage parades, broke down when faced with the seduction of 'intellectual power' in the form of Wilson's administration and the subsequent threat to socialist opponents of America's participation in World War I (Bourne, 1964: 3-14).

From the twenties on, many of the most outspoken American intellectuals expressed renewed antagonism to the business class from which came 'dullness, stupidity, aggressiveness in commerce, conformity to the remnants of traditional morality, and a moral opportunism linked with certain blind convictions about the economic status quo' (Lipset, 1972: 161). In most cases their apocalyptic revulsion appeared to take the leftist form of reconstruction. In America, adherence to Marxism largely served as a method of 'cultural protest'.

The Marxist sociologist, Tom Bottomore, has argued that beyond its manifest function of 'protest', Marxist 'criticism' largely helped American scholars to withdraw from the wider social arena, which he related is the inability of the intellectual to bridge 'political theory' to 'political action'. The lack of a 'two-way intellectual traffic' as Bottomore notes, signaled the absence of an effective radical platform in North America (1968: 39).

The break-down of American capitalism manifested by the Great Depression of the 1930s provided a test-case for Bottomore's hypothesis. Large segments of the intellectual and educated communities flocked to support of the Communist and Socialist parties. Yet, as in the earlier instance of Wilson's New Freedom, the appearance of a reform President of aristocratic origins, Franklin Roosevelt, who openly flattered intellectuals and incorporated some into his administration as experts, was able to win their enthusiastic support, particularly when they were able to combine interaction with 'anti-business' power in America with a pseudo-radical love affair with the Soviet Union.

As Nisbet notes in a different context, the behavior of the moralist critic reveals a 'fascination with power; especially the kind of power to be found in the leader . . . for in such power there is greater flexibility of use, less likelihood of its being rooted in and therefore hindered by ordinary social codes and conventions' (1973: 487).

Following World War II, the moralistic admiration for, contempt of, and fear of power, exhibited in the combination of involvement in radical-chic elites in Hollywood, New York, and Washington, while expressing a polemical disdain for American culture and a belief that the United States is a repressive society, led many to fear the consequences of continuing to question the functionings of the society particularly during the McCarthy Era. Leslie Fiedler and David Riesman and Nathan Glazer derided the 'loud fears of the intellectuals' and suggested that their exaggerated estimate of the strength of McCarthyism was linked to the 'outlived illusions of the Left' (Fiedler, 1954: 10-21; Riesman and Glazer, 1963: 87-114). Cold War heightened the intellectual's anxiety. As Christopher Lasch wrote of the behavior of many 'leftist' intellectuals of that time, they '. . . have not hesitated to criticize American popular culture or popular politics, but . . . they have [not] criticized the American government or any other aspect of the officially sanctioned order' (1969: 73).

Yet concern over McCarthyism was to provide the catalytic agent that helped to transfer the cultural critiques of the post-war era into the politicization of the sixties. For as Nisbet noted: 'Nothing that came out of the fierce disputes of the 1930's, not even the almost religious hatred of fascism among liberals and radicals, ever transferred itself so completely to the halls of the university, ever attached itself, so to speak, to the very roles of academics, as did the threat of McCarthyism, as this threat was almost universally perceived by university faculty' (1971: 143-144).

The politicization of intellectual life which flowed from McCarthyism was largely reflected in a strong identification with a relatively conservative political figure, Adlai Stevenson, a man who sought to de-emphasize economic and minority group issues, in favor of a stress on the decline of moral, cultural, and ecological standards in American society.

The linkage of cultural-academic concerns to national politics in the fifties made possible the intense politicization of intellectualdom in the ensuing decade. But it is interesting to note that the subsequent cultural-political folk hero of that period, John F. Kennedy, was not popular among non-policy involved intellectuals during his lifetime. Stevenson and to a lesser extent Hubert Humphrey were the preferred candidates of the politicized intellectuals.

Recognizing his difficulties with this constituency, Kennedy deliberately emphasized the 'public role of the intellectual' during and after his inauguration. And as Joseph Kraft indicated, this emphasis had 'a political purpose—as plain as the appointment of a Negro judge or a Polish Postmaster General. It is aimed to be specific, at the egghead liberals within the Democratic party ...' (1963: 112). But during the thousand days of the administration, Kennedy continued to meet with considerable rebuffs. Nine months after the young President took office, James Reston wrote a column in the *New York Times* discussing the 'discontented intellectuals'. He noted that the new regime was being described as 'the third Eisenhower administration', that the intellectuals were 'disenchanted by the absence of new policies, the preoccupation with political results, the compromises over education and the techniques of appointing conservatives to put over liberal policies and liberals to carry out conservative policies' (1961: 10E). And in an article published in November 1963, just before the assassination, Kraft reported that there was considerable tension between the administration and the intellectuals. 'Harsh criticisms have come from the novelists Norman Mailer and James Baldwin, the playwright Gore Vidal, and the political scientists Sidney Hyman and Louis Halle. "Where", the critic Alfred Kazin asked in a notable essay, "is the meaningful relation of intellectuals to power" ' (1963: 114,112).

Ironically, the tragic death of the young President and his succession by Lyndon Johnson, who appeared to typify the 'wheeler and dealer' politician, accomplished what Kennedy had been unable to do in life. This change was curiously prophesized before the 1960 election by James MacGregor Burns, who, after noting the lack of appeal of Kennedy's nonemotional pragmatic orientation, stated: 'If he should die tomorrow in a plane crash, he would become at once a liberal martyr, for the liberal publicists of the land would rush to construct a hero' (1960: 16).

During the mid-1960's, American intellectuals once again appeared to take over the role of polemical 'moralists' with respect to political criticism, denouncing the system for betraying its own basic democratic and anti-imperialist beliefs. Beginning with the faculty initiated teach-ins against the Vietnam War in 1965, they played a major role in sustaining a mass anti-war movement out of which a number of radicals emerged. A variety of statistical data serve to validate Kenneth Galbraith's boast about their political effect.

> It was the universities—not the trade unions, nor the freelance intellectuals, nor the press, nor the businessmen . . .—which led the opposition to the Vietnam War, which forced the retirement of President Johnson, which are forcing the pace of our present withdrawal [1971] from Vietnam, which are leading the battle against the great corporations on the issue of pollution, and which at the last congressional elections retired a score or more of the more egregious time-servers, military sycophants and hawks (1971:52).

Yet with the decline in American military participation in the Vietnam War, and the end of mass forms of political protest, the support for moralistic *political* perspectives also has been undermined. Working within a society, in which no left-wing third party has secured more than two percent of the vote since World War I, American intellectuals, like American students, have returned to an emphasis on cultural and educational criticism.

Their principal spokesmen continue to challenge the society for preserving inequality, but largely from the vantage point of its failure to live up to traditional American ideals of equality of opportunity. Their predominant political issue is the ancient American progressive cause, the corruption of the environment, one which they again blame on American business, on the monopolies (née trusts), and the inherent greed of commercial civilization.

In a larger sense, however, the emphasis on the 'moralist' as distinct from the 'gatekeeper' role among American intellectuals in recent times may reflect the fact that unlike revolutionary intellectuals in other places, and other times, they have not known what they want.

Hence once more we return to our earlier emphasis on the intellectuals' source of authority and their integration into the larger social milieu. The absence of large numbers of American intellectuals who have applied innovative intellect to politics has reflected the nation's professed philosophic 'outlook', its liberal egalitarianism. However, the extent to which intellectuals have been unable to adapt to the larger political system has been largely due to the conflicting 'rights' in interpreting their authority as between 'scholarship' and 'art' or 'ideas' and 'politics'. The 'messiah' disavows his potential 'following'. He becomes the 'watchdog' for the social system. For him, the task of the Grand Inquisitor never ends.

Type C: Preserver

Aron has noted that behind all 'doctrines' and all 'parties' are intellectuals who translate 'opinion or interests into theories' (1962: 235). In this role of preserver he may often be a tradition-maker helping to frame the legitimation for authority, old or new. As Eisenstadt puts it:

> They participate in the symbolic and institutional frameworks of such traditions, or as performing their functions as the conscience of society within the framework of existing traditions (1972: 1).

In contributing to system maintenance, however, intellectuals become integrated themselves as part of the cultural system, often fostering what Weber called the 'National Idea'. In a highly differentiated society, this role becomes the 'expression of a special craft' (Ascoli, 1936: 17-41). They apply reason to the organized institutional frameworks of society. As Shils noted:

> Alongside these institutions for the formation of skills, the guidance of dispositions, and the preliminary exercise of the capacity for judgment, there are also the institutions in which these skills, dispositions, capacities are to be brought into serious operation . . . (1969: 336).

This attitude is derived from world-historic culture roots. Thus Znaniecki rightly asserts that in order for intellectuals to perform this role, they must be able to explicate the knowledge of past to present society. (1968:39). Their power lies largely in their ability to narrate human destiny. They integrate the ethos of their society.

The articulative powers of Japanese intellectuals in helping to reconstruct their society during the Meiji Restoration illustrates the significance of this role. As Jun Eto remarked:

> No matter how radically they differed from one another in their literary or political opinions, Meiji writers shared in the dominant national mission of their time: the creation of a new civilization that would bring together the best features of East and West, while remaining Japanese at its core (1965: 603).

Although the key Marxist intellectuals, as formulators of original concepts and strategies fostering fundamental change properly fall under the category of those who have applied intellect as gatekeeping innovators, they also should be seen as the formulators of new traditions which have served to create a new legitimation for hierarchical relationships in post-capitalist society (Coser, 1965: 141-142). Various critics have even argued that Marxism emerged as an ideological expression of the 'class-interests' of the intellectuals who foresaw socialism as a social system dominated by them as the spokesmen for the incompetent masses. Jan Machajski, a Polish former Marxist, writing at the turn of the century, paralleled the interpretation which Marxists presented of the role of populist and equalitarian slogans of the American and French Revolutions in legitimating bourgeois class rule in his analysis of the consequences of successful socialist revolution. Like the anarchist theoretician, Michael Bakunin, he argued that it would result in a society controlled by the mandarins. And he suggested, predating the similar thesis of Robert Michels, that concepts of participatory democracy, of control of the machinery of complex industrial society by the masses, in a system in which opposition politics and protest were ruled out, were utopian and would only serve to conceal the fact that such a society would be severely stratified with respect to power and privilege.

As might be expected, Machajski's writings about the preservative functions of Marxist ideology have not been allowed to circulate in the Communist world, but there is some reason to believe that his analysis and predictions have bothered the leaders of the Soviet Union. Machajski and his teachings were subject to vitriolic attack in *Pravda* in 1926 when he died, and again in 1938, when they were condemned as 'outrageous, hooligan, and dangerous to the Soviet state' (Shatz, 1967: 45-57; Nomad, 1961: 97-117; Avrich, 1965: 66-75).

In recent years, a number of neo-Marxists have openly called for and supported the role-type of the intellectual formulator of revolutionary ideals, a position explicated in semi-disguised form much earlier by Lenin in *What is to be Done?* (Lukacs, 1971: 299-329). Lefebvre has suggested that the 'control of ideas . . . is the only judge and supreme criterion of knowledge' (Lefebvre, 1969). Marxist theorists have never faced up to the implications for communist society of entrusting such power of narration. and preservation to intellectuals. Kostas Axelos, a Marxist analyst, has pointed to the need for 'a critical examination of the Bolshevik theory of the role of the intellectual . . . in formulating the class consciousness of the proletariat . . .' (Axelos, 1968: 419).

Marx himself, of course, rejected this role, though he can be cited as a prime example of an intellectual 'tradition-maker'. He criticized as bourgeois 'utopians', those socialists who think that 'the working class is incapable of its own emancipation . . . [that] it must place itself under the leadership of educated . . . bourgeois' (Marx and Engels,

1968: 626-633). Hence, from such a point of view every intellectual must be viewed with suspicion. This is precisely the source of Marxist anti-intellectualism (Man, 1927: 298-304; Spargo, 1911: 67-106).

The growing impact of post-revolutionary intellectuals and the university community on the *Body Politik* of various nations is a result of more than just an increased demand for trained talent. The intellectuals articulate 'modernity'. In the developing nations, they have been the 'only initially available modern elite' whose assignment has been to establish a rationalistic argument between 'protest and change' (Eisenstadt, 1966: 158). The developed societies have equally provided a role for them as a 'mirror of conscience' (Dahrendorf, 1963: 20).

We have noted earlier arguments that endemic in the occupational role of 'intellectual' is a strong preference for working outside the system. As Coser notes: 'When intellect is harnessed to the pursuit of power it loses its essential character . . .; to harness it to the chariot of power is to emasculate it' (1965: 185). Yet, intellectuals also feel that they alone should be the 'special custodian' of basic system values like reason and justice (which are related to the nature of their occupational role), striking out passionately when they fear the national identity is threatened by some gross abuse (Hofstadter, 1963: 28-29).

Even though for the most part, intellectuals see themselves in a world 'they never made', they have been 'bound' by an 'unexpungible identity' with the nation, since it has been the raison d'être of the literary and scholarly intellectuals.

In their role as tradition-maker, intellectuals become participants. The critical intellectuals (both type A and B), though, continue to deny the possibility of participating in government, without betraying their ideals (Kissinger, 1959). They view the 'others' as conservationist and unholy. The growth in social importance of intellectual institutions and skills, e.g., the university and science, has made it possible for the 'caretaker' intellectuals to bring statements of their concerns to the attention of the public. The laity now read and take notice of intellectual products. From the point of view of the intellectuals, this gives them a chance to discuss and participate in a larger arena than previously was afforded. Such pragmatic attempts, interestingly enough, are often viewed by both the 'Gatekeepers' and the 'Moralists' as a source of anti-intellectualism. The avant-garde questions the 'clerisy' (Cunliffe, 1955: 23-33). For in large part, the fear expressed is perhaps that in becoming a spokesman, the intellectual might forfeit the right to question the main assumptions of his society. This would deny his elitism. In fact, however, we must recognize that intellectuals have often assumed the role of spokesmen for the society. Both Dahrendorf in his study of the German society, and Moddie in an analysis of development of Brahminical scholarship in India, have noted this role as a classical attitude of the group. Here the intellectual '. . . becomes part of the existing order of authority' (Dahrendorf, 1963: 263; Moddie, 1968; Buber, 1959: 83-103). Dahrendorf suggests that many Weimar ministers of state were of this type. Comparable roles are played by intellectuals in many of the 'new' and developing nations, as occurred in the early United States (Lipset, 1967: 84-85).

How and when does an intellectual conform to his society? This dilemma has often posed serious philosophical debate. Should the intellectual remain aloof, lest he lost his objectivity? As noted, a conformist outlook has often been looked at as a sign of cowardice. For much of the ability of the 'monk' to conform to his society largely depends on the extent to which he finds the social structure, including the polity, encouraging him to interact on an equal, full, and intimate basis with other sections of the elite, who show a regard for his opinions.

The answer in part, therefore, to the question of the varying patterns of 'conformity' among intellectuals lies in the different positions of the intellectual in social systems of different times and places. Although consideration of these comparative factors goes beyond the limited scope of this discussion, it is important to point up the need to pay attention to the larger structural context in which intellectual activity takes place. From Tocqueville on, assorted commentators on the comparative role of intellectuals have suggested that British intellectuals, though given little formal role recognition, the very word is regarded as un-English, have long been accepted as part of the Establishment, of that group of high level 'cousins', who attend the same schools, belong to the same clubs, and listen to each other, regardless of differences in opinion or roles. One who already belongs cannot 'sell out' (Coser,

1965: 350-353). In France, on the other hand, those intellectuals not directly involved in government, have extremely high public status, are fawned on by the press, but have almost no direct contact with the governing elites. In so far as the intellectuals can have a sense of full participation, it has been by cooperating with 'counter-elites' of the left currently, but in part of the right in the past.

In the United States, on the whole, intellectuals have perceived themselves as doubly 'outsiders', unloved by the governing elites and 'public opinion'. Conversely, America has provided more comfortable incomes and more provision for employment in universities and other institutions. As a society without the kind of social establishment derivative from aristocratic norms, it has not given diffuse elite status to intellectuals (or anyone else), and has sharply differentiated between experts and intellectuals. British intellectuals, handled more 'sensibly' than their compeers elsewhere, are better able to play the 'preserver' role, to explicate the national tradition in a positive fashion. The American 'outsiders', as we have seen, tend to transpose into moral conflicts controversies which are far more concerned with means than with ends, while the French, who are even more frustrated by their structural position, are prone to take on an even more intense moralistic role, which, according to Aron, leads them 'to ignore and very often to aggravate the real problem of the nation' (1962: 248, 234).

Type D: Caretaker

The critical understanding of this role can mainly be attributed to the advent of the Industrial Revolution. Society now needed functionaries who could maintain the scientific order, which began in the western societies as early as 1500. It was an intellectual revolution, for people sought to explain the world differently. 'The change' as Bronowski states, oriented people '. . . from a world of things ordered according to their ideal nature, to a world of events running in a steady mechanism or before and after' (Bronowski and Mazlish, 1960: 108).

The ensuing attempt towards a pragmatic definition of scientific theory gave rise to industrial development. This 'orderly' transformation was no mere coincidence of history. Intellectual conditions as early as the sixteenth century, notably in England and France, afforded a strong impetus to the emergence of industrial society. As evident in the American Revolution, Puritan understanding was more than an attempt at describing the mechanical functions of the universe (Butts and Davies 1972). The Paris Meetings by the 'scientists'—Descartes, Desargues, Fermat, Pascal, and other noted social thinkers began a *rational* dialogue in explaining social conditions. The Royal Society was established on 28 November, 1660, at a meeting in Gresham College, London. These men held Puritan sympathies (Merton, 1938: 360-632; Lyons, 1968).

The Protestant Ethic reflected the elementary belief that the social and economic conditions of rationality and opportunity would be met. Ascriptive hierarchy began to be replaced by achieved rights. This signalled the beginning of the Modern State which gave rise to the idea of objectivity—an institutional prerequisite to the development of legal-rational authority. As Crozier suggests, it diminished 'the uncertainty of social action' (Crozier, 1969: 204). The growth of the Nation-State ushered in the rapid development of 'public servants' now employed to administer the secular state (Barker, 1944). An essential task was the development of a codified legal system. Bendix notes that 'proper systematization was the work of university-trained judges . . . that gave a special impetus to the formal rationality of the laws' (1960: 407). The traditional exegesis replaced the consideration of the individual *(Einzel-individuum)*. Legal administrators now became the essential innovators of the political community, and literally for the first time, intellectuals systematically began to share in the maintenance of the bureaucratic structure. In this social dualism, the intellectual became the 'caretaker'. The 'monk' had discovered the New World.

Bureaucratic authority separated the sphere of 'public' and 'private' domain. It further estabished an institutional hierarchy where competency was to be based on occupational merit (Young, 1958; Gerth and Mills, 1946: 196-244). It emphasized achievement. Increasingly, in the industrial societies, this meant that individuals would educate themselves for a career and that qualified officers could maintain and manage social services. Educators were now called upon to train civil servants to manage bureaucracies. The 'felicific calculas' as Bentham called it, gave birth to the term 'utility' in the maximization of pleasure and the minimization of pain. The critical function for the government was hence proclaimed to be contained in the 'minimax' principle (Bentham 1948; Morgenstern, 1950: 113-139). The intellectual as educator became a social functionary.

The pluralistic conditions were now manifested in the emphasis on universalism and achievement. Intellectuals as social planners called for an examination and reduction of aristocracy. As Schumpeter noted:

> the state, its bureaucracy and the groups that man the political engine are quite promising prospects for the intellectual looking for his source of social power. As should be evident ... they are likely to move in the desired direction with not less 'dialectical' necessity than the masses (1950: 310-311).

Raymond Aron commenting on the advanced industrial society, has noted the spread of distributive roles as *scribes,* who make up the operational staff of public or private administrations, and *experts,* or those who make their knowledge available to others (1962: 203). These are then the accountants who manage the nerves of their society. They undertake the role of the custodian. In a techno-bureaucratic society, as noted earlier, the skills of these experts increasingly are called for in the implementation of policies. Shils points out:

> There must therefore be a body of persons capable of reproducing and transmitting this pattern of technical and specialized knowledge and skill. A body of persons different in the substantive content of their intellectual culture but having parallel functions, is not less necessary for providing the education requisite to administration and public discussion (1972: 175-176).

The increasing participation of intellectuals in government is, as Merton indicates, a process linked in their minds to their earlier commitment to change their society. He observes that the choice originated with the intellectuals themselves (1968: 267).

These professionals in a major way have assumed a leadership role. Schumpeter pointed to the increased 'direct relationship' between intellectuals and the bureaucracy (1950: 155). This trend has been resisted by the business professionals, who especially in America, have viewed themselves historically as a source of national leadership providing support for community values (Boorstin, 1967: 115-123). Not incorrectly, they see the bureaucratic intellectuals as maintaining strong ties with the more critical unattached ones outside of government, particularly in the university, who continue to act as 'gatekeepers' or 'moralists'. Ironically, the intellectual in his role as 'caretaker' often pays particular attention to these criticisms precisely because his fellow 'free' intellectuals argue that in his abandonment of innovation and intellect, he has given up his claim to be an 'intellectual'. Henry Kissinger was moved a decade and a half ago to a classic defense of the caretaker as intellectual in answer to such contentions (1959).

The increased power, status, and income of this technical elite have recently been the topic of an international seminar convened by Professors Bell and Dahrendorf. Their concern serves to highlight both the theoretical and practical significance of this prototypical role of the intellectual as caretaker. Bell's 'axial principles' (Bell, 1968: 145-246), of 'The Post-Industrial Society' emphasize the structural trends which have fostered these developments.

(a) in 'The Post-Industrial Society', economy (as measured in terms of GNP in the labor force) has shifted from the manufacturing to the services sector, which require a larger university trained group of professionals at the summits (Bell, 1973: Chapter 2).

(b) the increase in professional and mechanical class enhances 'technocratic forms of decision-making' (Bell, 1971: 1-24).

These trends which greatly benefit intellectualdom as a stratum are seen by some as reducing the historic tension between power and intellect (Lenski, 1966).

CONCLUDING REMARKS

Our attempt in this essay has been to develop the prototypical political roles of the intellectual. Attention in attempting such a paradigmatic analysis has been paid to discussing social conditions which contribute to the development of such roles.

The place of the intellectual in the society is neither inherently contradictory nor abusive. The fulfillment of the myriad of his roles lies in his capacity to assume responsibility and move away from interpreting the society from a particular ideological dogma. This is particularly true for the New Nations. The extent to which intellectuals, and other elites of such nations, are able to define their authority on a legal-rational basis will foretell the future stability of these countries. Intellectuals define the content of legitimacy. Any discussion as to the oppositional role of the intellectuals must take into consideration the role of the nation in providing a creative and critical dimension of the intellectual's own legitimacy. In his narrative role, he may have to become both 'monk' and 'messiah'.

Yet as John Ward has pointed out, the very nature of the intellectual role, even when perceived in conservative 'preserver' terms, presses those who fulfill it to undermine social stability (1965-66: 105-106).

In advanced industrial or post-industrial society, we would argue that the growth in the size and influence of an academic research establishment, and free-lance intellectualdom, which insists on being critical, is undermining the capacity for 'action-intellectuals' to maintain social equilibrium. Daniel Bell in presenting his analysis of post-industrial society contends 'the deepest tensions are those between the culture, whose axial direction is anti-institutional and antinomian, and the social structure, which is ruled by an economizing and technocratic mode. It is this tension which is ultimately the most fundamental problem of the post-industrial society' (1973: 44). As noted elsewhere:

> the basic tensions, the contradictions within the system, come increasingly from within the elite itself—from its own intellectual leaders supported by large segments of its student children. In Helgelian terms the contradiction of post-industrial society, whether Communist or non-Communist, may be its dependence on trained intelligence, on research and innovation, which requires it to bring together large numbers of intellectuals and students on great campuses and in a few intellectual communities located at the centers of communication and influence (Lipset and Dobson, 1972: 184).

Thus, we return at the end to Schumpeter's question, can an advanced industrial society win the allegiance of its intellectuals by being successful in material terms? He concluded that it could not, that all its achievements would be ashes in the writings produced by intellect, that intellect is inherently alienated. To gain the participation of the intellectuals, power must offer more than bread, it must allow access to a court of glory, Camelot?

REFERENCES

Aron, Raymond (1962), *The Opium of the Intellectuals.* New York: Norton

Ascoli, Max (1936), *Intelligence in Politics.* New York: Norton

Avrich, Paul (1965), 'What is "Machaevism"?' *Soviet Studies:* 17 (July)

Axelos, Kostas (1968), 'Des "intellectuels révolutionnaires" à "Arguments" '. *Praxis:* 4, nos. 3-4

Baran, Paul A. (1961), 'The Commitment of the Intellectual'. Monthly Review: 13 (May)

Barker, Ernest (1944), *The Development of Public Services in Western Europe.* London: Oxford University Press

Barzun, Jacques (1961), *The House of Intellect.* New York: Harper Torchbooks

Bell, Daniel (1973), *The Coming of Post-Industrial Society.* New York: Basic Books, Inc.

––– (1971), 'Technocracy and Politics'. *Survey:* 17 (Winter)

––– 1968, 'The Measurement of Knowledge and Technology', in Eleanor Sheldon and Wilbert Moore, eds., *Indicators of Social Change.* New York: The Russell Sage Foundation

Bendix, Reinhard (1960), *Max Weber: An Intellectual Portrait.* New York: Doubleday and Co., Inc.

––– (1946), 'Max Weber's Interpretation of Conduct and History'. *American Journal of Sociology:* 51 (May)

Bentham, Jeremy (1948), *Introduction to the Principles of Morals and Legislation.* London: Hafner Library of Classics

Berrigan, Daniel (1967), *False Gods, Real Men.* New York: The Macmillan Company

Birnbaum, Norman (1969), 'The Making of a Vanguard'. Partisan Review: **32**, no. 2

Bodin, Louis (1962), *Les Intellectuels*. Paris: Presses Universitaires de France

Boorstin, Daniel J. (1967), *The Americans: The National Experience*. New York: A Vintage Book

Bottomore, T.B. (1964), *Elites and Society*. London: C.A. Watts

――― (1968), *Critics of Society: Radical Thought in North America*. New York: Pantheon Books

Bouc, Alan (1970), 'Cultural Revolution Comes Full Cycle'. *Le Monde:* (October 7)

Bourne, Randolph (1964), *The War and the Intellectuals*. New York: Harper Torchbooks

Bronowski, J. & Bruce Mazlish (1960), *The Western Intellectual Tradition*. London: Hutchinson

Buber, Martin (1959), *Between Man and Man*. Boston: Beacon Press

Burns, James MacGregor (1960), 'Candidate on the Eve: Liberalism Without Tears'. *New Republic:* (October 31)

Butts, Robert E. & John W. Davis (1972), *The Methodological Heritage of Newton*. Oxford: Basil Blackwell and Mott Ltd.

Chun, Kung & Chao Hiu (1969), 'How To Look at Intellectuals Correctly'. *Peking Review:* 8 (February)

Cohn, Norman (1971), *The Pursuit of the Millennium*. New York: Oxford University Press

Coser, Lewis A. (1965), *Men of Ideas*. New York: The Free Press

Cox, Harvey (1966), *The Secular City: Secularization and Urbanization in Theological Perspective*. New York: The Macmillan Company

Crozier, Michel (1969), *The Bureaucratic Phenomenon*. Chicago: The University of Chicago Press

Cunliffe, Marcus (1955), 'The Intellectuals. The United States'. *Encounter:* 4 (May)

Dahrendorf, Ralk (1967), *Society and Democracy in Germany*. New York: Doubleday-Anchor Books

――― (1963), 'Der Intellektuelle und die Gesellschaft'. *Zeit:* 13 (March 29)

Dostoevski, Fyodor (1948), *The Grand Inquisitor on the Nature of Man*. New York: The Liberal Arts Press

Eisenstadt, S.N. (1972), 'Intellectuals and Tradition'. *Daedalus:* 101 (Spring)

――― (1971), 'Contemporary Student Rebellions―Intellectual Rebellion and Generational Conflict'. *Acta Sociologica:* **14**, no. 3

――― (1966), *Modernization: Protest and Change*. Englewood Cliffs, New Jersey: Prentice-Hall

Engels, Friedrich (1967), *The German Revolutions*. Chicago: The University of Chicago Press

――― (1957), *On the History of Early Christianity*. Moscow: Foreign Languages Publishing House

Eto, Jun (1965), 'Natsume Soseki: A Japanese Meiji Intellectual'. *American Scholar:* 34 (Autumn)

Feuer, Lewis S. (1969), *The Conflict of Generations.* New York: Basic Books, Inc.

Fiedler, Leslie (1954), 'McCarthy'. *Encounter:* (August)

Frankel, Edith B. (1971), 'Alexander Tvardovski: The Loyal Rebel'. *The Jerusalem Post Magazine:* (December)

Galbraith, John Kenneth (1971), 'An Adult's Guide to New York, Washington and Other Exotic Places'. *New York:* 4 (November 15)

Geiger, Theodore (1949), *Aufgaben und Stelling der Intelligenz in der Gesellschaft.* Stuttgart: Ferdinanc Enke Verlag

Gerth, H.H. & C. Wright Mills (1946), *From Max Weber: Essays in Sociology.* New York: Oxford University Press

Gittings, Anthony (1971), 'Shift in Chinese Education Policy'. *The Guardian:* (September 26)

Grana, Cesar (1964), *Modernity and Its Discontents.* New York: Harper Torchbooks

Hamilton, Alastair (1971), *The Appeal of Fascism: A Study of Intellectuals and Fascism, 1919-1945.* London: Anthony Blond

Hansen, G. Eric (1969), 'Intellect and Power: Some Notes on the Intellectual as a Political Type'. *The Journal of Politics:* 31 (May)

Hoffer, Eric (1968), 'Where the Real Rat Race Is'. *San Francisco Examiner:* (December 23)

Hofstadter, Richard (1963), *Anti-Intellectualism in American Life.* New York: Knopf

Israel, John (1966), *Student Nationalism in China, 1927-1937.* Stanford: Stanford University Press

——— (1969), 'Reflections on the Modern Chinese Student Movement', in S.M. Lipset and P. Altbach, eds., *Students in Revolt.* Boston: Houghton Mifflin

Kessler, Jascha (1969), 'The Censorship of Art and the Art of Censorship'. *The Literary Review:* 12 (Summer)

Kissinger, Henry (1959), 'The Policymaker and the Intellectual'. *The Reporter:* 5 (March)

Knight, Everett (1960), *The Object Society.* New York: George Braziller

Kolegar, Ferdinand (1965), 'Literary Intellectuals and the Politics of Perfection'. *Indian Sociological Review:* 3 (October)

Kraft, Joseph (1963), 'Washington Insight: Kennedy and the Intellectuals'. *Harper's:* 227 (November)

Ladd, E.C. and S.M. Lipset (1975), *The Divided Academy: Professions and Politics.* New York: McGraw-Hill

——— (1973), *Academics, Politics, and the 1972 Election.* Washington, D.C.: American Enterprise Institute for Public Policy Research

Lasch, Christopher (1969), *The Agony of the American Left.* New York: A Vintage Book

Lefebvre Henri (1964), 'S'agit-il de penser'. *Le Monde:* (January 29)

Lenin, V.I. (1963), *What Is To Be Done?* Oxford: Clarendon Press

Lenski, Gerhard (1966), *Power and Privilege.* New York: McGraw-Hill

Lipset, S.M. (1969), 'The Possible Political Effects of Student Activism'. *Social Science Information:* 8, no. 2

——— (1967), *The First New Nation.* New York: Doubleday-Anchor Books

——— (1963), *Political Man.* New York: Doubleday-Anchor Books

——— (1972), *Rebellion in the University.* Boston: Little, Brown

——— & Richard B. Dobson (1972), 'The Intellectual as Critic and Rebel: With Special Reference to the United States and the Soviet Union'. *Daedalus:* 101 (Summer)

Lively, Jack (1965), *The Works of Joseph DeMaistre.* New York: The Macmillan Company

Lukacs, George (1971), *History and Class Consciousness.* London: Merlin Press

Lyons, Sir Henry (1968), *The Royal Society: 1660-1940: A History of Its Administration Under Its Charters.* New York: Greenwood Press

Malia, Martin (1961), 'What is the Intelligentsia', in Richard Pipes, ed., *The Russian Intelligentsia.* New York: Columbia University Press

Man, Henri de (1969), *The Psychology of Socialism.* New York: Henry Holt

Mandel, Ernest (1969), 'The New Vanguard', in Tariq Ali, ed., *The New Revolutionaries.* New York: William Morrow

Marx, Karl & Friedrich Engles (1968), *Selected Works II.* New York: International Publishers

Matejko, Aleksander (1966), "Status Incongruence in the Polish Intelligentsia'. *Social Research:* 33 (Winter)

May, Henry F. (1964), *The End of American Innocence: A Study of the First Years of Our Own Time.* Chicago: Quadrangle Books

Merton, Robert K. (1968), *Social Theory and Social Structure.* New York: The Free Press

——— (1938), 'Science, Technology and Society in Seventeenth Century England'. *Osiris: Studies on the History and Philosophy of Science, and on the History of Learning and Culture.* Bruges: The St. Catherine Press, Ltd.

Moddie, A.D. (1968), *The Brahminical Culture and Modernity.* New York: Asia Publishing House

Moller, Herbert (1966), 'Youth as a Force in the Modern World'. *Comparative Studies in Society and History:* 10 (April)

Molnar, Thomas (1961), *The Decline of the Intellectual.* Cleveland: Meridian Books

Montaigne (1948), *The Complete Essays.* Stanford: Stanford University Press

Morgenstern, Oskar (1950), 'Die Theorie der Spiele und des Wirtschaftlichen Verhaltens', Part 1, *Jarbuch für Sozialwissenschaft.*

Mornet, Daniel (1967), *Les Origines intellectuelles de la revolution française, 1715-1787.* Paris: Armand Colin

Moynihan, Daniel Patrick (1970), 'Text of a Pre-Inauguration Memo from Moynihan on Problems Nixon Would Face'. *New York Times:* (March 11)

Nettl, J.P. (1969), 'Ideas, Intellectuals, and Structures of Dissent', in Philip Rieff, ed., *On Intellectuals.* New York: Doubleday

Nisbet, Robert (1973), "The Myth of the Renaissance'. *Comparative Studies in Society and History:* 15 (October)

––– (1971), *The Degradation of the Academic Dogma.* New York: Basic Books

Nomad, Max (1961), *Aspects of Revolt.* New York: Noonday Press

O'Brien, Conner Cruise (1971), 'Thoughts on Commitment'. *The Listener:* 86 (December)

Onis, Juan (1971), 'Cubans' Ordeal Arouses Artists.' *New York Times:* (September 9)

Paléologue, Maurice (1955), *Journal de l'affaire Dreyfus.* Paris: Plon

Pares, Bernard (1962), *Russia Between Reform and Revolution.* New York: Schocken Books

Pike, James A. (1967), If This Be Heresy. New York: Harper and Row Publishers

––– & John W. Pyle (1955), *The Church, Politics, and Society: Dialogues on Current Problems.* New York: Morehouse-Gorham Company

Preston, R.H. (1971), *Technology and Social Justice: An International Symposium on the Social and Economic Teaching of the World Council of Churches from Geneva 1966 to Uppsala 1968.* Valley Forge: Judson Press

Rawin, Solomon John (1968), 'The Polish Intelligentsia and the Socialist Order: Elements of Ideological Compatibility'. *Political Science Quarterly:* 83 (September)

Reid, Whitelaw (1873), 'The Scholar in Politics'. *Scribner's Monthly:* 6

Reston, James (1961), 'Washington on Kennedy's Discontented Intellectuals'. *New York Times:* (October 8)

Riesman, David & Nathan Glazer (1963), 'The Intellectuals and the Discontented Classes', in Daniel Bell, ed., *The Radical Right.* New York: Doubleday

Röpke, Wilhelm (1960), 'National Socialism and the Intellectuals', in George B. deHuszar, ed., *The Intellectuals.* New York: Free Press

Schumpeter, Joseph (1950), *Capitalism, Socialism, and Democracy.* New York: Harper Torchbooks

Schwartz, Benjamin (1961), 'The Intelligentsia in Communist China: A Tentative Comparison', in Richard Pipes, ed., *The Russian Intelligentsia.* New York: Columbia University Press

Shatz, Marshall (1967), 'Jan Waclaw Machajski: The "Conspiracy" of the Intellectuals'. *Survey:* no. 2 (January)

Shils, Edward A. (1968), 'Intellectuals', in David Sills, ed., *International Encyclopedia of the Social Sciences,* 7. New York: Macmillan and The Free Press

––– (1969), 'The Intellectuals and the Powers: Some Perspectives for Comparative Analysis', in Philip Rieff, ed., *On Intellectuals.* New York: Doubleday

––– (1972), *The Intellectuals and the Powers and Other Essays.* Chicago: The University of Chicago Press

Snow, C.P. (1955), *The New Men*. New York: Scribner's

Solzhenitsyn, A.I. (1968), 'Letter to the Fourth All-Union Congress of Soviet Writers'. *Bulletin of the Munich Institute:* 15 (August)

Soucy, Robert J. (1966), 'The Nature of Fascism in France', in Walter Laqueur and George Mosse, eds., *International Fascism 1920-1945*. New York: Harper Torchbooks

Spargo, John (1911), 'Anti-Intellectualism in the Socialist Movement: A Historreal Survey', in John Spargo, *Sidelights on Contemporary Socialism*. New York: Huebsch

Teitelboim, V. (1968), 'Problems Facing Latin American Intellectuals'. *World Marxist Review:* 11 (December)

Tocqueville, Alexis de (1956), *Democracy in America*. New York: Vintage Books, vol. 2

Troeltsch, Ernst (1960), *The Social Teaching of the Christian Churches*. New York: Harper Torchbooks

Tse-Tsung, Chow (1960), *The May Fourth Movement: Intellectual Revolution in China*. Cambridge: Harvard University Press

Venturi, Franco (1960), *Roots of Revolution*. London: Weidenfeld and Nicolson

Waelder, Robert (1962), 'Protest and Revolution Against Western Societies', in Morton A. Kaplan, ed., *The Revolution in World Politics*. New York: John Wiley

Walker, Richard (1963), 'Students, Intellectuals, and the Chinese Revolution', in Jeanne J. Kirkpatrick, ed., *The Strategy of Deception*. New York: Farrar, Straus & Giroux, Inc.

Wang, Y.C. (1966), *Chinese Intellectuals and the West*. Chapel Hill: University of North Carolina Press

Ward, John (1965-66), 'Cleric or Critic? The Intellectual in the University'. *American Scholar:* 35, no. 1

Ways, Max (1967), 'Intellectuals and the Presidency'. *Fortune:* 75 (April)

Weber, Max (1954), *On Law in Economy and Society*. New York: Simon and Schuster

––– (1958), *The Religion of India*. New York: The Free Press

––– (1963), *The Sociology of Religion*. Boston: Beacon Press

Werner, Ernest (1964-65), 'Remodeling the Protestant Ministry'. *American Scholar:* 34 (Winter)

World Marxist Review (1968), 'Upsurge of the Youth Movement in the Capitalist Countries'. 11 (July)

Young, Michael (1958), *The Rise of the Meritocracy*. London: Thames and Hudson

Znaniecki, Florian (1968), *The Social Role of the Man of Knowledge*. New York: Harper Torchbooks

II

REVOLUTIONARY MOOD AMONG THE
CONTEMPORARY INTELLIGENTSIA

THE HUMANISTIC INTELLIGENTSIA

Harold M Hodges Jr
San Jose State University

We hypothesize—more accurately, we contend—that there is a profound unease, a sense of disquietude in the air. It is taking hold for the most part in the West, and particularly in the United States among many intellectuals and enlightened laymen alike. It defies a recognizable label or a ready definition. All the same, it is inescapably there, its roots are deep, and it is surely no small thing. It may portend, we venture, nothing less than a revolution—a quiet revolution. A 'quiet' revolution? Precisely. For it may not be what we commonly take to be a revolution: a sudden, perhaps violent, and dramatically overt effort meant to topple a dominant socio-political-economic structure. Nor will it be invested with such other familiar corollaries of revolutionary change as an explicit and fervent ideology or leaders who have emerged from the underground to rally mass support among the ranks of the alienated and the disenfranchised.

The growing number of the participants in this ferment constitute something like an international stratum which has most in common with the old intelligentsia from Eastern Europe. The latter also wanted to abolish the burden of the past. The classical predecessors of today's intelligentsia wanted, however, to achieve their goals in a more positivistic way, while their western cousins appear to be revolting *against* the positivist tradition.

All the same, what we are alluding to is strikingly akin to a revolution-in-the-making: a movement which, if it succeeds, seems destined to wrench and reshape our familiar configurations of norms, ideals, values, patterns of leisure, styles of life, and workaday worlds just as surely as the classical revolutions have supplanted new dynasties for old (or, to be more apposite, perhaps, just as the Renaissance redefined the Western world). If, then this incipient upheaval is taking hold with little fanfare, even the remotest possibility of its success demands immediate and serious attention from those in the intellectual community.

We propose that at one level, the more popular level (among, say, many who are attending or have recently attended universities and among many of their elders who are professionals or semi-professionals), this disquietude reflects a still-latent yet increasingly conscious and overt unhappiness with the nature and quality of everyday life. More specifically, it is an uneasiness with the nature and quality of the social roles, career options, leisure, institutions, and interpersonal relationships which appear to enmesh us in the technobureaucratic Western world. Moreover, this restlessness in the face of the status quo shows many signs of generating an unprecedented antidote: an alternative way of life which for many if not most Westerners will differ in a striking manner from the mainstream way of life which we take for granted.

At still another level (the level which will constitute the major focus in this paper), this disquietude is attracting increasing attention among intellectuals, in particular many younger scholars in the social and behavioral sciences, not to mention a considerable number of physical scientists.[1]

We have suggested that the malaise to which we refer cannot be readily defined; yet if it is still too amorphous, many-faceted, and mutable for that, we can, for want of a working title, label the recognition of it the 'new humanism'.[2] In one sense, the adjective 'new' is misleading. For the roots of the new humanism are venerable. Its lineage can be traced to such seemingly disparate philosophies and social movements as Taoism, Zen and Ch'an Buddhism, Sufism, romanticism, and anarchism, and such individuals as Lao Tsu, Meister Eckhart, the nineteenth-century American transcendentalists (Ralph Waldo Emerson, Henry Thoreau, William James), the founding fathers of

existentialism (Friedrich Nietzsche and Soren Kierkegaard in partic-
ular), early-day and latter-day figures in the depth, humanistic, and
transcendental psychologies (Carl Jung, Wilhelm Reich, Victor Frankl,
Fritz Perls, Abraham Maslow, Carl Rogers, Roberto Assagioli, Rollo
May), spokesmen for the Eastern philosophies in the West (Sri Auro-
bindo, J. Krishnamurti, Idries Shah, Aldous Huxley, D. T. Suzuki, Alan
Watts), and such people as Henri Bergson, Michael Polanyi, T. S. Kuhn,
Rene Dubos, R. D. Laing, Eric Fromm, Norman O. Brown, Herbert
Marcuse, Paul Goodman, and Carlos Castaneda.

Before delving further into the matter of the new humanism's
progenitors and guiding lights, however, it will be instructive if we
tender a brief synopsis of its major tenets and points-of-view. Accordingly, we will allude first to what many of those we call new humanists
take to be the major failings in the traditional conceptions of social life
and social man, and next to some representative personal goals (idealized self-conceptions, personal attributes, and ways of perceiving and
acting) correlative with the philosophical stance of the new humanism.

SOME REPRESENTATIVE NEW HUMANIST CRITICISMS
OF CONVENTIONAL CONCEPTIONS OF SOCIAL LIFE . . .

1. Whatever the sciences of man might proclaim, social life and
social man are still unfathomed (and perhaps unfathomable) mysteries.
We may *think* that we have fashioned paradigms, theories, conceptual
apparati, and modes of analysis which are accurate if not yet definitive,
but we delude ourselves—perhaps in the same way that the defenders of
Ptolemy argued on the eve of the Copernican revolution that the earth
was indeed the hub of the universe.

2. Our standard models of man, heirs of a Western intellectual
tradition that would rely almost exclusively upon cognitive, rational,
categorical, analytical, schematic, objective, and conceptual modes of
inquiry, analysis, and depiction, have filtered out certain aspects—perhaps crucial aspects—of social reality. More specifically,

a) in championing, as we have been prone to do, the Cartesian conception of cogito ergo sum—in one-sidedly focusing, that is, on man as a *thinking* animal—we have grievously underestimated the role enacted by the more subjective, latent, spontaneous, idiosyncratic, unconscious, and 'unprogrammed' facets of man. We have, for instance, overplayed what such students of 'bimodal consciousness' as Deikman (1971) Tart (1972), Ornstein (1973), and Bogen (1969), assert to be the functions primarily enacted by the 'left-hemispheric' portions of the human brain [i.e., the (i) verbal, (ii) logical, (iii) directed or explicit, (iv) cautious, and (viii) active functions]. We have simultaneously *depreciated* the functions associated with the right hemispheres of our brains [i.e., the (i) nonverbal or nonlineal, (ii) intuitive, (iii) tacit or oblique, (iv) relaxed or nonchalant, (v) diffused, (vi) affective or emotional, (vii) impulsive or hunch-playing, and (viii) passive functions].

b) relatedly, in conceiving man as an intrinsically norm-abiding, role-playing animal, we have slighted the very significant fact that the human is simultaneously acted upon *and* selfactuating, role-playing *and* at frequent and fundamental odds with the roles imposed upon him, norm-abiding *and* norm-evading, a conforming, pliable, 'tribal' being *and* a stubbornly unique, self-assertive individual who never succumbs to the pressures exerted by a never-ending socialization process. He is at once a consonance-seeker and a dissonance-seeker, a being in quest of equilibrium and a being in quest of tension.

If at least some of the new humanists have one-sidedly championed the essentially Dionysian ideals inherent in many of the 'right-hemispheric' qualities listed above, the majority have called instead for something more like a focus upon a synthesis or fusion of the Apollonian and the Dionysian as constituent elements in our self-makeups. They have urged in effect that the social and behavioral scientist (a) attend to man as both a phenomenological and a sociological animal—as an intentional and self-conscious actor who creates much of the social reality which surrounds him and as a being who is also inescapably shaped and bound by a configuration of social matrices and processes; (b) recognize that humans (and their social milieux) are simultaneously characterized by processes making for change and 'becoming' *and* constancy, cohesion, and predictability, and (c) acknowledge that the human animal is as much—or more—a creature actuated by subconscious or unconscious as by conscious elements.

It is urged, in sum, that serviceable as it often is to picture humans in terms of such social ties as age, sex, race, ethnicity, religion, nationality, or social class, it is imperative that we also pay heed to their stubbornly *unique* and *mutable* qualities. To attend too exclusively to one facet of man at the expense of another is to be dangerously simplistic and reductionist. Worse, the new humanist would argue, it is to be parochial and unrealistic. For is it not our intentions as students of man and society to comprehend them?

To some new humanists, it seems profitable to visualize the socialization process (particularly in the middle-class precincts of Western society) in terms of a 'channeling' procedure which, in shaping the infant into an adult, commonly entails the movement of such qualities as those portrayed in column A, below, toward those listed in column B:

Column A:	Column B:
spontaneous, unrestrained	self-restrained/inhibited/impulse-controlling
risk-taking/adventuresome/change-seeking	cautious/fearful of unfamiliar/security-oriented/stability seeking
gestaltic, holistic/open-ended	categorical/dichotomy—and either- or oriented/time-bound
senses oneness, unity with animals, nature and other humans	fearful, indifferent, hostile, or exploitive re. nature, animals, other humans
intuitive/affective	logical/cognitive
open or empty-minded	closed-minded
demonstrative, uninhibited, extroverted, enthusiastic	staid, impassive, reticent, reserved
innovative/exploratory	conventional/custom-bound, tradition-oriented
at ease with chaos, complexity, disorder, mystery	fearful of the unstructured, anarchic, undefined

can easily regress, get in touch with "primitive" or subconscious feelings, impressions	wary or unaware of primitive or subconscious currents within self
easily captivated, fascinated, filled with awe, wonder, and curiosity/ quests for new experiences	easily bored, blase, sensitive to monotony, and surfeited/quests for certitude
present-centered/lives for the "now" and savors the moment	future-oriented or past-oriented

These are, of course, crude or ideal-typical approximations meant to convey the essence of the distinctions instead of their precise nature. They are more impressionistic than empirical in coloration. Yet they do vividly portray the notion that the characteristics which dominate us in infancy and early childhood are, for the most part, effectively erased by the process of "growing up". Yet, we are asked, *are* such traits and impulses erased in *fact?* Or are they merely muted or subdued—so that they lurk beneath the visible surface 'reality' that we display (and are conscious of) in our taken-for-granted everyday social encounters and self definitions? In other words, *far from being obliterated in consequence of the socialization process, is it not possible that these 'childish' characteristics remain as central and quite significant features of our 'grown-up', self or personality configurations?*

They are invisible, it may be argued, because they have been variously repressed, disowned, and denied by the agencies of socialization (the family, peers, schools, and the mass media), not to mention by the 'super-ego' controls of the individual actor and his more conscious self-perceptions and self-evaluations. Repressed, disowned, or denied, yes. But inactive and inoperative? Far from it. For the 'primitive' in each of us, it may be argued, is at continual and now-conscious, now-unconscious odds with the 'civilized' veneer which we display when we are engaged in what Erving Goffman calls 'onstage' behavior. Thus, too, we are reminded, the *dialectical* nature of individual—and social—life. Just, then, as every society (every urban society in particular) witnesses a perennial give-and-take conflict between what Georg Simmel identified as the impulses toward 'life' (innovation, spontaneity, freshness, creativity) and the impulses toward 'form' (rigidity, institutionalization, formalization, conservatism, staleness), so also in the words of Walter Weisskopf,

Every society permits only certain human propensities to be realized and suppresses others. It bottles up certain drives, inclinations and capabilities which then, like the forces of the unconscious, clamor for realization and bring about social change (1971: 12).

Two related conceptions will come to mind here: Sigmund Freud's notion, voiced in his *Civilization and Its Discontents,* that the never-ending struggle between the 'instincts' of life and destruction 'is what all life essentially consists of' (1962: 69), and Nietzsche's allegation that social life is characterized by a perennial contest between the Dionysian and the Apollonian. Threading their way through the history of every society (and every individual as well) such Dionysian drives as impetuousity, spontaneity, daring, sensuousness, and life-affirming joy are conceived to be at constant odds with such obverse Apollonian drives as calmness, self-control, caution, self-repressiveness, and self-constraint (1956). Just, then, as societies contain both Dionysian and Apollonian elements (viz England's Elizabethan era zest and Cromwellian sobriety or its Neoclassical celebration of harmony tradition, order, and equilibrium and the Romanticists' championship of adventure, daring, diversity, and the expression of emotion), so does every human being. So too, of course, whole peoples (the Scots, say, or the Prussians) have been characterized by some as essentially Apollonian in inclination and some (the Sicilians, for instance, or the Lebanese) as more Dionysian.

To suggest another—and sociologically more relevant—parallel, it can be safely alleged that two of our central sociological orientations, the equilibrium and the conflict models of society (see Coser, 1964, and Horowitz, 1968) are in essence non-dialectical and dialectical conceptions of social life. So, too, with what Horowitz calls the 'domain assumptions' undergirding our major theories of socialization. Borrowing from a distinction suggested by Gordon Allport (1955), we will label these the Lockian (or sociological) and Leibnitzian (or existential) theories of the social self.[3]

John Locke, we will recall, assumed that the mind of the human is at birth an utter blank, a *tabula rasa*—a passive, mirror-like entity that acquires content, structure, and self-consciousness only through association with other humans. Gottfried Leibnitz urged, in contrast, that from earliest infancy onward the human mind is forever active in its own right, given to grappling with and interpreting the stimuli that bombard it, and bent on manipulating sensory data according to its own needs. The self, to Locke, was altogether a social product; the self, to Leibnitz, was at once compliant, submissive, and pliable and self-indulgent, autonomy-seeking, and stubbornly unique—forever at odds with culturally-stamped pressures to conform exclusively to the 'dictates of the tribe'. If, then, for Locke the self is reactive when stimulated, for Liebnitz it is self-propelled; for Locke, existence determines consciousness and for Leibnitz, consciousness—our perceptions of what is happening 'out there'—shapes and structures reality. Locke, then, was a progenitor of the sociology of knowledge, Leibnitz of the phenomenology affirmed by Alfred Schutz (1953).

In urging that students of social life pay far more heed to the Leibnitizian emphasis, the new humanists are contending that the social self is something far richer, more subjective, less predictable, more complex, and in frequent conflict (overt and covert, conscious and unconscious) with pressures to conform to societal norms, role-sets, and values—and less amenable to pigeonholing or categorical definitions—than is commonly assumed. In arguing for something approaching what T. S. Kuhn would label a 'paradigmatic' breakthrough (1962), they ask that we attend to the primacy of human consciousness and thus to the human as a *self-actualizing, self-conscious being who continually constructs and reconstructs 'reality' according to his own, idiosyncratic definitions.* While agreeing that 'free will' is more a myth than a reality, they contend that man is nonetheless continually changing, forever in a process of becoming and responding to new situations rather than cast in a predictable and readily cognizable mold. Never precisely the same from one moment or social encounter to the next, he possesses not one single and coherent self, but a multiplicity of protean selves (Lifton, 1968, and Gergen, 1972).

To sum up, and reiterate, the gist of the new humanist dispute with out standard conceptions of social life amounts to this: (1) because life consists of much that is rich, complex, forever changing, mysterious, and illusive, we must continually re-examine the worth or adaptive flexibility of our conventional paradigms, theories, concepts, and modes of analysis; (2) in doing so, we must admit that we have been prone to attend too exclusively to human beings as cognitive, rational, thinking animals—thus overlooking the more intuitive, affective, irrational, subjective, and subconscious elements of their makeup; moreover we (3) have customarily neglected the truth that man is simultaneously a compliantly norm-abiding 'tribal' being *and* a stubbornly idiosyncratic norm-opposing or norm-flaunting being—that the socialization process whereby he is inducted into the normative animal we take him to be represses but does not eliminate his more 'childlike' or Dionysian qualities; and in disregarding such conflict-ridden facets of self-makeup we (4) have belittled or ignored the fundamentally tension-infused, dialectical nature of both individual and social life. In sum, our standard 'oversocialized' conception of social beings and our normative, equilibrium-oriented conception of social life has bypassed the inherently amorphous, discordant, and mutable aspects of social reality.

In doing all of this, the member of the humanistic intelligentsia would add, we have often unwittingly taken the 'normal' to be functional, good, or suitable and the disruptive or the deviant to be dysfunctional or somehow 'wrong'. Small wonder, too, many of them would remind us, that we have frequently depreciated the pervasive role of power (vis-a-vis have/have-not or superordinate/subordinate groups or relationships) in sustaining what we take to be such 'normal' arrangements as structured social inequality, the family, educational institutions, political and economic life, and norms which regulate sex-graded, race-graded, and age-graded behavioral expectations. Given our conventional biases, we have also depreciated the sources, geneses, and importance of collective behavior.[4] We have all too often become, they conclude, students of a fictive social life which is fictional because it is infinitely too simplistic and reductionist.

So much, then, for a sampling of the indictments leveled against orthodox sociology by what we have chosen to call the new humanists. But what of their idealized (and often actualized) self-conceptions, personal attributes, and ways of perceiving and acting? What, also, of the links between such convictions and the philosophies, movements, and individual spokesmen, past and contemporary, which have helped shape, support, and sustain this 'revolution of consciousness?'[5] We have chosen to portray the gist of such qualities by outlining the characteristic beliefs or convictions in the left-hand columns and indicating some of the relevant philosophies, sources, or spokesmen in the adjacent columns. If some of these positions seem less sociologically relevant than others, it is because it is our intent in this last portion of the paper to convey the elemental 'flavor' of this emergent and not-to-be-lightly-dismissed consciousness. It would be less than candid to deny that this attempted synthesis is provisional, impressionistic, and quite subjective. We must acknowledge, too, that it is retrospective or *ex post facto* in that the inferences are drawn from the philosophies, movements, and individuals who appear to have been particularly influential in shaping the ethos of the humanistic intelligentsia. The new humanists, finally, must not be construed as an organized or self-conscious social group possessing an explicit ideology or uniform principles. It is less a social movement, then, than an amorphous, many-stranded, asymmetrical, still-germinating, and inconstant impulse. All the same, it is a vital impulse which demands, as we remarked earlier, immediate, open-minded, and serious attention from those in the intellectual community.

The Beliefs and Convictions:	Roots and Antecedents:	
It is crucial that we strive to re-achieve what was originally ours: aliveness, spontaneity, vitality, flow, freshness. We must relearn how to fantasy, to delve into the seeming chaos of our unconscious or subconscious minds. We must recover our native sense of wonder and curiosity and be open and ready to engage in new experiences. . . .	Lao Tzu	Abraham Maslow
	Gabriel Marcel	Henri Bergson
	Ortega y Gasset	Norman O. Brown
	Jacques Barzun	Clark Moustakas
	Taoism	Existentialism
	Sufism	
	Romanticism	Zen Buddhism
We must learn, in effect, to be 'born anew' . . . We must become, metaphorically, 'as little children:' open-ended, expressive, less bound by others' definitions of reality. This amounts to attaining a 'second naivete', to be-	R. D. Laing	Eric Fromm
	Joseph Chilton Pearce	Maslow
	Bernard Gunther	Peter Marin

coming more expressive and more open to our inner urgings. It means, too, that we must 'unlearn' much that we have acquired in the process of growing up, that we must transcend much that is habitual, stale, stereotyped, and hidebound; we must supplant a tunnel vision which is too exclusively defined by tribal norms with a more artless or innocent peripheral vision. . . .

By the same token, our freedom is on perpetual trial in the sense that we are in constant danger of becoming 'robotized' and 'inhuman', of 'selling out' ('I am as you want me') for the sake of acceptance or popularity. We thus cannot take our freedom for granted . . . for freedom is difficult and slavery— self-induced slavery to others' definitions of situations—is easy and tempting. Similarly, our behavior can readily become patterned and thoughtlessly repetitive; most humans are in fact 'asleep' and herdlike. We must, then, be forever wary of becoming bound by a habit or a situation. . . .

Don't Pretend! Shun facades, pseudoness, 'plasticity', 'pseudo-Gemeinschaft', and slavish role-playing; be 'yourself', not what others want you to be. Have the 'courage to be'; 'express your intrinsic self' . . . Disclose your 'true' self to others . . . Be honest with yourself. Preserve your authenticity, your freedom, and your vitality. Shun 'oughts', 'shoulds'. Create more of your own rules and rely more on your intrinsic conscience. . . .

Zen Buddhism

Taoism

Vedanta

Sri Aurobindo

Friedrich Nietzsche

Carl Jung

Wilhelm Reich

Rollo May

F. S. Perls

Nietzsche

Perls

Maslow

Zen Buddhism

Existentialism

Paul Tillich

Brown

Karl Jaspers

Jean-Paul Sartre

Soren Kierkegaard

Nicolai Berdyaev

Maurice Merleau-Ponty

Gabriel Marcel

Martin Buber

Clark Moustakas

May

Jung

Nietzsche

T. S. Eliot

Maria Ranier Rilke   Paul Goodman

Kierkegaard

Shakespeare

Claudio Naranjo

Carl Rogers

Sidney Jourard

Maslow

Zen Buddhism

The responsibility is ours: *we* give the world meaning. We can 'make our lives work.' We have the choice of whatever we feel; we can choose to enjoy or not to enjoy any situation, but this obligates us to choose, to commit ourselves, to dare, to take risks. Humans, in a word, are—or can be—much more self-determined. 'We are our own choices. . . .'

We are in never-ceasing danger of stifling, misdirecting, or repressing our fundamental fount of energy—our 'elan vital' or 'life force'. We easily lose our inherent aliveness, gusto, and spontaneity and become cold, dry, empty. . . .

Since much that is fundamental can only be experienced first-hand—since 'truth' is essentially experiential—wisdom must be attained as much or more by self-awareness as by reliance on external authority. Truths, then, must be intuited and grasped subjectively, for they lie in our subconscious or unconscious. If we are to 'reach' or 'look within' we must be wary of perception which is lopsidedly symbolic, abstract, conceptual, categorical, and word-bound. . . .

There is an essential symmetry or 'oneness' between man and nature, between man and the cosmos. Thus, dichotomies are man-made conceptual devices that falsify much of reality. We cannot split reality into discrete parts but must, instead, sense or grasp things holistically. There is,

phenomenology	
	Existentialism
Merleau-Ponty	
	Sartre
Nietzsche	
	the Upanishads
Laing	
	Romanticism
Jourard	
	Rogers
May	Maslow
Perls	
	Bergson
Zen Buddhism	
	Reich
Laing	Herbert Marcuse
Aldous Huxley	William James
Gautama Buddha	
	Meister Eckhart
D. T. Suzuki	
	Krishnamurti
Mary Baker Eddy	
	Marshall McLuhan
Bergson	
Jung	Rogers
Kierkegaard	Taoism
Sufism	Huxley
Alan Watts	
	Carlos Castaneda
Nietzsche	Perls
Maslow	
Fritz Pappenheim	Brown
Watts	Andrew Weil
Ruth Sasaki	
	Suzuki
Yung-chin	Jung
Laing	Marcuse
	Maslow
Nietzsche	
	Clark Moustakas

then, an underlying unity inherent in all dualities, all opposites. . . .

Paradoxically, life is also rife with dynamic give-and-take tensions—with an unremitting struggle between polar opposites (the conscious and the unconscious, yin and yang, the intellect and intuition, control and spontaniety, the Dionysian and the Apollonian). Humans and the social fabric in which they are enmeshed may be conceived as a fragile synthesis of contending forces or impulses which are working their way toward unity and equilibrium. Such tensions are at once the source of the energy which impels our lives and the necessary antecedents to ultimate fusion. . . .

The fundamental reality is change. All is impermanent and in a constant state of flux and metamorphosis. Life is not static and rigidly fixed, but dynamic and fluid. It is never precisely the same from one moment to the next. Everything is new. . . .

We must live for the 'now' and savor each moment rather than dwell in the past or the future. We must live from moment to moment; we must constantly evolve instead of stagnating. This entails continual alertness to all that is habitual or stereotyped within us. The stale and the routine can become anchors which impede growth and newness; we can as readily become prisoners of our own minds— our own rigid mental constructs— as prisoners of our cultural norms.

Reich
Zen Buddhism

George Leonard
Taoism

Gordon Allport

Pearce

Nietzsche

Jung

Sam Keen

Bergson

Jourard

Romanticism

Freud

Esther Harding

Taoism

Lao Tzu

Zen Buddhism

Vedanta

Jesus
Buddha

I Ching

Brown

Romanticism

Bergson

Revelations

Krishnamurti

Rogers
Sufism

Taoism
Idries Shah

Claudio Naranjo

Reich

Bergson

Zen Buddhism

Gurdjieff

Watts

William Blake

Maslow

Romanticism

Gestalt psychology

Ralph Waldo Emerson
Sufism
Perls
Colin Wilson

St. Augustine
Frankl
Shah

We are often our own worst oppressors; we are so prone to
fear life and spontaneity—to
repress or bottle up our feelings—that we become self-alienated,
self-imprisoned. We tend,
in a word, to throttle our native
aliveness. We vegetate, preferring
safety and familiarity to
adventure. . . .

Awareness, alertness, are crucial
to our well-being. We must be
self-aware, self-observant, self-
witnessing and we must be masters,
not slaves, of our drives. We are
far more capable of self-mastery
or self-overcoming than we admit.
True learning amounts to self-
discovery, to realizing and tap-
ping our own potential; imitation
is 'death'. . . .

Existence, life, are mysteries: we
must not oversimplify them. We
must, in fact, court and seek out
mystery rather than shun it. Similarly, we must be wary of traditional definitions of reality or
truth; we must take nothing for
granted. We must be open, skeptical,
curious, daring—continually questioning the purpose of life.

Reich

Perls

Rene Dubos   Goodman

Sartre

Franz Kafka

Nietzsche   Laing

Fromm   Brown

Jourard   Emerson

El-Ghazali   Ibn El-Arabi

Romanticism

George Bernard Shaw

Krishnamurti

Nietzsche   Robert Ornstein

Lao Tzu

Suzuki

Robert De Ropp

Buddha   Maslow

Taoism   Perls

Naranjo   William James

May

Ram Dass

Brown

Shaw

Nietzsche

Maslow

Existentialism

Saadi of Shiraz   James

Buber   Heidegger

Kafka   Walter Kaufman

Arthur Koestler

If many of the antecedents of the new humanism are ancient, it is
also apparent that its dominant thrust is a counter-thrust: that it is a
dialectical response to a contemporary phenomenon—a technobureaucratic ethos and milieu which is perceived (for the most part rather
dimly perceived) to be a threat to our very 'humanness'. In fact, the
dissent which we have labeled new humanism may be directly traced to
the 'countercultural' dissent which was so explosive an ingredient

among Western youth in the late 1960's. Now, as then, this dissent is actuated by an unwritten bill of particulars leveled against the pervasive mix of rationalism, technology, and bureaucratic organization which are the dominant elements of our 'postindustrial' age. It is instructive to isolate certain central themes which undergird this humanistic counter-thrust. These include:

1. *An essentially anarchistic celebration of participatory democracy* (and, correlatively, opposition to a distant, centralized form of government; the conviction that power should rest with the people; the feeling that there should be minimal external checks on individual freedom—that the real checks should be internal, stemming from the individual's sense of responsibility and willingness to cooperate with others, and a basic distrust of hierarchical authority and the regulation of people by bureaucratic norms.)

2. *An existential penchant for 'authenticity' and 'commitment'* (there is a restlessness that often amounts to open disgust with 'role-playing': selling out for the sake of acceptance or popularity, lacking the courage of one's convictions, and inability to speak frankly. What is more, authenticity is proved by commitment: lip-service profession of ideals will not do. One must do, not merely profess).

3. *An admiration for moral purity*—a morality with a two-edged nature. On the one hand it involves an idealistic conviction of what things should be; on the other (and more confidently) of what they should not be. If the former is concerned in the main with authenticity and commitment—with acting out one's professed moral beliefs—the latter would blame the 'other morality' (conventional middle-class morality) for being falsely virtuous and bypocritical.

4. *An emphasis on self-expression and spontaneity* materializes in a relaxed and come-what-may open-mindedness which is something quite different from a conscious yet falsehearted effort to be 'tolerant'; more spontaneous than contrived, it amounts to a readiness to accept others and their unique qualities on their own terms.

5. *A quest for 'community'*—for direct, informal, and intimate, *Gemeinschaft* (or *Wesenwille*) contact with others. This need for primary-like relationships has often been realized in practice. The profusion of

rural and urban communal living arrangements and the relaxation of traditional 'puritanical' restraints are familiar cases in point. At still another, yet surely related level, this search for community (which is at heart a repudiation of the many social, organizational, and technological pressures making for estrangement, social distance, and anonymity) is echoed in efforts to shatter such traditional barriers to interpersonal equality as race, sex, age, and social status. Much of this impulse, finally, recalls the long-time romantic desire (celebrated, for instance, by Rousseau and the English Lake Poets) for a 'primitivization' of society—creation, that is, of a society comprised of small, decentralized, communal 'tribes'.

6. *A profound distrust of authority-qua-authority.* This anti-authoritarian inclination is at least partially egalitarian and populist in nature and is thus linked to the ideal of participatory democracy. It is marked, too, by a deep-seated dislike for dominant-submissive, super-ordinate-subordinate interpersonal relationships and commitments. This theme, reflecting as it does, a strong distaste for powerlessness, is one of the more enduring of the animating impulses behind the growth of 'liberation' movements among minority Americans (Blacks, Asian-Americans, Mexican-Americans, and native-American Indians), women, homosexuals, and the aged.

What, then, does all this mean? It amounts to this: There is indeed a revolution—a *revolution of consciousness*—afoot. And, it behoves us as 'intellectuals' to pay heed, careful heed, to its roots, contours, dynamics, and ramifications. For it will surely ultimately (and radically) restructure the normative and value systems which we so take for granted as enduring (albeit glacially changing).

We failed—abysmally!—to predict the new humanism's more vocal, visible, and dramatic progenitor, the 'youth counterculture' of the 1960's (Hodges, 1973, Topics 24 and 25 and Hodges, 1974, chapter 16). Will we now fail to admit that this new humanist counterculture is very much alive—and far more massive, irreversible, and more significant than its predecessor? If we respond as we have traditionally responded, we will, for the most part, dismiss this emergent social movement as yet one more ephemeral fad. This will be a mistake.[6]

NOTES

1. Among the growing number of social and behavioral scientists who have championed a humanistic approach were the late Pitirim Sorokin, Florian Znaniecki, C. Wright Mills, Abraham Maslow, Roberto Assagioli, Stanislaw Ossowski and Michael Polanyi, and such contemporaries as Jack D. Douglas, Alvin Gouldner, Bernard Rosenberg, Randall Collins, Peter L. Berger, Irving L. Horowitz, Stanford M. Lyman, Stanislaw Andreski, Lewis Coser, Philip Slater, Andrew Greeley, John Horton, Alfred McClung Lee, Ted Goertzel, John Leggett, Sidney Willhelm, John Howard, Henry Anderson, David Arnold, Peter Manning, Rollo May, Carl Rogers, Robert E. Ornstein, Charles T. Tart, Dorothy Lee, Arthur J. Deikman, Edward Tiryakian, Marvin Scott, Sidney M. Jourard, Clark Moustakas, Huston Smith, Walter A. Weisskopf, James F. Bugental, James Fadiman, Stanislav Grof, John White, Stanley Krippner, and Ira Progoff. Among physical and life scientists supporting a new humanist *Weltanschauung* have been Willis W. Harman, Neils Bohr, P. W. Bridgeman, Arthur Eddington, J. Jeans, P. Schrodinger, James Fadiman and Rene Dubos.

2. We borrow this label from Barry Schwarts, author of *The New Humanism* (1974), New York: Praeger Publishers.

3. For an extensive analysis of 'sociologism' and existentialism, see Edward A. Tiryakian (1962), *Sociologism and Existentialism*, Englewood Cliffs, N.J.: Prentice-Hall.

4. 'Sociologists, in their preoccupation with social structure and institutionalized types of behavior,' Lewis A. Coser advises, 'often tend to neglect those forms of social behavior which are relatively unorganized and lack the stability and predictability of cohesive social groups. Yet collective behavior arising spontaneously, and not based on pre-established norms and traditions, should be studied closely if only because such behavior may enlighten us as to how an old order dies and a new social order emerges.' Coser (1963), *Sociology Through Literature*, Englewood Cliffs, N.J.: Prentice-Hall, 328.

5. The revolution of consciousness involves infinitely more than we have alluded to here. In addition to increasingly intensive explorations into the sources and ramifications of right- and left-hemispheric cognition—of bimodal consciousness—there is renewed interest in the scientific community (including the social and behavioral sciences) with such related (if until-now-beyond-the-academic-pale) phenomena as these:

i) *Altered states of consciousness* (studies of qualitative shifts in patterns of mental functioning which differ substantially from our normal, 'waking' states of consciousness; there is concern with the meditative practices of Eastern disciplines and with chemical and biofeedback techniques used as means of induction into latered states; there is equal concern with the characteristics, corollaries, and consequences of such 'ASCs').

ii) *Creativity and self-actualization* (studies of the psychodynamics and sociodynamics of those 'fully human' individuals who actualize their latent potentials).

iii) *Alpha-wave consciousness* (studies of the generation of sustained, electrically charged currents of brain energy which produce altered states of consciousness which deeply affect our perceptions and bodily functioning).

iv) *Nonallopathic or homeopathic medicine* (studies of healing accomplished by powers latent in the individual as opposed to the standard focus upon bacterially-induced illnesses and the treatment of symptoms).

v) *Dreams, hypnotic, hypnogic and sleep consciousness* (studies of nonwaking and non-normal types of consciousness).

vi) *Parapsychologic and psi phenomena* (studies of such phenomena as extrasensory perception, precognition, telepathic communication, clairvoyence, and psychokinesis).

6. The theme of this paper is elaborated in two books by this author: *Search for Self: The Sociology of Consciousness,* Sàn Jose, Spartan Books, 1975, and *On Becoming Fully Human: The Revolution in Human Consciousness,* (in process).

REFERENCES

Allport, G. (1955) *Becoming.* New Haven, Conn.: Yale University Press

Bogen, J. E. (1969) 'The Other Side of the Brain: An Appositional Mind', *Bulletin of the Los Angeles Neurological Societies,* 34: 135-162.

Coser, L. (1964) *The Functions of Social Conflict.* New York: Free Press.

Deikman, A. J. (1971) 'Bimodal Consciousness', *Archives of General Psychology,* 25: 481-489.

Freud, S. (1962) *Civilization and Its Discontents,* John Strachey (trans.) New York: Norton, paperback ed.

Gergen, K. J. (1972) 'Multiple Identity', *Psychology Today,* 5: 20-27.

Hodges, H. M. (1974) *Conflict and Consensus: An Introduction to Sociology* (2nd ed.). New York: Harper & Row.

Hodges, H. M. (1973) *Conflict and Consensus: Readings Toward a Sociological Perspective.* New York: Harper & Row.

Horowitz, I. (1968) *Professing Sociology.* Chicago: Aldine

Kuhn, T. S. (1962) *The Structure of Scientific Revolutions.* University of Chicago Press.

Lifton, R. J. (1968) 'Protean Man', *Partisan Review,* 35: 242-256.

Ornstein, R. E. (1973) *The Nature of Human Consciousness* (ed.). San Francisco: W. H. Freeman.

Schutz, A. (1953) 'Common-Sense and Scientific Interpretation of Human Action', *Philosophy and Phenomenological Research,* 14: 63-97.

Tart, C. (1972) *Altered States of Consciousness* (ed.) Garden City, N.Y.: Doubleday, Anchor Books.

8

FILMMAKERS AS PART OF A REVOLUTIONARY INTELLIGENTSIA

Leonard Henny
University of Utrecht

I INTRODUCTION

When speaking of the impact of technology on revolution in society one has to acknowledge that the communications technologies are today of great revolutionary potential; not only in the period of the actual seizure of power, but also in the pre-revolutionary and post-revolutionary stages.[1] At the height of a revolutionary take-over the radio and television stations are of prime importance, because, as Adorno has pointed out: 'heute herrscht wer uber das Bewustsein der Massen verfugt' [in today's society he rules who controls the consciousness of the masses].[2] When considering the role of the film and the filmmaker in the process of revolutionary social change, it is well known that there is an ever-increasing trend towards audio-visualization in the communications industry: film- and video-technology are gaining in importance over printing, phone and radio. There is no doubt that revolutionaries are turning more and more to the use of film-technology as a means to communicate with their (potential) constituency. At the same time it is also clear that in most countries the ruling establishment are attempting to get a firmer grip on the media, either through increased government control or through corporate monopolization. At this point it is important to take a closer look at the position of the filmmaker as compared to other categories of intellectuals in revolutionary movements. Unlike revolutionary poets, novelists, painters, musicians, actors, etc. filmmakers are heavily dependent upon a highly capital-intensive production system in order to produce a specimen of their work. Not counting subsistence expenses, a poet's investment in tools may range from 25 cents for a ballpoint to a couple of dollars for a fountain pen. A filmmaker however has to count with an initial investment of tens of thousands of dollars to produce a 'low budget' film. In addition, the filmmaker is highly dependent on the cooperation of camera crews, laboratory technicians and the availability of films stock and studio facilities. It is one thing to write a revolutionary pamphlet in the attic of a cottage in the mountains; it is quite a different thing to transfer a soundtrack of a revolutionary speech in a government-owned sound studio!

In spite of these difficulties, revolutionary filmmakers have been producing and are still producing oppositional films, sometimes clandestinely, within the studios of the establishment; sometimes in underground studios from 'liberated territories'.

In this paper I will present a description of the ways in which revolutionary movements have used and are using the medium of film to foster their cause, and how filmmakers function within the context of a revolutionary intelligentsia. It is my hypothesis that in the past, films have been effective primarily in helping to consolidate successful revolutions rather than in helping to bring about revolutions (e.g., USSR, DRV, Cuba). Today however we can see the emergence of revolutionary cinema in the West, which points to the growing importance of the role of film in the process of revolutionary social change (Europe, USA, Latin America, Africa).

II THEORETICAL CONSIDERATIONS

In the context of this paper I will limit myself to a study of the role of film in revolutionary movements which support a change from some form of capitalism to some form of socialism.

(a) Political Economy of Filmmaking

Film technology was developed under capitalism, and from the outset the means of production of the film industry were under the control of private businessmen (Prokop, 1971: 23-24). In terms of the Marxist dichotomy between 'substructure' and 'superstructure' we can say that film is typically tied both to the societal substructure (the economics of the means of production: 'hardware'), as well as to the societal super-structure (the ideology of the owners of the means of production: 'software'). Consequently, in capitalist society the importance of the film-industry is both as a *source of profit* as well as *a carrier of ideology*.

(b) Historical Stages in Revolutionary Filmmaking

As has been argued in the above, the electronic media, and particularly the film industry, tend to form a system-dependent entity. Generally speaking, films with a content that runs counter to the predominant ideology can rarely be produced within the official film-industry. By the same token it is obvious that insurgent groups tend to lack the financial resources to produce their own 'counter productions' on a large enough scale to meaningfully offset the 'all is well' ideology of the predominant system. Thus, revolutionary filmmaking has in the past primarily developed *after* the means of production of the film industry were brought under the control of the new rulers. This was true in Soviet Russia, where the great revolutionary filmmakers made their films after 1917. It was also true in the Democratic Republic of North Vietnam and in Cuba where, before the revolution all filmmaking was controlled by the corporate film-industry (mainly French and American), but where since the victory of Ho Chi Min in Vietnam and of Castro in Cuba a strong socialist film production has been established.

III FILM UNDER POST-REVOLUTIONARY SOCIALISM

(a) USSR: The Use of Film after the October Revolution

Lenin was one of the first, if not the very first, among revolutionaries to assess the revolutionary potential of film technology. In a now famous interview with Lunatscharski (Lunatscharski, 1971) Lenin called film 'the most important of arts', and during a brief period (between the successful October Revolution and the beginning of repression during the Stalin era in the thirties) film blossomed in Soviet Russia along with the other forms of art. On the second day after the seizure of power, Lenin decreed the establishment of a revolutionary film industry which supported such filmmakers as Serge Eisenstein, Dziga Vertov, Medvedkin, and Pudovkin (LEYDA, 1960: 121). Mayakowski, the Soviet poet described the function of the young industry as 'the carrier of the movement'. Film was first a means to counter the 'false consciousness' which had been shaped by the films imported from the USA and Germany, and secondly a tool to create a new consciousness. Dziga Vertov, the founder of the Soviet Newsreel studio, writes in the 1922 manifesto to the filmmakers:

Pre-revolutionary so-called artistic images are still dangling in your mind, like icons. You're still confused by the obsolete relics of foreign film dramas which come, covered with a sauce of excellent film techniques, from western countries. But Spring is coming! We're ready to start from scratch in our new film factories. . . ! Hail the poetry of moving machines, the poetry of turning wheels and turning rods; wings of steel, the iron cry of movement, the blinding light of glowing beams. . . . To reveal the soul of the machine, to exite the worker, make him fall in love with the work-bench. . . . The farmer will relate to the tractor, the machinist will call the locomotive his friend. We bring creative joy to mechanical work, we unite man and machine, we educate new people. The new man, free of pessimism. The rhythm of man and machine. What better subjects for our camera.[3]

The early Soviet film breaks in an absolute way with the 'Kinematographic' foreign import film: 'don't approach', 'don't look', 'dangerous for your eyes', 'beware of contamination'. 'The death of the kinematographs', is the pre-condition for life of 'Kinoglaz', or revolutionary cinema as defined by Vertov:

The film drama irritates the nerves, but Kinoglaz helps people to see. The film drama clouds the eyes and the brain; Kinoglaz opens the eyes, clarifies observation. The film drama gives you a pain in the neck, Kinoglaz brings a fresh wind from the woods and from the fields; it brings the wealth of life itself. (Vertov, 1973: 25-26).

The new cinema Kinoglaz was to achieve a fundamental reconstruction of the process of film reception. Its task was to foster community feeling, instead of individualistic satisfaction of the senses; it should expand the consciousness of the new socialist man to become aware of the relations between facts. 'Yes comrades, we bring the arts to the periphery of our consciousness.' (Vertov) The major contribution of the early Soviet film to film art is the development of the techniques of montage, and the use of film as a tool to create consciousness (agitation). The essence of the new montage is the dialectic juxtaposition of events (scenes), which leads to a syntheses: a new event, namely the fact that the spectator no longer sees the events as disconnected, but has begun to understand the relationships between the events. In an example by Vertov:

> Coffins of national heroes go down into the earth (filmed in Astrakan 1928), earth is being shovelled over the graves (Kronstadt 1921), salute of the cannons (Petrograd 1920), commemoration, comrades uncover their heads (Moscow 1922).

The major contribution of the early Soviet film to the usage of film is the newsreel (Kino-pravda). Here again both Vertov and Medvedkin have been pioneers. Vertov was director of the nationalized newsreel department. Not only did he direct the productions, but he also brought the films to the people in the outer states. So he organized a tour on the river Volga with the steamship Red Star, and a 19 month tour with the 'Lenin train' (agit train), which brought not only films, but also political speakers, and a theatre group to all states of the union (April 1919-November 1921). Medvedkin took this initiative one step further in that he not only brought Soviet films to the people in the provinces, but also made instant reportages at the stations where the train would stop long enough to allow the making of a film on local conditions. The train had a full laboratory, animation studio, and an editing room on board. This was 1932! (Cine Cubano, 1973: 88-91). The films which were made on the way fulfilled a function of 'criticism and self-criticism' in the construction of the new socialist state. Some of the films were highly critical of workers morale. ('Let Us End Impersonalization', a film to induce worker-responsibility for their machines). Other films lashed at inefficiencies in the production process ('The satirical journey of a camel in the repair shop for traincars in Dniepropetrovsk', an animation film made in a few days during a delay at the station).

Most of the films were made on the spot to show workers better ways of handling machines and/or organizing the work (Cine Cubano 1973:94-97). In the thirties, the disciplining of artists into the mold of 'socialist realism' began to have its devastating effects on creative people like Vertov and Medvedkin. As David Bordwell states: 'Few artists of Vertov's generation opted for the alternatives offered by Mayakovsky's suicide and Meyerhold's death in a labour camp. Most of them simply adhered to policy. For Vertov there was only the quiet humiliation of obscurity. What could be more shameful for the Vertov of the awful manifesto than cranking out Stalinist newsreels? Writing of himself in the third person, he observed, with both humor and self-pity: 'The tragedy of Vertov is that he did not know how to grow old" (Bordwell, 1972).[4] Yet the experiments with film technology by both Vertov and Medvedkin have had a great influence on film making in revolutionary Cuba (Santioago Alvarez) and also on various revolutionary film groups which emerged as a result of the May 1968 events in Paris (e.g. the founding of the 'Dziga Vertov Group' by Jean-Luc Godard, in Paris 1969, and the founding of the Medvedkin collective in Bordeaux).

(b) The Use of Film in Post-Revolutionary Cuba

The first strips of film came to Cuba with the US soldiers in 1898; and since then film has remained tied to the US hegemony, until the successful revolution in 1959. In the pre-revolutionary period the Cuban film theatres presented 'an overkill of US, Mexican and Argentinian amusement films' (Cine Cubano, 1969:41). For various reasons the Mexican and Argentinian films were only shown in the big cities, and only the middle classes and the rich were in a situation to go to the cinema. Commercial distribution to rural areas was not economical. But many outlying areas were being served by USIS* films, which covered all corners of the country except for the mountainous regions. Immedi-

*United States Information Service.

ately after the revolutionary takeover, the first law that Fidel Castro signed, was the decree to nationalize the film industry and to establish the Instituto Cubano del Arte y Industria Cinematográfica (ICAIC). This national Film Institute was headed by a group of self-educated filmmakers who during the Batista dictatorship had been active in the film club of Nuestro Tiempo, the literary organization which united many intellectuals, who obtained leading positions after the revolution of 1959.

> The first thing we decided to do was to initiate a Latin-American newsreel service to provide counter-information against the two capitalist news services which continued to operate, even after the revolution. Since 1959 we have made some 600 news documentaries, for some of which we have obtained international awards at film festivals outside Cuba. We made these films without any technical schooling. None of us has been at a film school. We learned to film by making films! After the first two years the ICAIC started to make also didactic documentaries: films about the agrarian reforms, about health programs, and training films for the workers. Shortly thereafter we began to make political documentaries. To raise political consciousness of our people; and finally we also began to make feature films, some of which even became very popular among progressive people in Europe and the United States ('Memories of Underdevelopment' for example, and 'Los Dias del Agua'). In the beginning we had no laboratories, and there were no sound engineers. All those technical services had to be obtained from abroad, because the Yankees had never invested capital equipment in Cuba. However, as time went by we were able to build our own film industry and at last we became independent from foreign domination. (Alvarez: 1972).[5]

The films of the ICAIC clearly have their roots in the cinematic tradition of the Soviet filmmakers (particularly Dziga Vertov and Rom). Artistically they show inspiration from cubism and surrealism: using animation, calligraphy, and graphic effects, like for instance the montage of headlines, newspaper clippings, and historic drawings. Particularly in the later years some of the longer newsreel-documentaries became real lessons in history—for instance the report on Castro's visit to Chile, and the guerilla instruction film 'Third World-World War III'. By now, the ICAIC has established one of the very best film archives in the world, which serves revolutionary filmmakers from all parts of Latin America. In many of the films the spectator can recognize a certain dialectic composition of scenes; alternatively they may present 'open' (informative) and 'closed' (interpretative) images or sequences.

'Our films are to inform, to denounce, to mobilize, to testify and to urge upon analysis of the need to struggle', writes Jorge Fraga, one of the ICAIC newsreel producers (Fraga, 1972). In addition to the inspiration derived from early Soviet filmmaking the ICAIC also rejuvenated the old idea of the 'Film train' (Vertov/Medvedkin). In 1961 the ICAIC started an experiment to send out film projection teams in mobile units. Though at first handicapped by rough roads, which destroyed much of the sensitive projection equipment, it did not take more than one year to work out a liquid cushioning system to protect the projection lamps and sound system from breaking on the bouncing roads. While in 1962 there were 4,500 projections, reaching more than one million spectators in the region of Havana, by 1969 some 75,000 projections were held, reaching more than 7 million spectators in all corners of the island.[6] These projections are being held in schools, hospitals, factories, parks, and on farms. As a rule the projectionists make a 10-day tour and then come back to the same villages with a new program. Recently the 'cinema-by-truck' has been extended with the 'cinema-by-donkey'. Since 1969 some 12 projectionists have started to go to the remotest sections of the country in the mountains by donkey train, showing films to people who have never seen a film before, and who have never left their region (Cortazar, 1967). In Cuba, as in the USSR, cinema has been used as a revolutionary tool only in the post-revolutionary era. In Vietnam, however, we will see that for the first time film technology has served to help revolutionaries in bringing about revolutionary social change even before the completion of their revolution.

(c) Filmmaking in North and South Vietnam

The history of Vietnamese film making is closely tied to the history of the long wars against French colonialism in the 1950s and against US intervention in Vietnam in the sixties and early seventies. Ho Chi Minh, poet, statesman, and revolutionary, who himself had worked as a photographer during his youth in Paris, has continuously stimulated the development of the arts as in integrated element in the Vietnamese liberation movement. Already in 1936, Phan Trong Tue, one of Ho Chi Minh's associates, set up the 'Cameramen's Friendship Association', which concentrated solely on the documentation of the underground resistance against French colonialism. In 1945, immediately after the defeat of the Japanese forces, the Tele-Cine-Photo Section of the Ministry of Information and Propaganda of the Provisional Government, set up a mobile cine-photo unit which moved from village to village along Highway 1 to show films and photographic displays of the Vietnamese resistance against of the return of the French. On 15 March, 1954, after the retreat and defeat of the French at Dien Bien Phu and after the separation of the country between North and South along the 17th parallel, Ho Chi Minh signed a bill to establish a National Film Institute, later to become 'Studio Hanoi'. Ho gave great importance to the revolutionary power of the cinema. At the occasion of the many film showings that he had with filmmakers he used to say: 'to make good films it is not enough to be an artist and to learn to master the techniques of filmmaking, it is also necessary to be a good fighter.' (Pham Ngoc Truong, 1972). After the partition of 1954 it took until 1960 until the resistance movement in the south established the National Liberation Front. One year later South Vietnamese artists founded the 'Association of Art and Literature for the Liberation of South Vietnam', and one year later South Vietnamese filmmakers founded Studio Giai Phong (Studio Liberation), and the studio of the Liberation Army. In the 10 years following its birth Studio Liberation has been of great importance, not only in the villages in the liberated zones (some 60 million entrances a year), but also in international diplomacy. South Vietnamese films won many film prizes at international festivals,[7] and in many cases Studio Hanoi and Studio Liberation were able to provide international TV stations with film footage that contradicted the material coming from American networks (Sylvester, 1972). The making of films under the conditions of the war has met with extreme difficulties. Most Vietnamese filmmakers have had only a three-month course at the studio. There is a constant shortage of equipment and of film material. Developing of the films is almost always done in the fields—in ceramic jars, using a flame and ice cubes to achieve the correct temperature for the chemical baths. When a camera breaks down one might have to wait for months to obtain a spare part. In many cases cameras have been repaired with parts from watches and clocks. Though not all filmmaking is concerned with the battlefield, there are many reports of instances of exceptional heroism on the part of cameramen and camerawomen. In the internationally acclaimed documentary 'The Bihn Gia Victory on Highway 2' there is a sequence that was made by a cameraman who had jumped on the road to film an oncoming US tank. 'A GI, who had been hiding in the tank suddenly aimed his gun at him. But the cameraman cut him down with his pistol, while filming with the other hand how the GI was hit and fell back in the tank' (National Liberation Front, 1972:5). The surprising thing about many of the Vietnamese films is their artistic quality. They reflect the poetic mood of the Vietnamese culture. From the midst of a war scene the camera may suddenly turn to a branch of a tree full of flowers mirrored in a clear pond, which drew the attention of the cameraman on the side of the highway. As Charles Forniau writes: 'These war films in which we see the numerous faces of suffering women and of self-determined women soldiers, they are of the magnitude of the literary masterworks of the nineteenth century. (Forniau, 1972).

> Our films are a weapon, they are a weapon to fight an ideological battle. But at the same time our films help to inform our people what really happens. When we show our films in the Mekong area we have to go hundreds of kilometers, on foot or on bicycle; carrying the projector, the generator to generate electricity in the bush, and the films. But whenever we show our films the people are extremely relieved and generous. They understand that our films help to improve the health conditions in the country, because they show the population how to prevent diseases, and how to help the wounded. At the same time our films are a moral support for our soldiers who fight the foreign aggressors (Thep Hong, 1974).

The showing of films in Vietnam has often been almost more difficult than the making of them. Very few villages have electricity, and even if they have, there has been the problem of how to keep the enemy from being alerted. During war time there were never more than 150 people allowed to attend a screening. Many of the screenings were being held underground. There is a certain hierarchy in the way in which films of various categories are being brought to the people. The spearhead is the newsreel—to sharpen the consciousness and to motivate the people. Then there are the documentary, the popular science films, and the animation and puppet films. Their function is to deepen the understanding of the problems of the resistance and to guide the building of socialism. Finally the feature film is to affirm the joy of living and to be part of a movement which creates a new society. Aside from reaching the Vietnamese, the films of Studio Hanoi and of Studio Liberation also have had a definite effect on the many young Americans and young Europeans who saw some of the Vietnamese films that have been shown at the anti-war meetings around the world. In this way these films helped to create an international consciousness, which is clearly reflected in the words of US antiwar delegates in Hanoi 1972: 'Your struggle, courage, culture has forced us to recognize certain truths about our own country and what will be necessary to change it. . . .''[8]

V REVOLUTIONARY FILMS IN THE THIRD WORLD

(a) The Emergence of 'Third Cinema'

The concept of 'third cinema' was developed by Fernando Sonalas and Octavio Getino, the filmmakers of the three-hour documentary film 'La Hora de Los Hornos' ['The Hour of the Furnaces'], which documents, analyses, and criticizes neo-colonialism in Latin America. In their article 'Towards a Third Cinema' (Solanas, 1969) Solanas and Getino distinguish between three categories of films. The 'first cinema' (The 'Hollywood' cinema) serves to satisfy the need of the ruling classes (i.e. capital accumulation and the spread of the ideology of consumer values). They state that in the first cinema, 'the image of reality is more important than reality itself'. First cinema shows a world full of phantasies and spooks, in which awfulness is wrapped in beauty. There is the image of the hero, who has succeeded in the world: he is self-controlled, smooth, sophisticated, learned; then there are the thousands of do-nothings, the lazy people, the underdeveloped people who swarm the streets. These people are pitiful and stupid. However, whenever they resist they are pictured as wild beasts, as lunatics, as dangerous people. The first cinema films that come to an 'underdeveloped country' serve as dope to the masses. They destroy whatever national consciousness still exists. In 1969 there were in Argentina 26 television stations, one million sets, and nothing but 'fair weather' programs. The first alternative which developed as a reaction to the 'first cinema' was the so-called 'cinema d'auteur', 'expressive cinema', 'Nouvelle Vague' (France), 'Cinema Novo' (Brazil), or in short: the second cinema. It represented a liberation on the part of the filmmakers. They developed new cinematic techniques (cinema verité) and explored new subjects. Yet their films catered to a select audience: intellectuals, liberals, progressive clergymen. These films kept their audiences in a spell of psychological introspection. They took the viewer through complex emotional affairs, involving humanistic dilemmas with flashbacks to Freudian reminiscences. Second cinema typically referred to societal problems, but it did not raise questions concerning the politics of changing society. However, in the late sixties the contradictions in society intensified. By May 1968 even Godard himself who had been in the midstream of the development of the Nouvelle Vague (second cinema) realized that the filmmakers of the second cinema had become 'trapped in the fortress that they thought to have conquered'. Second cinema films had become a small business inside big business, and were almost completely incorporated in the system.

'Third cinema' as Solanas and Getino define it, is revolutionary cinema. It developed as a part of the liberation movements in the third world. Its origins lay outside the film establishment. The first 'third cinema' film, 'Me Gustan Los Estudiantes' was shot by students during a rebellion in Montevideo, Uruguay. It was financed by film clubs and with money from uncles and aunts of the students. Many of the revolutionary films were financed by wealthy progressives, or, in a number of cases, money was advanced by German, Swedish and Dutch television. 'La Hora de Los Hornos' was financed partly from the income of TV commercials and partly from fund raising among left-leaning Peronists. 'The Blood of the Condor', by Sanjines, a film which gives a devastating criticism of the Peace Corps, was financed through a fund raising campaign among physicians who discovered that Peace Corps volunteers were carrying out a program to sterilize Indian women. As Solanas and Getino point out, third cinema is 'guerilla warfare with a camera'. It could not have developed if it had not been for the change in film technology: lightweight 16mm cameras and tape recorders; improved sensitivity of film emulsions which made it possible to film indoors without flood lights; automatic lightmeters; improved systems for sound synchronization . . . all these technological changes helped to demystify the filmmaking as a 'profession' only to be mastered by artists and geniuses. In fact a number of well known 'third cinema' films were debuts, made by laymen who had not made major films before. But most of the third cinema films have been, and are now being made by professionals, a number of which received international recognition by winning awards at major film festivals.[9] The production of these films takes place under the most difficult circumstances. In 'The Hour of the Generals' there is a documentary sequence of an execution of strike leaders in the desert. After the workers were shot one by one, the cameraman was shot as well. The film was saved by bribing the soldiers who performed the execution. As Solanas and Getino point out:

guerilla cinema means constant flexibility; combining 'legal' and 'illegal' productions, changing labels on film-cans, wiping out your traces, hiding 16mm equipment. Likewise the showing of third cinema films takes place in hiding: in basements and on attics, rarely in theatres. These are 'meetings' on decolonized, liberated territory hidden from the "consumptive society." To quote Fanon: such meetings have liturgic elements; they create a privilege for people, to listen and to be heard. The person who participates can no longer look upon himself simply as a viewer. From the moment that he enters the screening he crosses the line from observer to participant in the revolutionary struggle. He becomes an actor, who is more important than the actor on the screen. Any moment the police may come in and arrest him. Yet by taking these risks he is able to liberate himself from the loneliness and the state of non-communication, which is the reality of everyday life.

(b) The Dialectics of Oppositional Filmmaking

At the same time third cinema filmmakers take certain risks which are exemplary for the risks which oppositional intellectuals take when taking sides on political issues. Many Latin-American filmmakers have been jailed for their films. It is known of a number of Chilean film-makers that they have been tortured after their arrest following the end of the Allende regime. In some cases however, the imprisonment of the filmmaker may have an impact on public opinion, which may equal if not surpass the effect of the film. Many people around the world have become informed about the political repression in Colombia as a result of the imprisonment of the Colombian filmmaker Carlos Alvarez—in spite of the fact that very few people have actually seen his film, entitled 'What is Democracy?', which was the reason for his imprisonment. There is indeed a dialectic process which starts with the film-maker making a critical film, which, once it is banned, creates even wider circles of criticism. In the case of Carlos Alvarez the banning of his film and his imprisonment became an international rallying point not only at film festivals, but also through organizations like Amnesty International.

VI RADICAL FILM IN THE WEST

(a) Militant Cinema in France

The rise of the militant cinema in France cannot be understood without referring to the structure of the established film industry, and the events of May 1968, when students and workers came close to changing the very structure which controls the cinema in its present form. The French film industry is strongly monopolized by cartels, which in turn are closely tied to the government. In 1970 55 percent of the films on TV were US films (not counting the films of US subsidiaries made in

Europe). Less than 35 percent of the films on TV were French films, and the majority of these still tend to be produced by only a few big firms. In the field of theatre distribution it turns out there are 121 distributors. Only seven are American, but those seven account for 33 percent of the business. The industry is highly commercialized and highly competitive. Scripts are being judged on their potential commercial return and on their ability to placate state censorship. In 1972 there were still 40 films, made by militant filmmakers, waiting for clearance at the censor. These films are being denied distribution even in the non-commercial circuit (Degand, 1972). During the first weeks of May 1968 it seemed for a moment that many of the checks and controls over capitalist society and thereby over the film-industry were toppling. For instance, only one week after the first demonstrations in the streets of Paris, there was already a meeting of more than 1500 film workers in Suresnes. Among them were dozens of big name stars and directors, proclaiming solidarity with the revolutionary students and workers. From the Suresnes meeting stemmed the famous Delcaration of the 'Etats Généraux du Cinéma'. The signers of the declaration soon formed an instant filmmakers pool, which led to many impromptu productions documenting the strikes and demonstrations in which at one time more than ten million people were on strike. Furthermore, in many factories (including some studios) workers had occupied their plants. Along with the production of the militant films sprang up a spontaneously formed network of distribution points. Hundreds of films were shown in schools, universities, factory canteens, in churches and youth centers, not only in Paris, but also in the provinces and abroad. For many people these films were definitely a radicalizing experience. In fact, whenever a film show on the street or in a school was prohibited, the reality of the appearance of the police on the scene was obviously more revealing to the audience than the contents of the film (i.e. the film which the police had come to seize). For most of the filmmakers, however, their participation in the 'Etats Généraux du Cinema' was in fact no more than a romantic experience. No sooner was the incipient revolution under the control of the government than most filmmakers were already back on the set to make the same commercial films that they had denounced in the Declaration at Suresnes. However, a few filmmakers did continue to exert their energies for the revolution. The four most prominent groups are:

- —the 'Dziga Vertov Group', founded by Jean-Luc Godard and Jean-Pierre Gorin
- —MK5 (Marin Karmitz)
- —Slon (Société pour le Lancement d'Oeuvres Nouvelles)
- —Dynadia, later Canal 10 and Cinecité, both linked with the French Communist Party.

All groups had participated in the Etats Généraux. The founders of three of these groups, Godard, Marker and Maret had already worked together on a film made before May 1968—'See you Soon', at the Rhodiaceta factory in Besançon. Both Godard and Marker had worked on 'Far from Vietnam' (1967). In addition to the four groups a number of other groups developed as well, among which are: 'Cinéma Libre' (which took over what was left of the Etats Généraux) and Crepac/Scopcolour which consists of TV workers who were sacked during the 1968 upheaval. Even for 'insiders' it is almost impossible to present a clear picture of the similarities and differences between the various groups and their films. The matter becomes even more complicated when one consults French critics, because the journals and reviews are at least as split up, along political lines, as the groups, and they tend to criticize films and filmmakers according to their line which again, tends to shift as time goes on. Ironically the more Maoist 'Dziga-Vertov Group' is the only group which continues to produce their films with 'big money' from the film-establishment. Observers speculate that financiers are still fascinated by the name of Godard, the 'one-day-court-joker-jester' of the French cinephile bourgeoisie, whom the boulevard-press later called a fool, as soon as he became serious. (Groupe Cinétique, 1973:173). Financiers of the period seemed to feel that anything would go, as long as it was new, and as long as it carried the name of Jean-Luc Godard. The films that have been produced by the Dziga-Vertov Group definitely carry on the issues that were brought up during the many discussions of May 1968. In one of his latest films 'Tout va bien' ('Everything is OK') which Godard and Gorin made independently of the Dziga-Vertov Group, they ask the question of what happened to all the intellectuals who supported the revolution of

1968 but disappeared as soon as the streets were cleared. Though most critics do contradict each other when it comes to interpreting Godard, there seems to be a general consensus that he is one of the very few really revolutionary filmmakers of the seventies.[10]

The filmmaker who is probably politically most akin to Godard, is Marin Karmitz even though the filmmaking of Karmitz is in many ways very different. Karmitz who founded the collective MK5 has most clearly developed the idea of the manifesto of the Etats Généraux; that is, that the people themselves should make their films. Particularly in the independently produced film 'Coup pour Coup' [Blow for Blow] we see how a group of women workers replay the sequestration of the director of their company. Only three parts of the film were played by professional actors, all other participants (almost a hundred) are workers who helped in the take-over of their factory in 1968. Besides production, MK5 also takes care of its own distribution which nowadays not only includes their films, but also slide and tape reportages of ongoing political events.

Closer to, but still independent of the 'official' line of the French Communist Party is the film collective SLON, which was founded by Chris Marker. Since 1968 the SLON group has made some 50 films. Most of the films are made with workers in the factories; they have learned to handle the camera by themselves. The films are close to reality; people speak for themselves. SLON has two branches, one in Besançon, which is called the Medvedkin collective, and another, the Sochaux group from Sochaux (Hennebelle, 1972).[11]

The Dynadia group (or Canal 10) and later Unicite, are both 'party-line' filmcompanies that produce and distribute films for the official Communist Party (Moscow Line). Scopcolour, finally, is a commercial firm, composed of filmworkers who formerly worked with the state owned television corporation (ORTF). Most of them were fired in 1968, and since then have produced a number of socially engaged documentaries; for instance 'Strange Foreigners' about Portuguese and Algerian immigrant workers. The spectrum of filmgroups as described above is incomplete. Besides, I have focused only on the groups which operate outside the established film industry (even Godard's films, though financed by the industry are not distributed through commercial channels). There are a number of producers in the established film circles who have been moving into the domain of the political revolutionary film: Costa-Gravas for example with his film 'Z' on the Greek dictatorship and 'State of Siege' on the Uruguayan Tupamaros (Hennebelle, 1974).

(b) Radical film in the United States

The coming into existence of 'Hollywood' is probably the best example of the development of what Enzensberger has called 'the consciousness industry' (Enzensberger, 1968). The extent of the penetration of the US media in other countries of the West and in the third world has been extensively documented by Thomas Guback and Herbert Schiller (Guback, 1969; Schiller, 1973). In most countries there has been a development of some form of counterforces under various names: 'alternative cinema'.... The common denominator of these various movements is cinema' ... The common denominator of these various movements is probably best defined by stating that they all present an alternative to the 'hollywood' type cinema (Paquet, 1973). We can now ask the question: to what extent has there been a development of a counter-force in the United States itself? An early alternative to the Hollywood entertainment film has been developed by the 'Workers Film and Photo League of America', which was founded in 1928. Originally it was part of an international workers movement cinema, led by Bela Balazs. Some of the members of the league later founded Frontier Films, which produced a number of films that dealt with the problems of the Depression and the New Deal. When the US became engaged in World War II, Frontier Films petered out and it took until the upsurge of the New Left in the 60s before political filmmakers began again to resist the dominance of entertainment in the film industry. (Nichols, 1972). The rise of the New Left was in many ways a response to the doctrine of the 'American Way of Life' as it is promoted every day by the media, particularly by the illustrated journals and by the new medium: television. The first underground newspapers began to appear in 1965/1966. The first New Left film was by Fruchter and Machover:

'The Troublemakers' (1966) about the efforts of some white radicals to do organizing work in a black community in Newark NJ. Among the organizers was Tom Hayden, one of the leading figures in the New Left. A year later Fruchter and Machover, together with Robert Kramer and some other filmmakers founded Newsreel, a filmgroup which had as its purpose to provide "the movement" with films for internal discussion and for the propaganda of movement ideology, and to influence media groups. In the late 60s and 70s Newsreel went through a series of in-house revolutions. At its very beginning the core of Newsreel had consisted of a number of relatively wealthy white male film-professionals. Later, the women members and members with working-class background, who had begun to learn the skills of filmmaking, demanded a greater share in internal decision-making. By 1973 almost all the original members had left, and the leadership had moved to the hands of predominantly working class people. By 1973 there were only a few branches left; one in San Francisco and two in the Mid West. The group in New York was renamed in 'Third World Newsreel'. It is now professionally run, by blacks and people with other minority back-grounds (Chinese, South American). Women play an important role in the new management.

I have dwelt rather extensively on Newsreel, because it has probably been the most influential among the alternative media groups, and it has existed during the longest span of time. Besides Newsreel there have been (and still are) other radical media groups. American Documentary Films started as a production group under the leadership of Jerry Stoll. Its very first film 'Sons and Daughters' was completed in 1967 and gave a very early picture of the anti-war movement on the West Coast. ADF expanded considerably during the period 1968-70. Its catalogue listed some hundred titles of films from all over the world. In the beginning ADF primarily served movement groups but later it also rented and sold films to colleges and universities. Though the demand tended to be fluctuating it had managed to build up enough volume as a base for its survival. As Tom Brom states: 'At the height of the Vietnam struggle in 1969-70, as each demonstration day approached, every print of every film remotely concerning Indochina was booked at ADF to high schools, colleges, churches, community groups, YMCA . . . I swear there were days when I thought the Revolution was upon us' (Brom, 1973). In 1972, however, the group organized a Cuban film festival in New York. Due to government seizure of the Cuban films the festival had to be cancelled.[12] The incurred debts broke ADF and the company went bankrupt. A number of the ADF associates however joined with the Filmworkers Union which started in San Francisco in 1972, which became one of the most active film groups on the West Coast. A number of other groups started to operate in the 1970s, for instance 'Solidarity Films', 'Films for Social Change', and 'Tricontinental Films'. In addition to these more 'radical' groups, a number of smaller commercial distributors have begun to include films of the New Left perspective in their catalogues, such as Impact Films, New Yorker Films, and New Line Cinema. Here we see a rather typical phenomenon: namely that as soon as there appears to be some evidence of a 'market' films stop being politically dangerous and become a lucrative commodity. This rarely happens however to radical films. Some of the films made by Emile De Antonio and by Frederick Weissman have reached audiences beyond the radical cine-club milieu. In some cases imported foreign films with some revolutionary contents seem to have done rather well in the theatre, as for instance, 'Memories of Underdevelopment' (Cuba) and some of the 'less radical' films, as for instance, 'Z' and 'State of Siege'. Overlooking the situation in the United States one has to conclude, however, that the alternative cinema occupies a very marginal position in the overall media structure. The groups which produce and distribute films that offer basic criticism on the 'American Way of Life' lack the resources and the talent to operate on a competitive level. Even though stars like Marlon Brando and Jane Fonda support radical causes, nobody has yet been able to get them involved in producing a film with a radical perspective of the quality of 'Salt of the Earth' or 'Battle of Algiers'. This failure to develop the radical film in America is partly due to the very conservative climate in the film industry at large (remember the 'Hollywood Ten'), but is primarily due to a lack of organization among the radical media groups in building an alternative production and distribution system. This organization could eventually evolve from alternative media conferences, such as the Alternative Media Conference in Montreal 1974, and also from joint ventures among filmmakers along the lines being developed in Germany (Verlag der Autoren), in Holland (The Free Circuit), and in Sweden (Folkets Bio).

VII OPPOSITIONAL FILMMAKERS: A WORLD-COMMUNITY OF INTELLECTUALS

At the beginning of this paper I defined revolutionary filmmakers as those filmmakers who work towards a transition of society from some form of capitalism to some form of socialism. Whenever I speak of oppositional filmmakers I refer to a wider category: those filmmakers who play an active role in criticizing the inhuman conditions in their own country or elsewhere in the world. In this paper however, I have not specifically looked at those filmmakers in the West and in the capitalist societies who criticize from a moral rather than from a political point of view. Neither have we been able to document the work of filmmakers who, within the socialist countries, attempt to correct inadequacies. But it should be clear that oppositional film-makers are more and more playing an active role in building progressive social forces around the world. In this sense they are part of a 'world intelligentsia', on the basis of a common understanding of the crucial problems of their society . . . and of world problems . . . despite differences in opinion as to how to resolve them.[13]

During the last 10 years there has clearly been a growth in cohesiveness among oppositional filmmakers around the world. First there has been a growth in mutual solidarity, which found its climax in the international campaigns to free Carlos Alvarez in Colombia (Freunde der Deutsche Kinematek, 1974), and in 1975 in the campaign to put pressure on the Chilean junta of General Pinochet to free two Chilean filmmakers, Marcelo Romo and Guillermo Cahn. Secondly, there is a definite growth in mutual material support. Several groups of film-makers in the West have collected substantial amounts of funds and equipment in support of Vietnamese filmmakers. At the same time many Chilean filmmakers in exile obtained material support from colleagues in Berlin, Leipzig, Moscow, Paris, and Mexico City to complete the films which they had started at the National Film Organization, Chile Films, during the period of Allende's rule. Finally, there is a demonstrable growth in international organization among oppositional filmmakers which found its culmination in the meeting of some 50 filmmakers from more than 20 countries during the 'Rencontres Internationales Pour Un Nouveau Cinéma" (Alternative Media Conference), in Montreal, Canada, 1974. This meeting became a starting point for the establishment of international cooperation at the level of production and distribution as well as an exchange of experiences and ideas. Obviously, most oppositional filmmakers still work in isolation 'against the routinized thinking of the "power establishment" ', (Gella, 1974) but as this paper has tried to indicate, they work toward common goals in order to support the establishment of a more just and humane society.

NOTES

1. This article is an adaption of a paper 'Film Technology and Revolutionary Change', presented at the World Congress of Sociology, Toronto, 1974. A film on the same subject, entitled "Towards a People's Cinema", by Leonard Henny, is available from Transit Media, PO Box 315, Franklin Lakes, NY 07417, telephone (201)891-8240.

2. Adorno, Theodore, 1971, quoted in H. K. Ehmert: *Visuelle Kommunikation, Beitrage zur Kritik der Bewustseinsindustrie,* Cologne 1971, p. 8.

3. Translated by the author from Vertov, 1973: 'From the manifesto, beginning 1922'.

4. For a more detailed description of the situation of filmmakers under Stalin see Leyda, 1960:399-402.

5. The most well-known films by Santiago Alvarez are: 'Now', 'Hanoi, Mares 27', 'Hasta La Victoria Siepre', 'Piedra Sobre Piedra', 'El Sueno De Pongo', 'Soy Hijo de America'.

6. Statistics of projections and spectators reached by the 'Cine Movie' units 1962-69

Year	Projections	Spectators
1962	4,603	1,239,528
1964	38,190	4,852,614
1966	57,257	5,855,468
1968	74,220	7,582,494
1969	74,980	7,284,975

7. Vietnamese films which won international prizes are: 'The Struggle in South Vietnam', 'Dong Xoai in Flames', 'Towards the Firelines', 'The Women Artillerists of Long An', 'A Small Village on the River Tra', 'Victory on Highway 9'

8. Fonda, Jane, 8 July, 1972, at the occasion of her visit to Hanoi (with former US Attorney-General Ramsey Clarke). Vietnam News Agency

9. Sanjines, Jorge, 'The Blood of the Condor', Bolivia, 'The Courage of the People', Boliva; Rios, Humberto, 'The Cry of the People', Bolivia, 'Mexico, the Frozen Revolution', (directed by Reymundo Gleyzer); Beato, Affonso, 'When the People Awake' (Chile); Littin, Miguel, 'El Chacall Del Nahueltoro' (Chili); 'The Promised Land'; Silva, Jorge and Rodriquez, Martha, 'The Brickmakers' (Colombia); Dente, Jorge, 'The Hour of the Generals' (Bolivia); Alvarez, Carlos, 'What is Democracy?' (Colombia).

10. Politically Jean-Luc Godard showed himself a revolutionary while facing the police in the streets of Paris. Aesthetically Godard builds further on the revolutionary theory of cinema of Dziga-Vertov. He states: 'Marxism has it, that the most important thing is the relationships between things. . . . Here are three separate shots: one shot of an assembly line in a car factory, one shot of a naked woman and one shot of workers on a construction site. To express the pressure for emancipation for both the woman and the workers these shots should be put into such a relationship to each other so that they lead to a synthesis. The emancipation of the woman cannot simply result from sexual freedom. After all the woman has a relationship to her husband who works in the factory. She will only be sexually free on the day that her husband has his freedom in the factory. . . . Cinema means that one has to try to make links between things and events. (Interview with Jean-Luc Godard by Wilfred Reichard and Georg Alexander, WDR-TV, 26/6, 1971.)

11. If this article Hennebelle makes the point that the films of the 'Z' series are in fact 'a front' to conceal the 'Colonization' of the French film industry by the American dream-factory.

12. The Cuban films were seized on the basis of a clause which prohibits trade

with the enemy. According to ADF the proper licence had been obtained in advance.

13. For a precise description of the role of a 'World Intelligentsia', see Gella, 1974:7.

REFERENCES

Alvarez, Santiago, 1974, quoted from an interview in the film 'Towards a People's Cinema'.

Bordwell, David, 1972, 'Dziga-Vertov' in *Film Comment,* Spring 1972

Brom, Tom, 1973, former office manager of ADF, quoted in *Cinéaste*, 4, no. 4, Summer 1973, p. 19

Cine Cubano, 1969, 'Viva la Revolucion', interview with Pastor Vega, December, 1969

––– 1973, 'Kino Medved', no. 76/77

––– 1973, 'Informe del Cinetren', (Information about the film train), 76/77, pp. 94-97

Cortazar, Ocatvio, 1967, 'Por Primera Vez', documentary film about the cinemobiles made at the ICAIC

Degand, Claude, 1972, 'Le Cinema. . . . Cette Industrie', Editions Techniques et Economiques, Paris

Ehmert, H. K., 1971, *Visuelle Kommunikation, Beitrage zur Kritik der Bewustseinsindustrie,* Cologne

Forniau, Charles, 1972, 'Vietnam, Cinéma d'un peuple au combat', introduction to the month of Vietnamese Film Showings in Paris, March-April, 1972

Fraga, Jorge, 1972, 'El noticiario ICAIC latino-americano: función politica y lenguaje cinematográfica' (The ICAIC newsreel: its political function and its cinematographic language), *Cine Cubano* 71/72, p. 27

Freunde der Deutsche Kinematek, 'Der Fall Carlos Alvarez', documentation, West Berlin, 1974

Gella, Aleksander, 1974, 'An Introduction to the Sociology of the Intelligentsia', paper presented at the World Congress of Sociology, Toronto, 1974

Groupe Cinétique, 1973, 'Filmische Avantgarde and Politische Praxis', *Rowolt,* 24, Hamburg, p. 173

Guback, Thomas H. Enzeusberger, 1969, *The International Film Industry: Western Europe and America Since 1945*, Bloomington: Indiana University Press.

Hennebelle, Guy, 1972, 'SLON: Working Class Cinema in France', *Cinéaste*, V., no. 2, New York

– – – 1974, 'Cinema of the Z series', *Cinéaste*, VI, no. 2

Hong, Thep, 1974, quoted from an interview in the film 'Towards a People's Cinema".

Kramer, Robert, 1969, 'Towards a Redefinition of Propaganda', *Leviathan*, 2, no. 6, Oct-Nov.

Leyda, Jay, 1960, *Kino, A history of the Russian and Soviet Film*, London

Lunatscharski, Anatol W., *Gespräch mit Lenin uber die Filmkunst*, München, 1971

Medvedkin, Alexander, 1973, '294 Dias sobre ruedas' (294 days on the rail), in *Cine Cubàno*, no. 76/77, pp. 78-84

Nichols, Bill, 1972, 'The American Photo League', *Screen*, no. XIII/4, Winter '72-'73, p. 90-107

National Liberation Front, 'Our First Footages', in *South Vietnam Struggle*, 1972, March 13th, Central Organ of the NLF.

Paquet, André, 1973, 'Cinema Alternative: Vers ume definition pratique', Montreal, August (Mimeo)

– – – 1973, 'Alternative Cinéma Groups, an inventory', August, Montreal (Mimeo)

Pham Ngoc Truong, 1972, "L'oncle Hoet le Cinéma Vietnamien", in *Dien A'nh, Bulletin de L'Association des Cinéastes Vietnamiens*, no. 2, p. 11

Prokop, Dieter, 1971, *Soziologie des Films*, Berlin

Schiller, Herbert I., 1973, *The Mind Managers*, Boston

Solanas, Fernando and Getino, Ocatvio, 1969, 'Hacia un Tercer Cine', *Tricontinental*, Habana, Cuba

Sylvester, Régine, 1972, Interview with Nguyen Duy Can, e.a., at the International Festival of Documentary in Leipzig 1972, *Protokoll*, p. 73

Vertov, Dziga, 1973, *Schriften zum Film*, München

– – – 'Kunstdrama und Kinoglaz', in Vertov, op cit. pp. 25-26

III

STUDIES IN THE NATIONAL INTELLIGENTSIA

9

THE CLASS OF THE INTELLIGENTSIA IN AFRICA

Zygmunt Komorowski
University of Warsaw

The term intelligentsia comes from the Latin word *intelligentia–* 'comprehension'. In sociology it has been accepted to use this word to describe a social class (stratum) of educated people, professionally connected with intellectual work, and characterized by the attributes of mind and character formed by education and general culture. This stratum is supposed to be characteristic of societies in which the transformation of the pre-capitalistic social structure took place before the formation of a numerous and strong bourgeoisie (middle class)–in a way different from what has happened in Western Europe. This term is sometimes replaced by other expressions, such as 'intellectual professions', 'intellectual workers' etc. Lately it has become fashionable to use the expression 'intellectuals', which, however, has a more selective meaning, and seems more adequate for the intellectually and culturally more active part of this class. The intelligentsia is a larger group, connected by bonds of solidarity resulting from similar habits and the feeling of a similar position in the hierarchy of social prestige.

The term 'intelligentsia', as a sociological designation, appeared for the first time in Polish literature in the first half of the nineteenth century (K. Liebelt, 1844). For it was in Poland, from about the end of the eighteenth century, that a new and vigorous stratum had been formed from that part of the nobility which was disinherited of its goods and offices after the partition of Poland. This class, having no analogy with other classes known at that time, had to be referred to and classified. The members of the intelligentsia settled mostly in towns, maintaining strong family and social relations with the nobility in the country, and were anti-bourgeois by tradition (Chalasinski, 1958: 12). Formed in the period of major catastrophy of their country, when the most outstanding figures of former power were suffering persecution, this new class did not succumb to the worship of success and wealth as was characteristic for the middle classes. Financial status was less important for those people than social standing. (Chalasinski, 1958: 71 passim and 142). Free of the psychological complex of inferiority (descent), and in accord with the typical Polish tradition of the 'gentry democracy', the members of the new class courageously undertook the cultural competition with the salons of the aristocracy (Chalasinski, 1958: 85; Bialkowski, 1939: 23ff.) They were still very sensitive to the problems of good manners and honour. While deprived of old privileges, they preserved the bureaucratic inclination and the respect for offices, as well as a kind of exclusivity, which is characteristic for social groups of many countries, an exclusivity producing the character of a 'ghetto' which an 'outsider' could hardly join. New members—among them many of peasant descent—were accepted only under the condition of giving proof of general culture. At the same time, the members of the intelligentsia in Poland, existing in the conditions of a foreign government's oppression, created by the partition of Poland, and pushed aside from normal participation in state affairs, felt responsible for and entitled to the spiritual leadership of the nation. At the same time, not encumbered with wealth, they were inclined to social radicalism. The intelligentsia of Poland was opposed to class feelings virtually by definition, and many of its representatives belonged to the Polish and international revolutionary movements (Chalasinski, 1958: 62 and 137).

The notion of the intelligentsia as a class was transferred in the first place to Russia. Towards the end of the eighteenth and the beginning of the nineteenth century in Russia, as a result of the disintegration of the corvee economy, the group of the so-called 'raznoczyncy' (meaning people of different ranks) came into being. It was formed by represen-

tatives of the poor nobility, some members of the middle-class, orthodox priests and a few peasants. This group grew in number in the
second half of the nineteenth century, after the corvee had been
abolished in 1861. Later on it also came to be called the intelligentsia.

A large part of the nineteenth century Russian intelligentsia lived in
poverty. Its financial status was much worse than that of the
commercial middle class and the capitalist bourgeoisie. It was, therefore, inclined to take part in revolutionary movements, and often
professed social radicalism. While the Polish intelligentsia of that time
was aspiring to participate in the culture of the salons, and considered
itself the defender of the highest spiritual values and refined manners,
the dominating characteristic of the new class in Russia was revolt
against everything coming 'from above'. In his *Diary,* well known all
over Russia, Lew Lubimow (1957) notes that 'A typical member of the
intelligentsia does not shave every day, eats with his knife, and does not
kiss the ladies' hands . . .' This opinion is fundamentally different from
that attributed to the intelligentsia in Poland, where its members were
rather accused of 'lordly aspirations' (Szczepanski, 1971: 71). Common
to both classes, however, was their anti-bourgeois attitude.

The formation of the intelligentsia in other countries of central and
eastern Europe took place later and developed along different lines,
resulting in different characteristics of this class in the particular countries. The intelligentsia has been formed in a different way in Slovakia,
Bulgaria, the Ukraine, and Lithuania, where the peasant element dominated from the beginning. It was different still in Bohemia, Rumania
and Hungary.

Since the middle of the twentieth century, more and more discussion has been taking place concerning the intelligentsia in Western
Europe and in America, and most of all in the countries of the Third
World, meaning the collectivity of different professional categories
concerned with cultural creation, the organization of work and of
collective life, and the solution of various problems, which demand
specialized education and theoretical knowledge (Szczepanski, 1971:
87-92). One of its characteristic features is supposed to be the basing of
prestige on education by placing the possession of knowledge at the
head of social values, over the possession of material goods (as individ-

ual property), which has been the basis of the prestige of the former bourgeoisie.

The class called the intelligentsia in the developing countries, among others in Africa, has in fact little in common with the urban property-owning classes, and is often in opposition to those newly formed classes. It is a heterogeneous group of people, consisting of those distinguished by education and of the growing groups of qualified employees. The application to this class of terms which had been used in this region during the colonial epoch, such as 'évolués', 'lettrés', 'assimilados', seems anachronistic and deprived of meaning. The term used formerly, 'new elite', is inadequate. It is justified only in a rather narrow sense in comparison with the 'old elites', or with respect to the actual members of the political and cultural leading groups. It would be misleading and confusing to apply the term 'new elite' to the groups of 'ordinary employees' or 'ordinary specialists' in different professional fields—groups which are presently becoming larger and larger and which have no 'pioneering' spirit.

According to H. and M. Smith (1960), who have been investigating Nigerian society, the 'new elite' is being formed by people who for some reason possess a position of higher prestige and influence in the community to which they belong. According to the authors, the status of this 'elite' is most often identified with the degree of 'westernization of life' and with bilinguity (H. and M. Smith, 1960: 4 passim).

This description is therefore adequate for most people having higher education, after some training abroad, or for those occupying higher positions, but not for every educated man who wants to marry an educated woman, to educate his children, and to belong to the society of other people having similar education and interests. The 'new elites' of the Third World have constituted the kernal of the intelligentsia, and are today its important and visible components; they are not however the same as this class. The intelligentsia is a group larger than the 'elite', being less selective.

The attractiveness of the social models cultivated by the intelligentsia consists, among other things, in the fact that everybody can adopt them, and become thus a member of the intelligentsia. While it is impossible to imagine a society composed only of rich people (millionaires), it is easy to imagine a future in which all people will be members of the intelligentsia. This notion of the intelligentsia is associated with a certain degree of wealth, derived from better paying occupations.

One of the characteristics of the intelligentsia, in all countries, in addition to its opposition to the bourgeoisie and inclination to radicalism, is its integrating function. The intelligentsia represents the idea called by J. Chalasinski 'the belief in the classless ideal of the Nation' (Chalaskinski: 1958: 42). It is also very often specifically engaged in the creation and development of the national culture, which begins when individuals begin to act in solidarity, independent of their personal connections, in the name of the moral purposes of a large group, seen as historically formed and historically constant, displaying a universal, cultural activity. The nationalistic aspirations of the developing countries, taking sometimes the form of extremist ideologies, are also, above all, the work of the local intelligentsia, a product of the strong growth of this class.

The intelligentsia of the African countries, however, is (making allowances for regional differences) especially interested in international cultural contact, and serves as spokesman for cultural 'openness'. Its nationalism, especially in the first phases, derives mostly from defensive positions. It is inspired, on the one hand by opposition to the 'uprooting', the complete detachment from the rest of the society, and on the other hand by the necessity of opposing onesided absorption by wealthier and stronger societies. In Algeria, Ahmed Taleb—a man deeply involved in two cultures—argued that the precondition for free dialogue with European culture must be the regeneration and development of Arabic culture. The regeneration should come first, and the search for synthesis next (Taleb, 1957-1961; Alger, 1966: 101). Leopold Sedar Senghor instead requires special care for those values of the national culture which, 'translated' into modern language, will permit the African cultures to enter, on an equal level, the greater task of reforming the Culture of the Universe (Senghor, 1964: 229, 296). The same opinions are expressed by J. Ki Zerbo, Boubou Hama and many other popular writers and journalists.

Among educated Africans there exists a popular conviction about the particular 'vocation' of the cultural heritage of Africa. Although materially poor and technically underdeveloped, they are convinced that in the area of human relations and in their concept of life they have at least as much to offer as to take from the world. This conviction does not come merely from the struggle with post-colonial feelings, nor from a lack of knowledge about the world. It is often based on experience and current observation, and on the confrontation of such values as solidarity, faithfulness and the ability to enjoy life with European or American arrogance and lack of tolerance, monopolistic attempts, hypocrisy, egoism, agitation, gloom, etc. The contact of Africans with the intelligentsia of much wealthier regions does not always, unfortunately, encourage them to imitate the latter.

At the same time the phenomenon of symbiotism of cultures is general among the members of the African intelligentsia, as well in North Africa as to the south of the Sahara. Not only particular individuals, but also whole groups of people, feel attachments to two cultures at the same time, deriving ideas from both and taking part in the everyday life of both. A proof of this fact can be found in a whole pleiad of writers and their heroes, from Jean Amrouche and Mouloud Mammeri to Chinua Achebe and Albert Luthuli. The African intelligentsia largely looks at its culture in the context of larger complexes of continents, regions, languages, etc. L. S. Senghor, quoted above, conceives it as a system of four degrees: the tribal 'patria', the super tribal nation, and then the race and the civilisation (Senghor, 1961: 22 passim). Others speak of the common vocation: African, Arabic and Mediterranean (Taleb, p. 87), or Negro and African, etc.

At present, much is being said about the culture and its different connections. It would, however, be wrong to think that the entire intelligentsia of Africa sets primary store by cultural values. The fascination with technology as a source of power formerly unknown together with the impossibility of adopting various subtleties in the new way of thinking and imagining, must leave special marks. It can be found in many characteristic declarations of the extreme technocrats (technophiles), who seem to carry on the depreciation of humanistic values even further than their American or European colleagues. A. Laroui from Morocco says that 'Culture will come after professional specialization' (Laroui, 1967: 26-27); Salama Musa from Egypt seems to be of the same opinion.

The followers of Arican practicality consider that in the modern world it is 'the efficient man' (Alger, 1961: 85-86)[1] who should have dominating importance. For in their opinion, only such a man is able to oppose the waste of time caused by meditation, ceremonies and the traditional loquacity. The 'efficient man', possessing utilitarian knowledge, energy and initiative, is to be the antithesis of the loquacious old man. His role is often simplified in a curious way. 'Everything that does not give practical effects should be put aside,' say the extremists. 'Science should be subordinate to technology . . . Civilisation today is an industry, and its culture is science, whereas literature, religion and philosophy are the culture of rural societies' (Laroui, 1967: 27).

The belief in technology and in industry, together with the expectation of the 'efficient man', does not, however, stand for 'technocratic' activity. This activity sometimes grows even smaller in spite of theories and slogans, when the believers in technology place too much confidence in 'novelties' and the perspective of 'economic miracles'.

The revolution of 'economic miracles' can make very doubtful the sense of any "traditional" professional specialisation. What is more, an overdependence on externally provided materials and human power, connected with technological novelties, has created a rather popular habit of watching passively all the new beginnings. J. Binet tells about a 'progressive' village, which, after declaring its readiness to cultivate cotton, waited idly all the season for the instructor, who was expected to do the sowing (Binet, 1965: 53). The instructor, a guest paid by the government, was considered responsible for the success of the pioneer enterprise, and the villagers were entitled to get the prize of the crop only for the fact of approving the 'technological novelty'. The members of the African intelligentsia are not villagers, of course, and they are not waiting for instructors; still, similar attitudes can also sometimes be observed among them.

In conclusion, it can be stated that in the African countries a new social class is now being formed, based on the fundamental criterion of education. This class is larger than the so-called 'new elites', and is growing quickly. In the future its importance will become even greater. At the same time its features are not yet clearly defined. It has, on the one hand, the tendency to make money as quickly as possible, and on the other hand, to oppose the property-owning classes. It wants to become national, but in a meaning often different from the models known in other countries. It wants to take part in the formation of national cultures, and at the same time does not abandon cultural symbiotism. It talks much and willingly about culture and humanistic values, and at the same time has a tendency for the apotheosis of 'technology only' and the 'efficient man'. This diversity and these contradictions form the particularity of this class and explain why the application of the same measures in studies of this class in Europe, America and Asia is often erroneous. If we use the term 'intelligentsia' it is, because a better name has not yet been found. However, in order to avoid misunderstanding, it should always be added that it is the African intelligentsia—*in statu nascendi.*

A notion formed in the last century in central and eastern Europe is now being applied on the Black Continent. However, as I have tried to show, in these African societies, with their very particular traditions, it has undergone, and is still undergoing, important changes. The presence of a similar 'comprehension' (intelligentsia) connected with education does not mean the identity of whole cultures.

NOTES

1. On Alger states see: 'De l' Algerie originelle a l' Algérie moderne, elements de sociologie culturelle au service de l' éducation de base,' Alger 1961, pp. 85-86.

REFERENCES

Binet, J. (1965) *Afrique en question.* Dakar 53.
Chalasiński (1958) *Przeszlośc i przyszlośé inteligencji Polskiej.* Warszawa 12.
––– and L. Bialkowski (1939) *Prawdziwe i falszywe tradycje.* Lublin 23.
Laroui, A. (1967) *L'idéologie arabe contemporaine.* Essai critique Paris 26-27.
Lubimow, Lew (1957) *Diary,* Polish translation Zycíe *Literackie.* 3.XI.
Senghor, L. S. (1964) *Liberté I. Négritude et humanisme.* Paris: 229 and 296.
––– (1961) *Nation et voie africaine du socialisme.* Paris: 22 passim.
Szczepanski, J. (1971) *Odmiany czasu terázniejszego.* Warszawa: 87-92.
Smith, H. and M. (1960) *The New Nigerian Elite.* Stanford, Cal.: 4, 58, 112.
Taleb, A. (1957-1961) *Lettre de prison* Alger 101 passim.

10

THE DEVELOPMENT OF THE INTELLIGENTSIA
BETWEEN THE WARS:
The Case of Czechoslovakia

Jan Hajda
Portland State University, Oregon, USA

Czechoslovakia between the wars was a society with a feudal hangover. The aristocracy was dispossessed but its legacy was preserved in the dominant social distinctions. In terms of popular designations, the society was divided into three broad social layers: the 'masters' *(páni)*, the 'people' *(lid)*, and a somewhat vague in-between category of 'neither-masters-nor-people', sometimes referred to as 'half-masters' (pulpáni) (Boček, 1940; Bláha, 1947). The category of 'masters' subsumed all persons in non-manual occupations (doing 'better,' 'easier', 'spiritual', as distinguished from manual, work), requiring a higher level of education (usually at least professional secondary school) and a 'master-like' style of life (wearing of business suit, tie, gloves; adherence to a rather elaborate etiquette; attendance at concerts, stage performances, lectures, etc.) and granting an official right to the exercise of command or influence over others. The status of 'masters' also guaranteed to its occupant the possession of an occupational and/or academic title, used by others as a term of address and by himself as a term of self-designation, a title always extended to the occupant's wife. Thus, a physician was addressed as 'Mr Doctor' and his wife as 'Mrs Doctor'; a factory owner was called 'Mr Factory Owner' and his wife 'Mrs Factory Owner'; a grammar school teacher earned the address 'Mr Teacher' and his wife 'Mrs Teacher', etc. (Boček, 1940; RCC files, n.d.). Although not all 'masters' conceived of themselves as being superior to the rest of the society, most of them regarded themselves (and were regarded by the lower classes) as persons obliged or predestined to lead, and had an attitude toward the lower classes similar to doctor's toward his patients, a lawyer toward his clients, an employer toward his employees, or a commanding officer to his soldiers, an attitude ranging from a deep humanitarian and reformist concern through a patronizing attitude to messianism and aristocratism (Bláha, 1937; Stefánek, 1944; RCC files, n.d.).

The category of 'people' subsumed persons in strictly manual occupations who seldom had any education beyond upper grammar school and who for the most part (although not always) received a subsistence-level income. The term 'people' referred to a social layer lacking certain qualities, as contrasted with social layers possessing these qualities—it lacked an 'honorable' occupation, 'good' education, 'proper' style of life, opportunity (or, as was frequently believed, ability) to lead, and also titles. The 'people' were regarded by the 'masters' as occupying the status of followers, pupils, apprentices—as a passive group or mass to be organized by an outsider, but sometimes also as a healthy social layer in comparison with social layers which were 'sick' or 'faulty' in some respects (Bláha, 1947). Without exception the 'people' were untitled. They were addressed by their last names or by their Christian names, or possibly as Mr or Mrs. The attitudes of 'people' toward their own status within the class structure were by no means uniform. Most of them resented the social subordination or refused to acknowledge it verbally, quoting the standard Czech proverb 'I am a "master", you are a "master" ' *(Já pán, ty pán),* and derisively criticizing persons who achieved prominence and leadership. Only a minority willingly did not aspire to culturally valued equality and accepted the unequal distribution of rights and privileges as 'natural'. Such an attitude was expressed, for example, in the Slovak version of the above-quoted proverb: 'I am a "master", you are a "master", but who will feed the pigs?' (RCC files, n.d., Stefánek, 1944).

The in-between group was characterized by a combination of properties typifying the 'masters' and the 'people'. It was vaguely acknowledged by designations such as 'half-masters', 'would-be masters', 'neither-masters-nor-people', 'people but not quite like the poor people'. It comprised two somewhat different groups: (1) persons whose occupation was predominantly but not exclusively, or was only partially, manual, and whose style of life resembled the style of life of the 'people' rather than that of the 'masters', but who were economically independent, employed others, enjoyed an intermittend association with persons of firmly acknowledged 'master' status, and had an opportunity to exercise communal leadership functions; (2) persons in low-skilled and low-paid white-collar and sometimes semi-manual occupations, who occupied a quite subordinate status in the bureaucratic hierarchy and derived social prestige from their membership in the given institution rather than from their own occupation. Typically, the occupational titles of the members of this category were not clearly acknowledged as marks of social distinction; this was particularly true in relations with persons of higher social status. The 'half-masters' attitude toward the class system was expressed by a mixture of egalitarianism and rank consciousness, usually with emphasis on the former (Boček, 1940).

Although it could be said that on the whole the 'masters' represented the higher income group, the 'people' the low income group, and the 'in-between' category the middle income level, income as such was a poor criterion of status, especially in border cases. A country teacher, an actor, or an accountant frequently belonged to a lower economic level than a middle-sized farmer, but such people regarded themselves and were regarded by others as 'masters', while this was not true of the farmer. Similarly, a well-to-do skilled worker was regarded, and regarded himself, as belonging to the 'people', in spite of his high income (Bláha, 1947, Boček, 1940).

These three categories of designation were universally recognized, in spite of the fact that prewar Czechoslovak society was composed of several distinct ethnic groups. However, there was a certain degree of variation in the meaning of these categories and in the type of expected, permitted, and forbidden behavior associated with them. Among Czechs and Germans who occupied the western part of the country, the three categories were viewed as a system of gradual ranks with almost imperceptible transitions; among the three eastern ethnic groups, the Slovaks, Magyars, and Ruthenians, these differences were frequently conceived of as differences of kind (A. Štefánek, 1944; B. Štefánek, 1947; RCC files, n.d.).

Superimposed on these universal popular categories of designation were a number of more specific terms of reference denoting occupational clusters, such as 'intelligentsia', 'big estate owners', 'new middle-class', 'bourgeoisie', 'petty bourgeoisie', etc. The groups subsumed under them were sometimes explicitly specified and sometimes vague and overlapping. This second set of terms of reference (1) specified the boundaries of the three above-mentioned categories of designation, and (2) subdivided them into a number of more inclusive layers both vertically and horizontally.

The core of the 'masters' was the 'intelligentsia'. Most of them preempted the right for themselves, but were not necessarily granted the right, to set norms for the whole society, a right derived from their exclusiveness in regard to consumption, distribution and organization of cultural products (Bláha, 1937). They constituted the most titled and etiquette-conscious groups in the whole society. The higher the status, the more distinguished the title. The intelligentsia comprised mainly intellectuals, members of professions and higher ranks of civil service, but sometimes it also included well-educated business executives, factory managers, and higher bank officials. Education in colleges or universities, classical secondary schools *(gymnasium, réalka),* or teachers' institutes was a requirement (Bláha, 1937: 31-35). One sociologist speaks of the intelligentsia as a 'class of people who make a living on the basis of their school diploma' (Rádl, 1928).

According to my estimate, the intelligentsia comprised about 400,000 individuals in 1930. Including family members, this stratum numbered about 810,000 persons, i.e., 5.5 percent of the total population of 15 million. About one-half of the intelligentsia belonged to the professions, about one-fifth were civil servants, and less than one-third were members of the so-called 'technical intelligentsia'. The class status, as defined by conventional sociological measures, of the members of the intelligentsia was not uniform: about five percent belonged to the upper class, the remainder to the upper-middle class. The white collar group *excluded* by reason of lack of proper education from the ranks of the intelligentsia was substantial; together with family members it comprised eight percent of the total population.

In terms of social origins, the intelligentsia was strongly middle class. Between four-fifths and three-fourths came from the 'master' and 'half-master' families. The children of workers comprised less than one-tenth of all university students and only seven percent of the students in classical secondary schools (Bláha, 1937: 163-164; Doležal and Ullrich, 1937). On the other hand, it should be pointed out that the low rank of parents was not always a block to their upwardly mobile children. The first two Czechoslovak presidents, both university professors by occupation, came from low-status families. Masaryk was the son of a coachman, and Beneš the son of a cottager.

The dominant process characterizing the inter-war period was the gradual loss by the intelligentsia of pre-eminence in social norm-setting and a progressive diversification of this stratum. This led to the loss of cohesiveness among the various subgroups composing the intelligentsia and a narrowing of the circle of those included unequivocally in its ranks. This heralded the emergence of a more modern class society and a gradual abandonment of the traditional notion of intelligentsia as a status group in favor of the more Western concept of intelligentsia as a cultural stratum. This process progressed much faster and further in the Western provinces of Bohemia and Moravia than in the Eastern provinces of Slovakia and Carpathian Ruthenia. Thus the analysis that follows addresses itself to the development in the two parts of the country separately.

The traditional role of the educated was different in the western and eastern provinces. In both west and east, the intelligentsia began to emerge as a separate group at the beginning of the nineteenth century. It constituted the second estate, ranking next to the nobility and above the burghers, artisans, and peasants. Its predecessors, merging more or less with the intelligentsia but preserving their autonomous character and special power position, were the clergy and civil servants. There, however, most of the west-east parallels end.

In the western provinces, the intelligentsia soon emerged as a competitor and, in larger urban communities, as a successor to the nobility. This phenomenon was as much due to the role of the aristocracy as to the composition and orientation of the intelligentsia. The Bohemian and Moravian nobility comprised mostly high aristocrats, few in number (in 1848 they totaled about 2,300, including family members), alienated from the national and liberal movements arising in the population, and separated from the lower estates by a considerable social gap. Furthermore, to most of the population (Czechs), the aristocracy was a foreign rather than an indigenous upper stratum, a group of intruders or invaders whose status was not legitimized by consensus. The nobility was, therefore, not acknowledged as a leadership group, but was looked on as a stratum standing outside, even though at the top, of the system of stratification (Raupach, 1938; Denis, 1903).

Except for the top ranks of the clergy and civil service, the intelligentsia was recruited from untitled estates. They came from the lowest groups considerably more often than did the intelligentsia in West European countries. Given the prevailing anti-aristocratic sentiment and the relatively low social origin of the recruits, the intelligentsia emerged as a group of legitimate spokesmen, opinion leaders, and organizers of the lower estates, first in the cities and towns and later in the countryside. Unlike the aristocracy, they had close and frequent contacts with the lower estates, facilitated sometimes by a common social background, emphasis on achievement, and always by the missionary nature of the work the intelligentsia did among and for the 'people'.

They started and carried out the National Renaissance Movement, founded and led political parties and national and community institutions and associations. They represented the nation abroad as self-appointed ambassadors. They formulated the political, social, and, to some extent, economic programs of the nation and of individual communities. They were the norm-setting group by virtue of the great prestige they enjoyed and the monopoly of leadership they possessed (Wiskemann, 1938).

Their quasi-sacred mission, their exclusiveness, and their relatively small number gave them a feeling of solidarity transcending professional antagonism, for the most part. Since the turn of the century, the changing structure of the society and changes within the intelligentsia itself brought an end to the monopoly of leadership and the estate character of the intelligentsia. The rapid spread of universal education and the almost complete disappearance of illiteracy, as well as growth in the number of and enrollment in professional and evening schools, began breaking down the barriers of exclusiveness based on higher educational status. The growth and competition of the bourgeosie, and in part also growing emphasis on entrepreneurship among bigger farmers, deprived the intelligentsia of its monopoly of norm-setting and, frequently, of community leadership. The big entrepreneurs' ability to distribute material rewards and to impose sanctions severely limited the control of the "educated" over community life. Profit-making became an alternative to education as a goal and standard of evaluation (Bauer, 1907).

The introduction of universal suffrage and the growing power and influence of workers', farmers', and small entrepreneurs' political parties and associations destroyed the intelligentsia's monopoly on political leadership, although the "educated" among political leaders continued to be the strongest and most influential group. But the ever-increasing political diversity divided the intelligentsia into several warring, antagonistic ideological camps. A similar effect was created by the growing popularity of sports and entertainment industries: They introduced new standards of prestige and new opinion leaders who competed with the educated for influence over the lower strata. The shift was part of a general trend toward a full class society, republicanism, greater urban concentrations, and steadily decreasing importance of agricultural occupations and the number of persons engaged in them (Bláha, 1937).

Changes within the intelligentsia were no less important. Higher education, and thus inclusion among the 'better educated', became accessible to an increasing number of people. The size of the membership in itself lessened the estate solidarity of the group, but even more important was the effect of increasing specialization and diversification of professional careers available to the educated. The growth of industry and banking brought higher technological education and industrial and commercial bureaucracy which, on the whole, lost its identification with the traditional role of the intelligentsia, although individual managers, executives, and other college-educated employees continued to feel themselves to be, and were regarded as, part of it. The majority of the high-ranking employees became 'hired entrepreneurs' or technicians identified and identifying themselves to a considerable degree with the grand bourgeoisie and middle bourgeoisie (Bauer, 1907). Membership in the intelligentsia was only half-heartedly extended or was refused outright to the fast-growing lesser white-collar workers. Because of the nature of their work, subordinate position, and technical rather than classical education, they were referred to as 'half-intelligentsia', 'new middle class', 'employees', and a variety of other terms.

The growth of the civil service and extension of the spheres of government bureaucracy to new areas (post office, railroads, city transportation, state-owned industry, etc.) had similar consequences. The lesser civil servants, particularly in predominantly technical services, also emerged as a stratum unto itself, parallel to and designated like the lesser white-collar workers in industrial and commercial occupations. Furthermore, political as well as social circumstances gave rise to the distinction between the 'higher' and 'lower' bureaucracy, a distinction based not on educational level but on superordination and subordination of the office (Mertl, 1937).

A small group, but one that contributed equally to the dissolution of the estate character of the intelligentsia, was the newly rising group of professional politicians and organizers—professional secretaries of political parties and their affiliated organizations and of similar mass associations. It was a group of people who bought and sold power and public opinion, and who regarded success as its highest goal. Their status was not necessarily based on educational achievement, but rather on accumulated power.

The liberal professions—the 'hard core' of the intelligentsia—were undergoing change too. A number of them became incorporated into bureaucratic or semi-bureaucratic organizations, the civil service, commercial and industrial corporations, publishing houses, hospitals, and similar organizations, and thus lost some of their traditional autonomy. Partly as a result of the loss of control of political leadership and partly because of changing standards of evaluation, there emerged an increasing emphasis on money-making, and entrepreneurship, particularly among members of the legal and medical professions in larger cities (Obrdlik, 1937). New professions came into existence—dentistry, veterinary, nursing, social work, etc.—which helped to bridge the social gap between the traditional professions and the 'less educated' (Bláha, 1937; A. Štefánek, 1944).

The 'educated' thus became a very heterogeneous group, more and more abandoning the collective self-designation. The traditional estate feeling was still preserved among some of the high-ranking professionals and among small-town notables, but the past cohesion of the 'educated' was gone. Instead, each occupational group tended to defend its own particularistic interests and to compete with other occupations for greater recognition and influence.

As a result of these changes, the term 'intelligentsia' became reserved primarily for members of professions and the college- and *gymnasium*-educated civil servants. Occupation and education, rather than education alone, became the prevalent basis of status evaluation. Education came to be regarded as the most legitimate means of social mobility, as a prerequisite for occupational status; only secondarily was it considered a goal in itself. Nevertheless, claims to a high social status based mainly on the university diploma continued to be sanctioned by consensus. The academic titles (Mr Doctor, Mr Professor, Mr Engineer) conferred by institutions of higher learning were universally acknowledged as symbols of distinction, irrespective of the occupational status of the title holder; they were frequently used as terms of address and self-designation in preference to or as alternatives to the occupational titles (RCC files, n.d.).

In the eastern provinces (Slovakia and Carpathian Ruthenia), the situation was somewhat different. The 'educated', a relatively small group, preserved a greater degree of estate character and the traditional control of leadership throughout the third decade of the twentieth century. Up to the time of the dispossession of the aristocracy (at the end of the First World War), the leadership of the nobility was more or less accepted. This was due partly to the fact that some of the intelligentsia were recruited from the numerous landless gentry migrating to towns and cities. The untitled members of the intelligentsia then accepted the norms of the gentry, their glamorous style of life, their generally conservative and traditionalist orientation, their contempt for the 'people', and an aristocratic conception of their leadership role. They thought of themselves as forming a society for and by itself, as the 'chosen ones' representing the society, as a part standing for the whole, rather than as 'ambassadors of the people' or 'missionaries of the people' or 'awakeners', as the Czech intelligentsia conceived of itself during the nineteenth century. The gap between them and the lower strata was also reinforced by the fact that most of the intelligentsia was, like the high aristocracy and the gentry, Magyar or Magyarized, while the lower strata spoke Slovak or Ruthenian. In fact, anybody who had not graduated from a Hungarian gymnasium or who did not speak Hungarian was not regarded as a member of the intelligentsia by the 'people' (Štefánek, 1944, 1934, 1939).

The dispossession of the nobility—and that also meant the end of Magyar rule and the beginning of rapid social change—elevated the intelligentsia to the top of the social ladder, since the indigenous high status groups which could compete for the leadership role were few, and frequently they strove to join the intelligentsia rather than for autonomy.

The supremacy of the 'educated' and their relatively high solidarity resulted from the general character of the society and its cultural ethos. The educational level of the population was low. In 1930, 11.99 percent of the population was illiterate (as against 1.32 percent in the western provinces), (Annuaire statistique, 1937: 11-12) in spite of a concentrated campaign by the Government and voluntary associations, the rapid growth of schools, and a universal opportunity for formal education. Only 22.7 percent of the population lived in communities with 5,001 and more inhabitants, as against the western provinces with 32.8 percent in communities of this size (Annuaire statistique, 1934: 9). The standard of living was generally low. A majority of the population was engaged in agriculture and forestry (58.51 percent), as against 25.56 percent in Bohemia and Moravia); only 14.62 percent of the total population of the country deriving a living from industry and handicraft were concentrated in the east (Annuaire statistique, 1934: 15-19). The propertied middle strata were numerically few and thus usually unable to mediate between the upper and lower classes. Most of the adult population had little or no previous experience in political participation.

Another factor contributing to the greater solidarity of Slovak intelligentsia was the influx of Czechs into the eastern provinces after 1918 and the growing opposition to this influx. The Czechs pre-empted many positions in universities and other educational institutions, provincial government and the management of the economy. This blocked upward mobility of the young Slovaks and aroused feelings of nationalism. As a result the Slovak intelligentsia still tended to view itself as an avant garde of a notion.

The differences between the western and eastern parts of Czechoslovakia could be roughly compared to the American distinction between North and South. The west traditionally placed greater emphasis on achievement. Status differences there were gradual and were becoming more and more flexible. The east traditionally placed greater emphasis on ascription of status. The differences between classes were perceived by most as differences of kind. Each class constituted a definite subculture with a rather unique style of life and world view. In the urban upper strata and among peasants and farmers, there prevailed a definite, strong emphasis on rank and on acceptance of social status as a relatively permanent distinction. The acquiescence to the existing system of stratification was usually legitimized by religious beliefs and family traditions.

The social change typifying the development of the western provinces took a similar direction in the east under the impact of political revolution. The civil service started expanding rapidly, bridging the gap between the 'educated' and the 'uneducated'. However, in other groups of white-collar employees and in the professions the pace of specialization was slow. It accelerated only with the establishment of the independent Slovak state in 1939 when the young generation of educated Slovaks took over many positions abandoned by the expelled Czechs.

The case of the Czechoslovak intelligentsia between the wars differs substantially from the situation in other East-Central European countries. But it can be argued that the Czechoslovak development anticipated changes that have occurred since the Second World War, i.e., the gradual 'decomposition' of the intelligentsia that has taken place in contemporary Eastern Europe and was described so well by Szczepanski (1970) in case of Poland. If my assertion has any merit it can be argued that this transformation was merely speeded up, not caused by, the Second World War and the subsequent Communist takeover.

REFERENCES

Annuaire Statistique de la République Tchécoslovaque (1934, 1937) Prague: Office de statistique.
Bauer, O. (1907) *Die Nationalitätenfrage und die Sozialdemokratie.* Vienna: Brand.
Bláha, I. A. (1937) *Sociologie inteligence.* Prague: Orbis.
—— (1947) *Problém lidu.* Prague: Petr.
Boček, L. (1940) 'Jsou obchodníci, zivnostnici, řemeslníci, nižší úředníci "pány" či "lidem"?' *Sociologická revue,* 9 (nos. 1-2): 73-82.
Denis, E. (1903) *La Bohème depuis la Montagne Blanche.* Paris: Laroux. 2 vols.
Doležal, Jr. and Z. Ullrich (1934) 'Výzkum abiturientů českých středních škol v zemi české a moravskoslezské ve školním roce 1933-34.' *Statistický obzor,* 16 (nos. 4-10): 117-124.
Mertl, J. (1937) *Byrokracie.* Prague: Orbis.
Obrdlík, A. (1937) *Povolání a veřejné blaho.* Prague: Orbis.
Rádl, E. (1928) *Krise inteligence.* Prague: Fastr.
Raupach, H. (1938) *Der tschechische Fruhnationalismus.* Essen: Essener Verlagsanstalt.
'Research on Contemporary Culture Files: Czechoslovakia' (n.d.) New York: Columbia University.
Stefánek, A. (1934) 'Novoslováci.' *Sociologická revue,* 4 (nos. 3-4): 272-277.
—— (1939) 'Syngenza a spoločenske "ja" '. *Sociologická revue,* 9 (no. 1): 85-98.
—— (1944) *Základy sociografie Slovenska.* Bratislava: Slovenská akadémia vied a umeni.
Stefánek, B. (1946) 'Maďarský pán'. *Sociologický sborník,* 1 (no. 2): 14-20.
Szczepanski, J. (1970) *Polish Society.* New York: Random House.
Wiskemann, E. (1938) *Czechs and Germans.* New York: Oxford University Press.

11

SOVIET SCIENTIFIC AND TECHNICAL INTELLIGENTSIA AND ITS SOCIAL MAKEUP

N N Bokarev and N B Chaplin
Institute of Sociological Research, Moscow

The XXIVth Congress of the Communist Party of the Soviet Union put forward the objective of integrating the achievements of the scientific and technological revolution and the advantages of the socialist economic system. This is an objective of historical significance. In a developed socialist society science begins to fulfil in an increased scope the function of a direct productive force. It becomes a mighty factor in the creation of the material and technical base of communism.

Socialism, the foundation of which is public ownership of the means of production, creates the most favourable conditions for rapid development of science and wide utilization of its achievements in industry, agriculture and other branches of economy. Socialism utilizes the achievements of scientific and technological progress in the interests of the entire society, for the benefit of every man.

As a result of the constant attention paid by the Communist Party of the Soviet Union to the development of science in our country the number of Soviet scientific and technical intelligentsia is constantly growing. Soviet scientists and engineers take an active part in the construction of the material and technical base of communism, greatly contributing to further increasing the efficiency and intensification of

Translated from the Russian by A. Zhiritsky.

social production; they are in constant search for new ways and possibilities of accelerating scientific and technical progress.

The progressive scientific and technical intelligentsia in capitalistic countries is well aware of the role being forced on it by state and monopolist bourgeoisie in a modern exploitive society. Hence, it decisively fights against technocratic conceptions, and more and more actively participates in the people's struggle for the triumph of such a social and political system capable of ensuring the constant growth of the material and cultural welfare of all members of society; it is fighting for the socialist transformation of economic, political and cultural life in their countries.

With the rapid development of the scientific and technological revolution various theoretical 'schools' and orientations have appeared which try to give their theoretical interpretation of the main social motive forces and laws of the scientific and technological revolution. The so-called technocratic school is known to be the most influential one in modern Western sociology.

According to Western scientists, 'technocracy' is a political system where dominating positions belong to specialists in administration and economy, hence, the 'technocrat' is defined as a man who, due to his scientific and technical knowledge, is exercizing social and political power in society.

As Daniel Bell asserts, since the scientific and technological revolution is the main factor of contemporary social progress, with scientists and engineers being leaders of this revolution, it would be logical to assume that all political and social power must be concentrated in the hands of scientists and engineers. Nevertheless, Bell, being himself a political leader, opposes the theoretical ideas of the 'technocratic society'. He contrasts to it the conception of a 'post-industrial society', where the power belongs to politicians leaning on the help of scientist-technocrats.

In spite of opposition from a considerable group of Western sociologists to technocratic conceptions, these conceptions are wide spread, and are included in political programmes of ultra-right extremists, utilized for the theoretical argumentation of various fascist social movements.

Technocracy is considered by some Western sociologists as the only force capable of bringing order into and organizing the governing of the modern world. In essence, technocratic conceptions are nothing but theoretical grounds of some circles of the contemporary state-monopolist bourgeoisie striving to establish their political domination. As technocracy develops, the technocrats declare the leading role goes to production, while everything else loses significance, and hence, must be eliminated if it impedes the achievement of this goal.

In other words, the matter concerns establishing the absolute power of the state-monopolist bourgeoisie and utilizing the scientific and technological revolution to consolidate its power. Thus, scientists and engineers are forced to play the role of a blind instrument in the hands of the state monopolist bourgeoisie. It becomes estranged from the people and hostile to their interests.

The experience of building socialism in the USSR shows that scientists and technical specialists are not a special social force with its own ideals and aims; on the contrary, they are an integral part of the united Soviet people, its social ideals and aims being common with those of the working class and peasantry, with all the working people of the country. Therefore, all talk about numerous groups of dissidents supposedly existing in the USSR among the intelligentsia are in our view absolutely unfounded. Soviet scientific and technical intelligentsia are as one with all classes and social groups of the Soviet people, in their common Marxist and Leninist ideology, in the unity of the social and political objectives in the communist construction.

Soviet scientific and technical intelligentsia as all Soviet people possess such moral and social traits as a high sense of civic duty, humanism, patriotism inseparable from internationalism, class solidarity and others. In a Soviet society where there is the hegemony of the working class, scientists and technical specialists are distinguished by lofty morals, by the feeling of their social usefulness, because all their activities serve the people.

Scientific understanding of modern socio-political, socio-economic and philosophical problems, social laws governing the development of society and science are a major feature in the make-up of the scientific and technical intelligentsia. Solid scientific grounds help the Soviet scientific and technical intelligentsia to be well oriented in new phe-nomena, to give them a correct evaluation and make well-grounded practical conclusions. The scientific and technical intelligentsia con-stantly enrich their social and political knowledge, closely linking it with the solution of practical problems in the interests of the whole people.

The specialty of an engineer-sociologist of an industrial enterprise has recently appeared in the Soviet Union. By now, such specialists already work in many enterprises. The engineer-sociologist should com-bine a knowledge of technological and production processes with an understanding of the social relations that exist among people engaged in production processes and with the ability to work out practical mea-sures for the improvement of production efficiency and productivity. The most important objective of an engineer-sociologist is to achieve an optimal combination of efficiency and productivity on the basis of systematic sociological research.

In order to solve this task, to ensure a steady growth of social production—a base for the growth of the material and cultural welfare of all members of Soviet society—the Soviet scientific and technical intelligentsia must comprehend the socio-political goals of our country. That is why industrial enterprises, research and design organizations pay great attention to the growth of the political knowledge of the scien-tific and technical intelligentsia. The improvement of the content, forms and methods of the political education of scientists and special-ists consists primarily in mastering scientific theory and the method-ology of social research; in the close link between these studies and the tasks being solved by collectives; in the formation of the communist world outlook; in the development of creative activity of people in paid and voluntary work; in raising the moral level of the people.

As the results of sociological research conducted in a number of Moscow research institutes show, a large majority of scientific workers and technical specialists have renewed, deepened and broadened their ideological and political knowledge. Nearly every third scientific worker attends various theoretical and methodological seminars. A large num-ber of scientists and technical specialists study Marxist-Leninist theory by themselves.

While mastering the socio-political theory of the function and development of our society, Soviet scientific and technical intelligentsia at the same time actively participate in the realisation of the Party programme which 'demands clarity and preciseness in ideological positions, the further raising of revolutionary vigilance, a consistent struggle against indifference to politics, against survival of private property, petty-bourgeoise mentality, against manifestations of any nihilistic attitude towards the gains of socialism, and the penetration of a bourgeois and revisionist view'.[1]

Many scientists and technical specialists fruitfully and successfully combine intensive scientific activity with intensive public activities.

In the research institutes where the above-mentioned research has been conducted, a large number of specialists (from 63 to 78 percent) actively participate in various voluntary socio-political and production activities. In answer to the question about the motives of satisfaction with these activities, about 50 percent of them emphasized first of all the social usefulness of the work. This motive has received the highest score of positive evaluation in the sum total of received answers.

The increase of skill and education is one of the important conditions for the successful creative activity of the Soviet scientific and technical intelligentsia. For this purpose various forms of training and education are used: the writing and presentation of theses, attendance at economic courses, theoretical and methodological seminars, and post-graduate correspondence courses. A systematic assessment of scientists and technical specialists is conducted to promote their professional growth.

Sociologists took part in working out typological methods of assessment in order to raise its efficiency. Today we widely use an assessment form where each specialist puts down the results of his activity, while the head of the section he works in makes an evaluation of his results as well as personal and professional qualities. The assessment form comprises a description of the results achieved by a specialist (both in theory and practice), it shows the degree of his personal participation (author, co-author, rank and file collaborator, post-graduate), points out the number of publications where the achieved results have been exposed, and gives a brief characterization of his scientific and organizational activity. The head of the section defines the degree of novelty of the work executed.

In some research institutes, the total result of the work fulfilled by various research units is summed up with the help of the methods of expert evaluation, the object of study being theoretical and practical results of completed research projects or of stages in their fulfillment. In this case it is easier for experts to evaluate the whole work, define the novelty of elaborated ideas as well as the potential or already achieved effectiveness of their application.

Selection of the expert group is made in a democratic way: expert candidates are announced by laboratories, then members of the Scientific Council and the heads of laboratories publicly vote for the total list of candidates. It gives an opportunity to make expert commissions both competent and objective, and at the same time to draw the broad scientific public into the decision-making process concerning the solution of important problems at the institute.

The research results, presented for examination, are reported to general seminars of scientists investigating the problems concerned. As our experience has shown, these seminars are actively attended not only by leading scientists but by scientific youth too. Expert evaluation helps to improve the exchange of scientific information among the units of research institutes and to establish mutually beneficial research contacts. The publicity of expert judgements and their educational significance serve as an important impetus for improving the quality of work as well. We had the chance to find this out while analyzing the results achieved by those units of the institutes that in the previous year got rather poor evaluation marks.

As practice shows, the research units of the institutes as a rule bring to the assessment seminars really interesting and important scientific works and experts give them objective and qualified evaluation. It turned expertise into one of the important elements of material incentive. Sociological methods thus become closely linked with the solution of production and economic tasks.

In collective research discords frequently occur as well as disputes and discussions. The conservative contradicts the contemporary. The leader of a research collective must be capable of timely support for important

conceptions. A creative climate in a research collective and its achievements depend considerably on the ability of the research collective leader
to create an atmosphere of creative relations between collaborators.

It is important to emphasize here the increased participation of
managerial and supervisory staff in the fulfillment of one of the
important management functions—the function of motivating a man in
a purposeful activity. To stimulate a man to put into his work all his
knowledge, to constantly increase this knowledge, to work with high
creative effort, to constantly show initiative in the improvement of his
and his colleagues' work and social and productive activity—these are
the tasks of social management being solved by supervisors.

L. I. Brezhnev, General Secretary of the Central Committee of the
CPSU, once emphasized that

> the best plans will not be fulfilled if those who work in machine tools or in the
> fields, on livestock farms, in research institutes or the service industries do not
> throw themselves into their work. The energy of highly organized labour
> multiplied by love of one's country, of the socialist Motherland, can work
> wonders![2]

The important task of supervisors consists in creating the conditions for
achieving a high level of organization of labour, in helping each worker
to fully utilize his skill and show his abilities.

The scientific and technological revolution exerts an influence not
only on the development of production, but on the progress of all
Soviet society, that lays on scientists tremendous social responsibility.
Today many fundamental scientific problems are being solved com-
plexly by the combined efforts of large research collectives headed as a
rule by leading scientists. Each of these scientists is not only a leader of
a theoretical 'school' but an organizer responsible for the political and
moral qualities of hundreds of his colleagues.

Soviet scientists do their best to educate their pupils and successors
in the spirit of Marxism-Leninism, to instill in them the feeling of
devotion to the Communist Party; the qualities that all leading Soviet
scientists have possessed. K. A. Timiryazev once wrote that he believed
and was sure that the Bolsheviks adhering to Leninist conceptions
worked for the happiness of the people and would make them happy
by all means.

Among the important social qualities of the Soviet scientific and technical intelligentsia are: collectiveness, and high creative activeness in research and socio-political activities. These qualities are inherent in all the Soviet people, they are founded in the whole socialist way of life, primarily, by the socialist means of production based on the public ownership of the implements and means of production.

The quality of collectivism is closely linked with socialist humanism and optimism. These traits are inherent in the make-up of the Soviet scientific and technical intelligentsia, who devote their life and strength to the great goals of the freedom and happiness of man. Respecting man's dignity, thinking about the satisfaction of man's vital material and intellectual needs, the Soviet scientific and technical intelligentsia and all the Soviet people spare no efforts to attain the harmonious and versatile development of Soviet man's personality. Real humaneness of thoughts and actions cannot exist without a firm belief in the implementation of the objectives which Soviet man strives for.

The Soviet scientific and technical intelligentsia possess rich scientific knowledge, organizational and political skills, and inexhaustible creative energy, which it entirely devotes to its socialist fatherland, to the further strengthening of its political and economic power, to multiplying the intellectual potential of socialism, and to the triumph of communist ideals. Socialism provides all the conditions necessary for the creative activity of the Soviet scientific and technical intelligentsia.

Not technocraticism, but socialism is the mainline of human progress; not technocraticism, but socialism solves all social problems put forward by the scientific and technological revolution and provides all the necessary socio-economic and socio-political conditions for creative work in the interests of a people building a communist society.

REFERENCES

1. 'Lenin's Ideal and Cause are Immortal'. Novosti Press Agency Publishing House, Moscow, 1973, 60-61. Theses of the Central Committee, Communist Party

of the Soviet Union on the Centennial of Birth of V. I. Lenin.

2. L. I. Brezhnev. 'The Fiftieth Anniversary of the Union of Soviet Socialist Republics', Novosti Press Agency Publishing House, Moscow, 1972, 75.

NOTES ON CONTRIBUTORS

B. N. Chaplin is Professor at the Institute of Sociological Research, Moscow.*

N. N. Bokarev is Professor and Head of Department of the Institute of Sociological Research, Moscow.*

Lewis S. Feuer is Professor of Sociology at the University of Toronto, Canada. He is the author of many works, most recent are: *Ideology and the Ideologist* (Harper Torchbook, 1975) and *Einstein and the Generations of Science* (Basic Books, 1974).

Aleksander Gella is a Pole, educated entirely in Poland, holding degrees in law, economics and sociology from: Jagiellonian University, Crakow; The Higher School of Planning and Statistics, Warsaw; and the Institute of Philosophy and Sociology of the Polish Academy of Sciences, Warsaw. He taught sociology at the Jagiellonian University and had a research appointment in the Polish Academy of Sciences. Since 1967 he has had visiting professorships in the USA at San Jose State and the University of California, and in 1970 he became Professor of Sociology at SUNY/Buffalo, N.Y. He has published books and articles in Polish, and in English he edited *Ward-Gumplowicz Correspondence* (N.Y. 1971). He is working on *Social Stratification in Eastern Europe*. He is also preparing a three-part empirical study of the Polish intelligentsia in the past, in socialist Poland and in exile.

Jan Hajda was born in 1927 in Czechoslovakia. He is Professor of Sociology at Portland State University, Oregon, USA. He obtained his B.A. from Willamette University, and his M.A. and Ph.D. at the University of Chicago, and has taught at John Hopkins University and the University of California at Riverside. He was a Fulbright Fellow 1966-67. He has edited *A Study of Contemporary Czechoslovakia* (University of Chicago, 1956).

*Requested biographical information was not received—Ed.

Leonard Henny is a sociologist/film-maker. He has lived in Holland, Venezuela and the USA. Some of his film productions are 'The Schizophrenia of Working for War' (defense engineers opposing the Vietnam War), 'Black Power' (with Stokeley Carmichael), 'Dead Earth' (with the ecologist Barry Commoner), 'Vietnam Veteran', 'Video-eyes, Video-ears' and 'Other Sides of the News' (1975). He is presently associated with the Sociological Institute of the University of Utrecht, where he teaches sociology and film-making.

Harold M. Hodges, Jr. attended Stanford University and the University of Southern California where he obtained his Ph.D. in Sociology in 1958. He has taught at the University of Wisconsin, University of California at Santa Barbara, Yale University and San Jose State University, where he is teaching at the present time. He was chairman of the Department of Sociology and Anthropology 1965-68. He is the author of many reviews and articles and his books include *Social Stratification: Class in America* (Schenkman, 1965) *Society and Education* (Merrill, 1965), *Peninsula People: Social Stratification in Suburbia* (Spartan, 1964), *Conflict and Consensus: An Introduction to Sociology* (Harper and Row, 1971, 2nd ed 1974), *Conflict and Consensus: Readings Toward a Sociological Perspective* (Harper and Row, 1973) and *Search for Self: The Sociology of Consciousness* (1975).

Tibor Huszar is Professor of Sociology at the Eotvos Lorand University, Budapest. He is co-editor of the journal of social sciences *Valosag*. He has written *History and Self-knowledge,* and *Problems of Juvenile Delinquency* and has edited the sociological and social-theoretical readers *The Sociology of the Young Generation* and *Gramsci's Social Philosophy.*

Zygmunt Komorowski was born in 1925. He is professor at the Institute of African Studies at the University of Warsaw and has specialized in the sociology of Africa. He is the author of several books in Polish including *Among the Legends and Truths of Africa* (1974), and has written on society and education in the Ivory Coast and Senegal.

Seymour Martin Lipset is Professor of Political Science and Sociology, and has been since 1975 Senior Fellow at the Hoover Institute at Stanford University, USA. He has taught at the University of California at Berkley and Harvard University. The author of many important works in sociology, he has recently published (with Everett Ladd) *The Divided Academy: Professors and Politics* and (with David Riesman) *Education and Politics at Harvard.*

Asoke Basu is Associate Professor of Sociology at California State University at Hayward.

Helena Z. Lopata is Professor of Sociology in the Department of Sociology, Loyola University of Chicago and Director of the Center for the Comparative Study of Social Roles. She has written several books including *Occupation: Housewife, New York* (OUP 1971), *Widowhood in an American City* (Schenkman, 1973), *Polish-Americans: Status Competition in an Ethnic Community* (Prentice-Hall, forthcoming), and *Marriage and Families* (Van Nostrand, 1973).

Peter C. Ludz was born in 1931 and educated at the universities of Mainz, Munich, Berlin and Paris. He has a Diploma in Economics and his Ph.D. (1956) from the Free University of Berlin. At present he is Professor of Political Science at the University of Munich and Theodor Heuss Professor of Political Science at the Graduate Faculty of the New School for Social Research, New York.

NOTES

NOTES

NOTES

NOTES